CLIVE BARKER'S
NEXT TESTAMENT™

VOLUME ONE

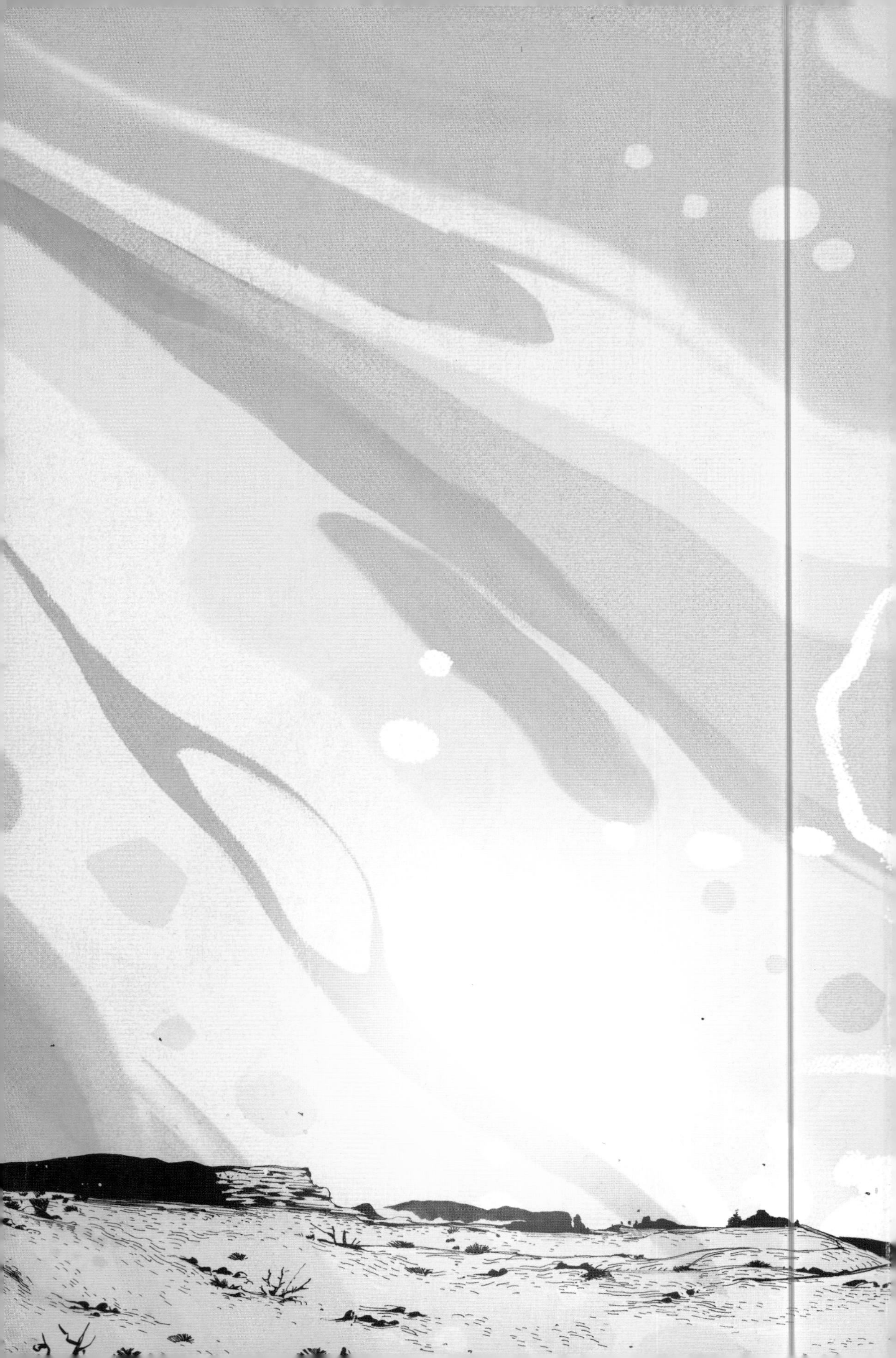

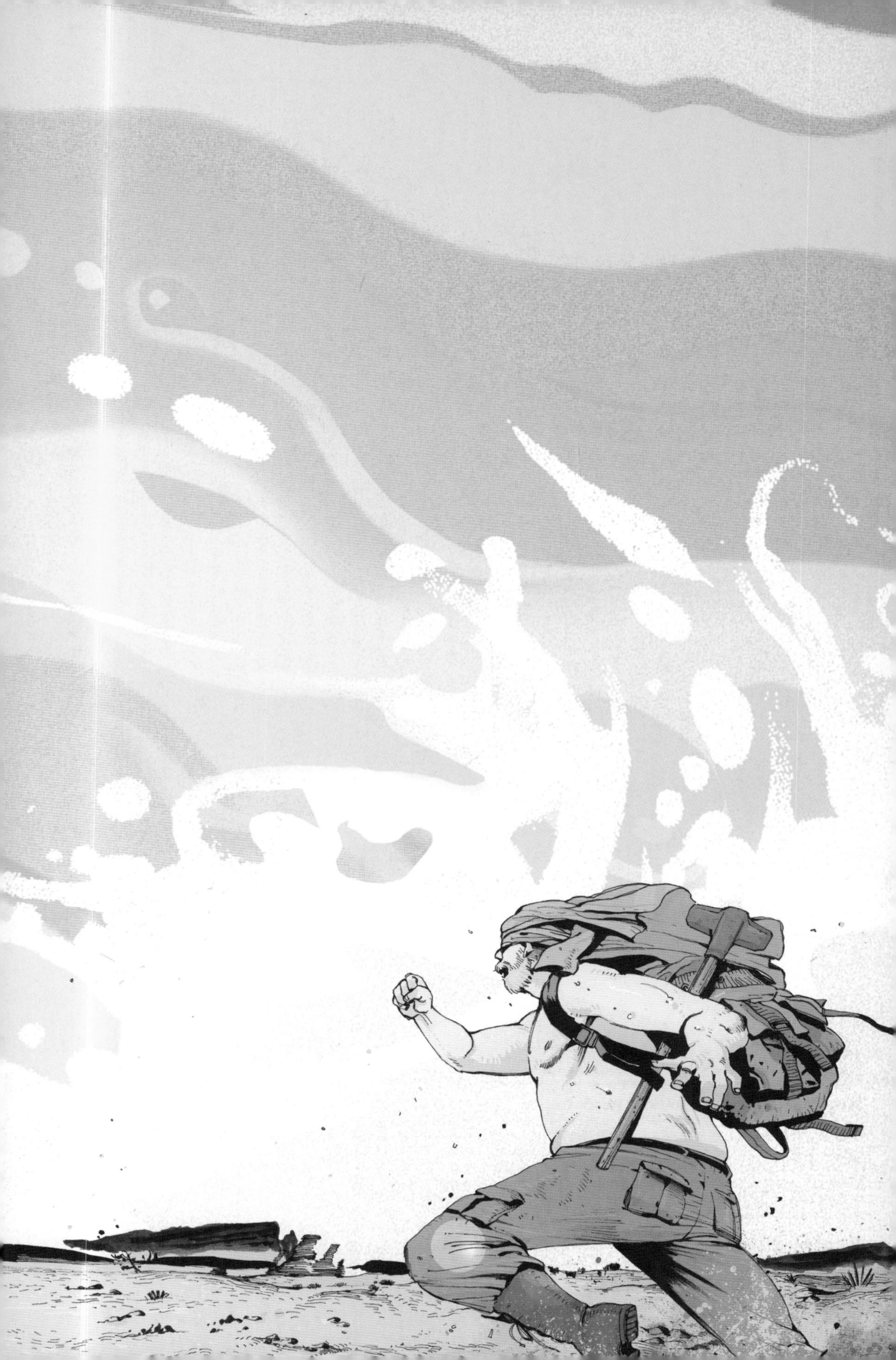

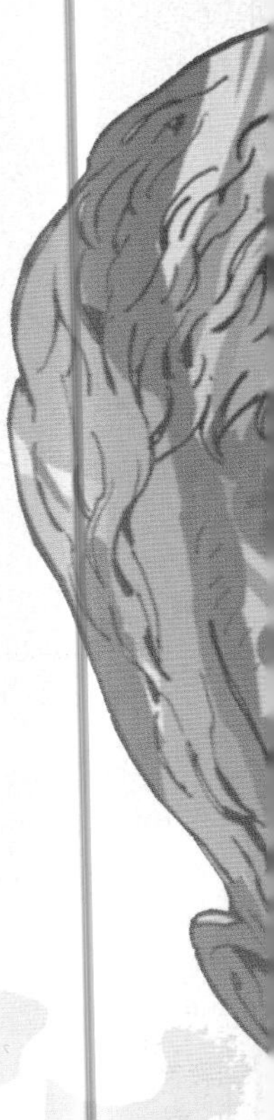

BOOM! STUDIOS

ROSS RICHIE CEO & Founder • JACK CUMMINS President & COO • MARK SMYLIE Chief Creative Officer • MATT GAGNON Editor-in-Chief • FILIP SABLIK VP of Publishing & Marketing • STEPHEN CHRISTY VP of Development
LANCE KREITER VP of Licensing & Merchandising • PHIL BARBARO VP of Finance • BRYCE CARLSON Managing Editor • MEL CAYLO Marketing Manager • SCOTT NEWMAN Production Design Manager • IRENE BRADISH Operations Manager • DAFNA PLEBAN Editor
SHANNON WATTERS Editor • ERIC HARBURN Editor • REBECCA TAYLOR Editor • CHRIS ROSA Assistant Editor • ALEX GALER Assistant Editor • WHITNEY LEOPARD Assistant Editor • JASMINE AMIRI Assistant Editor • CAMERON CHITTOCK Assistant Editor
HANNAH NANCE PARTLOW Production Designer • DEVIN FUNCHES E-Commerce & Inventory Coordinator • BRIANNA HART Executive Assistant • AARON FERRARA Operations Assistant • JOSÉ MEZA Sales Assistant • ELIZABETH LOUGHRIDGE Accounting Assistant

A catalog record of this book is available from OCLC and from the BOOM! Studios website, www.boom-studios.com, on the Librarians Page.

BOOM! Studios, 5670 Wilshire Boulevard, Suite 450, Los Angeles, CA 90036-5679. Printed in China. First Printing.
ISBN: 978-1-60886-367-9, eISBN: 978-1-61398-221-1

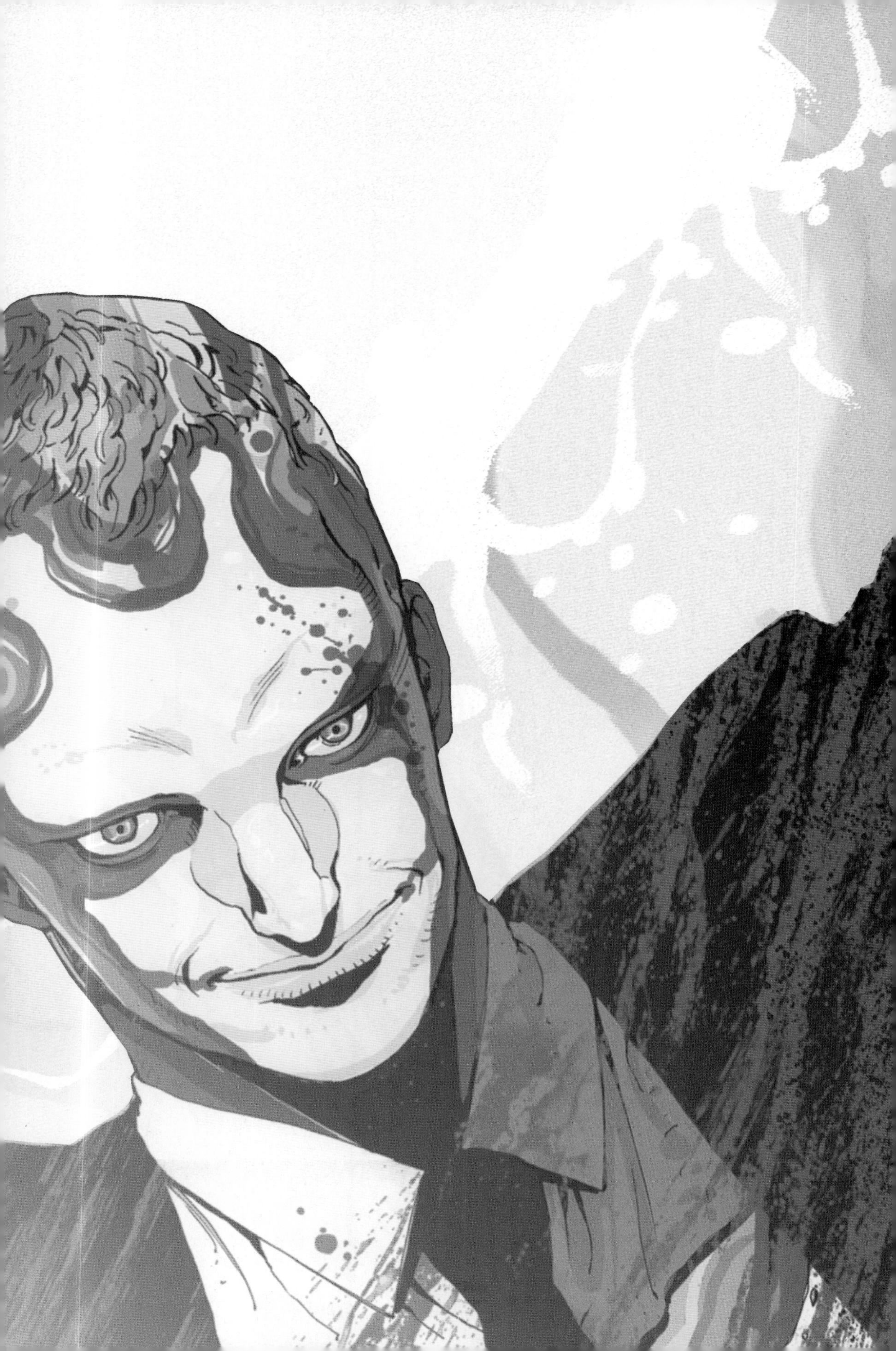

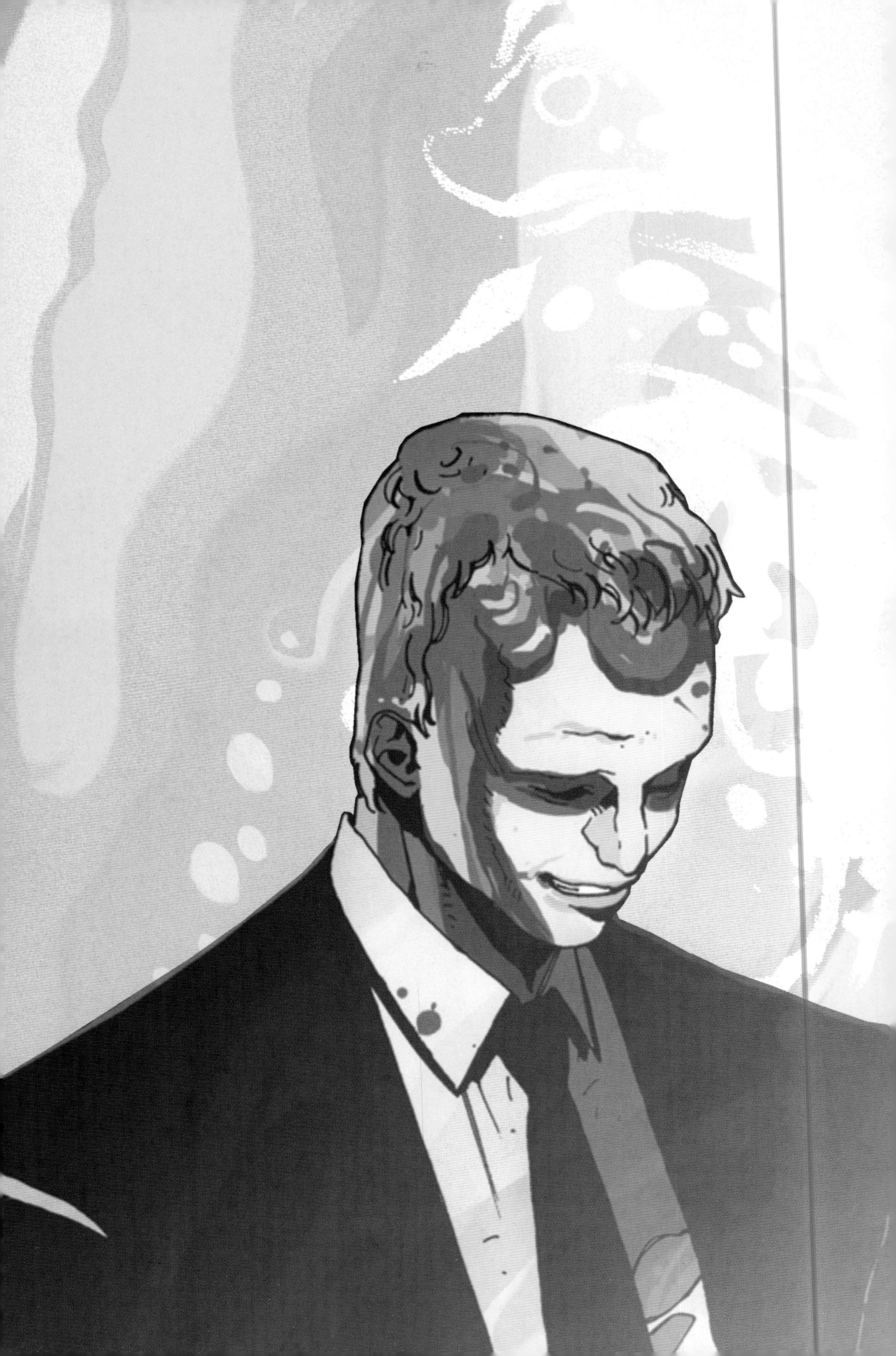

WRITTEN BY

CLIVE BARKER
& MARK MILLER

ART BY

HAEMI JANG

LETTERS BY

STEVE WANDS

COVER BY

GOÑI MONTES

ASSISTANT EDITOR

CHRIS ROSA

EDITOR

MATT GAGNON

TRADE DESIGNER

EMI YONEMURA BROWN

SPECIAL THANKS TO BEN MEARES

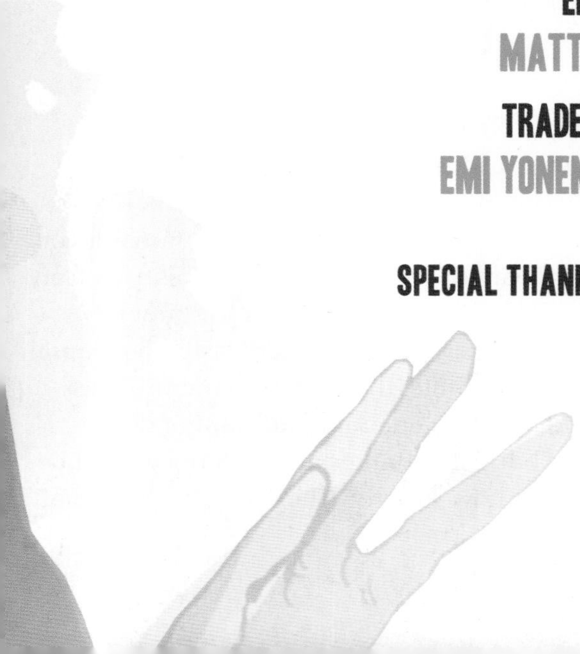

Introduction by Victor LaValle

"Homer opened the door."

If you get a chill when you read that line, the thrill of recognition, then let me salute you as a fellow old school Clive Barker acolyte. That sentence, of course, is the first line of Barker's classic, *The Great and Secret Show*, published in 1989. I picked that bad boy up then, a young man who had no idea of what he was about to experience. (And who, to my great embarrassment now, didn't even pick up the witty nod to that Greek granddaddy of every Western writer who ever penned an epic.) This was Barker's Odyssey, so to speak, the story of some ordinary men who sail into the extraordinary.

The Great and Secret Show begins in the Omaha Central Post Office but will, eventually, cross into many other states and states of being. Before this novel I'd read, devoured, Barker's infamous series of stories, Books of Blood, but that hadn't adequately prepared me for this. A war across time and dimensions, one where our dreams provide the foot soldiers. While there was much to horrify in the novel there was just as much to ponder. While Barker is, rightly, revered for his gruesomeness he couldn't possibly have lasted this long, or remained this popular, if his only trick was bloodletting.

Think of some of his masterworks and one of the threads running through so many of them. In *The Great and Secret Show* we meet "Kissoon" and the Iad Ouroboros; in *The Damnation Game* we encounter the relentless evil of Mamoulian; and of course there are those Cenobites. There is evil in the world and it is fucking cosmic. That's what I've often taken from Clive Barker's stories. Cosmic horror. Cosmic meaning "of or relating to the whole universe." Cosmic meaning "infinitely or inconceivably extended; vast." It makes sense that H.P. Lovecraft is an author often invoked when discussing Clive Barker, but there is a vital difference between the two. Lovecraft's "Great Old Ones" and all their eldritch terrors are cloaked in shadows, glimpsed from the corner of a madman's eye, evil too tremendous to behold. Barker, on the other hand, drags his evils into the light. Rather than reducing their power this only adds to it. Barker's many sinister faces are never simply grotesque. His evil is sensual, seductive, a demon with whom you'd foolishly consent to spend the night.

Which brings us to Next Testament. Collected here are the first four issues of Barker's series, created with the talents of Mark Miller, Haemi Jang, and Steve Wands. In Next Testament God is back and he's a motherfucker. You might say that's one of the running themes of Clive Barker's career. The divine, the all-powerful is tangible, attainable, but mere human beings rarely grasp the cracked complexity of its design. This inability to truly comprehend or even control reality tends to cause a lot of trouble. In Next Testament a vision comes to a man in a dream and in following this vision that man unleashes a celestial beast, a being that claims to be the Lord of the Hebrew Bible, the Old Testament badass himself, back to wreak havoc on the modern world. Smiting enemies and raining death from the sky. God as a terrorist. Holy shit. Nobody but Clive Barker and his crew would be wild enough to tell this story. Even more impressive is how superbly they pull this heresy off.

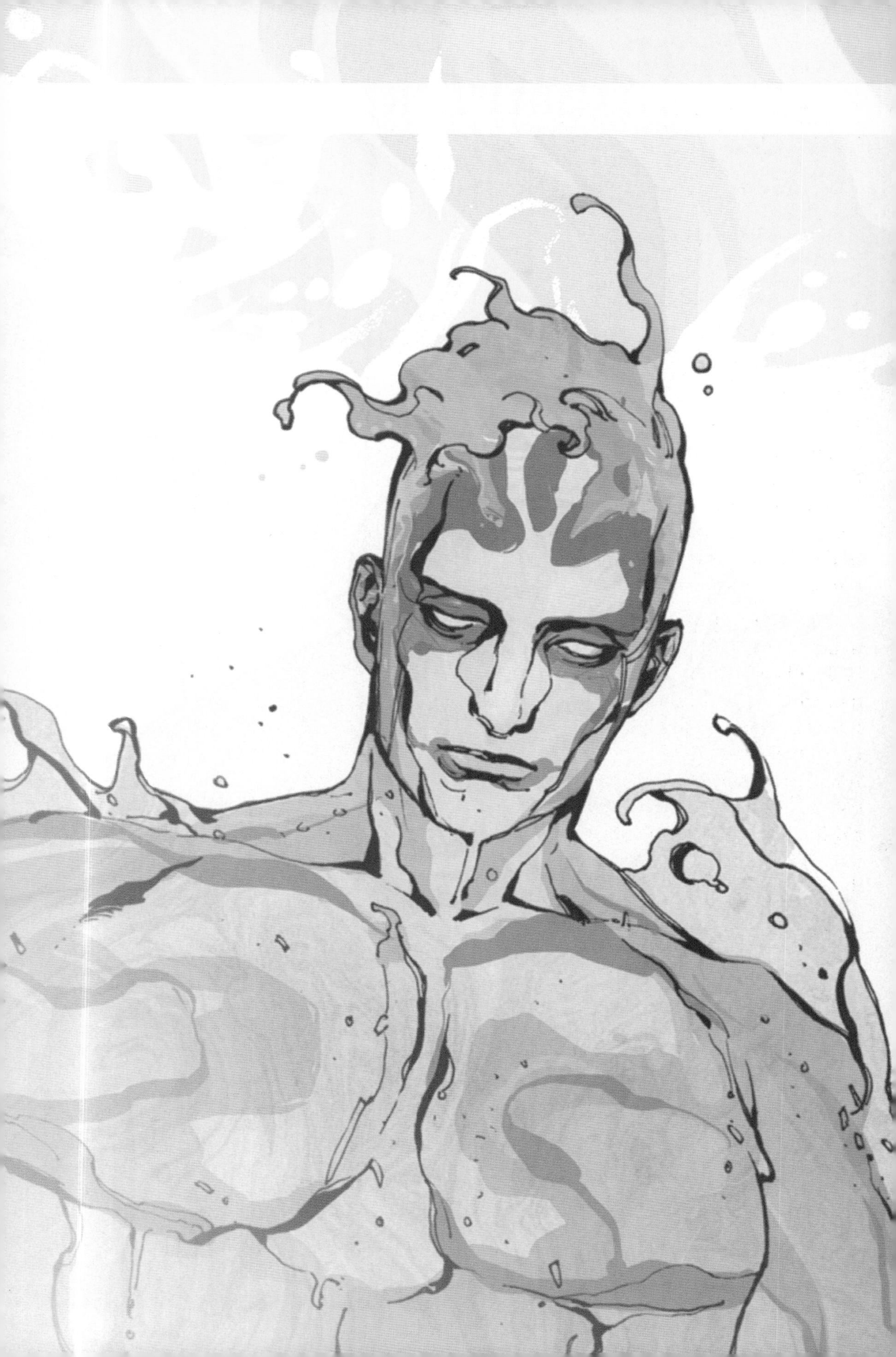

CHAPTER ONE

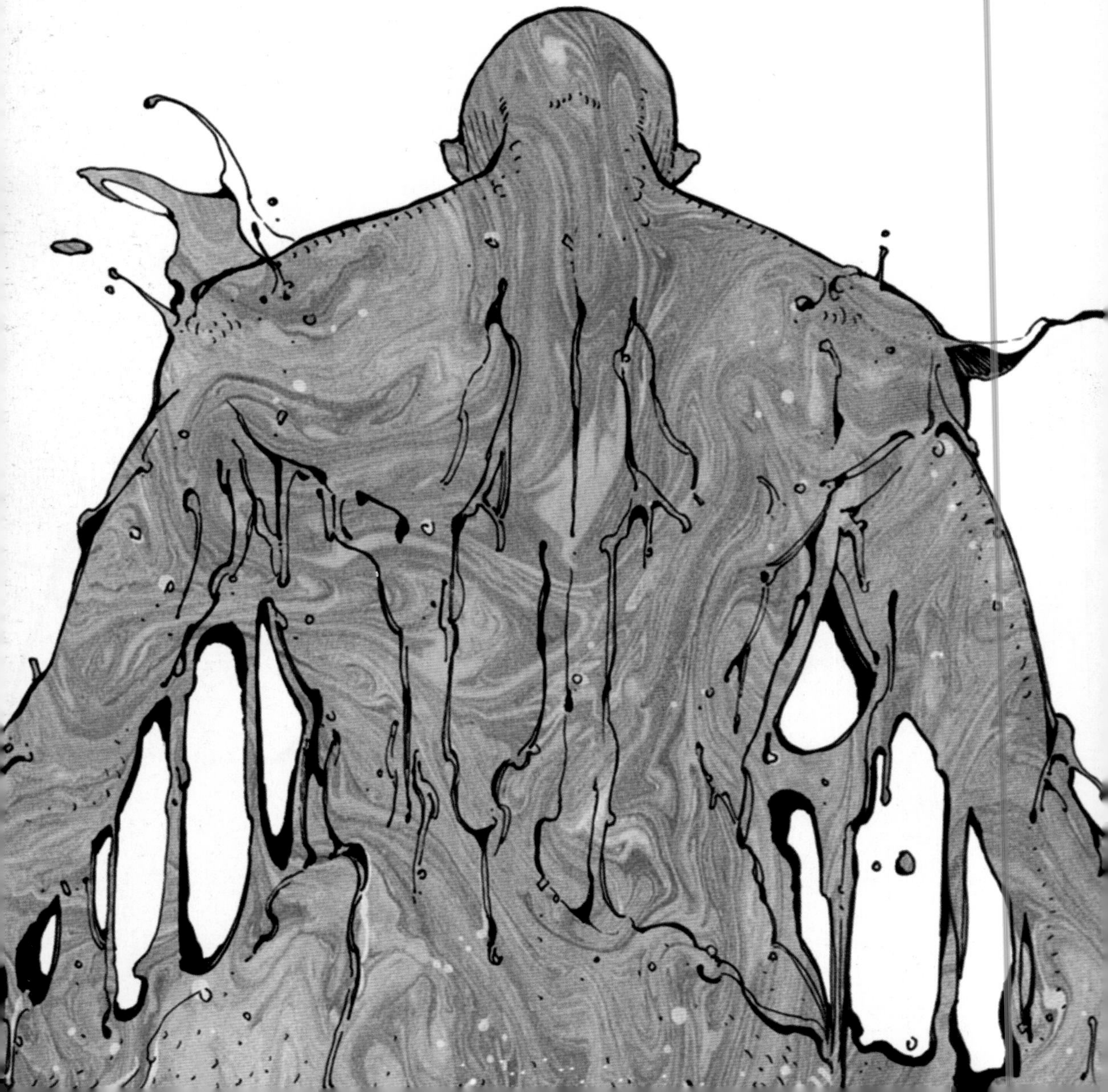

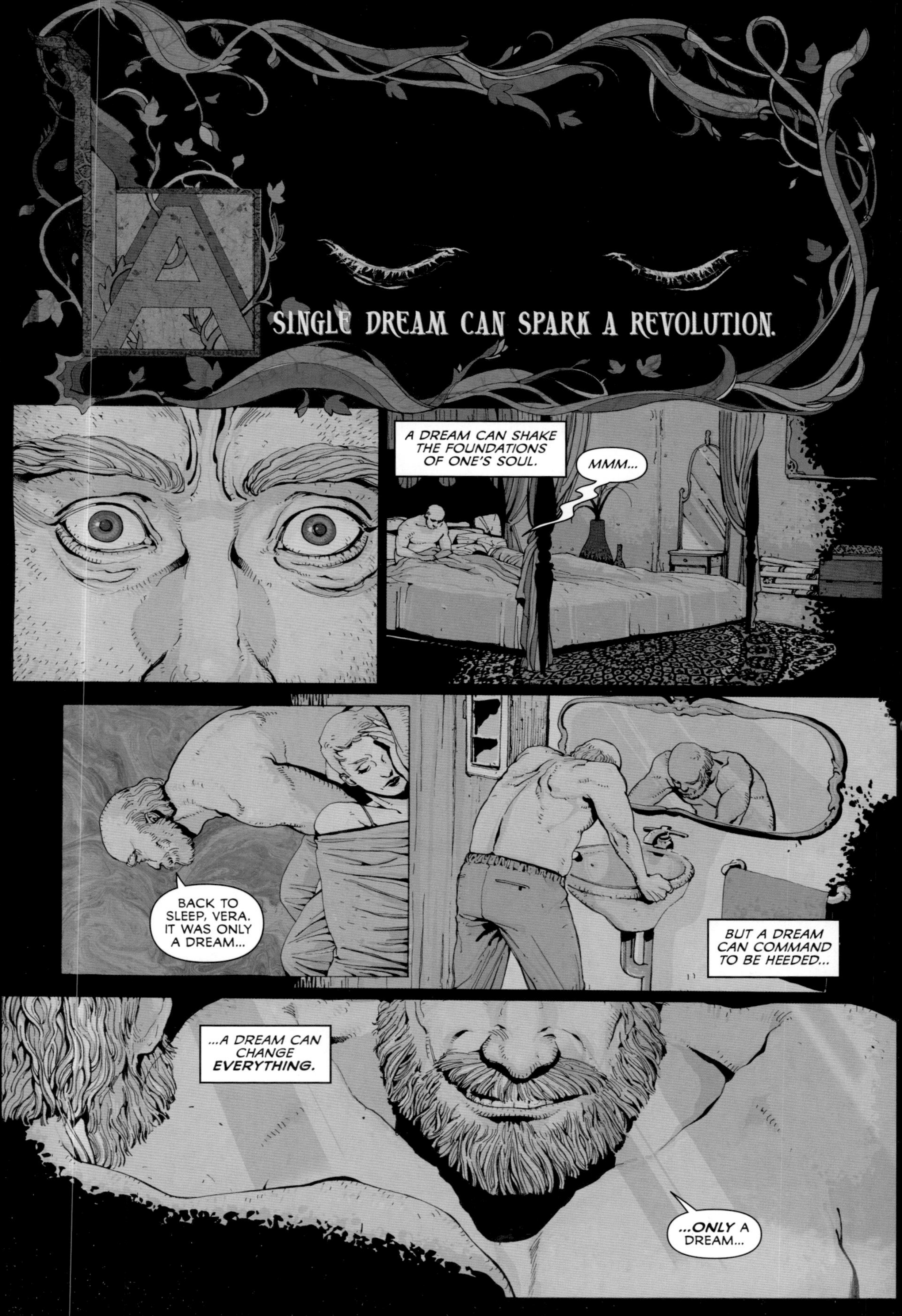
A SINGLE DREAM CAN SPARK A REVOLUTION.
A DREAM CAN SHAKE THE FOUNDATIONS OF ONE'S SOUL.
MMM...
BACK TO SLEEP, VERA. IT WAS ONLY A DREAM...
BUT A DREAM CAN COMMAND TO BE HEEDED...
...A DREAM CAN CHANGE EVERYTHING.
...ONLY A DREAM...

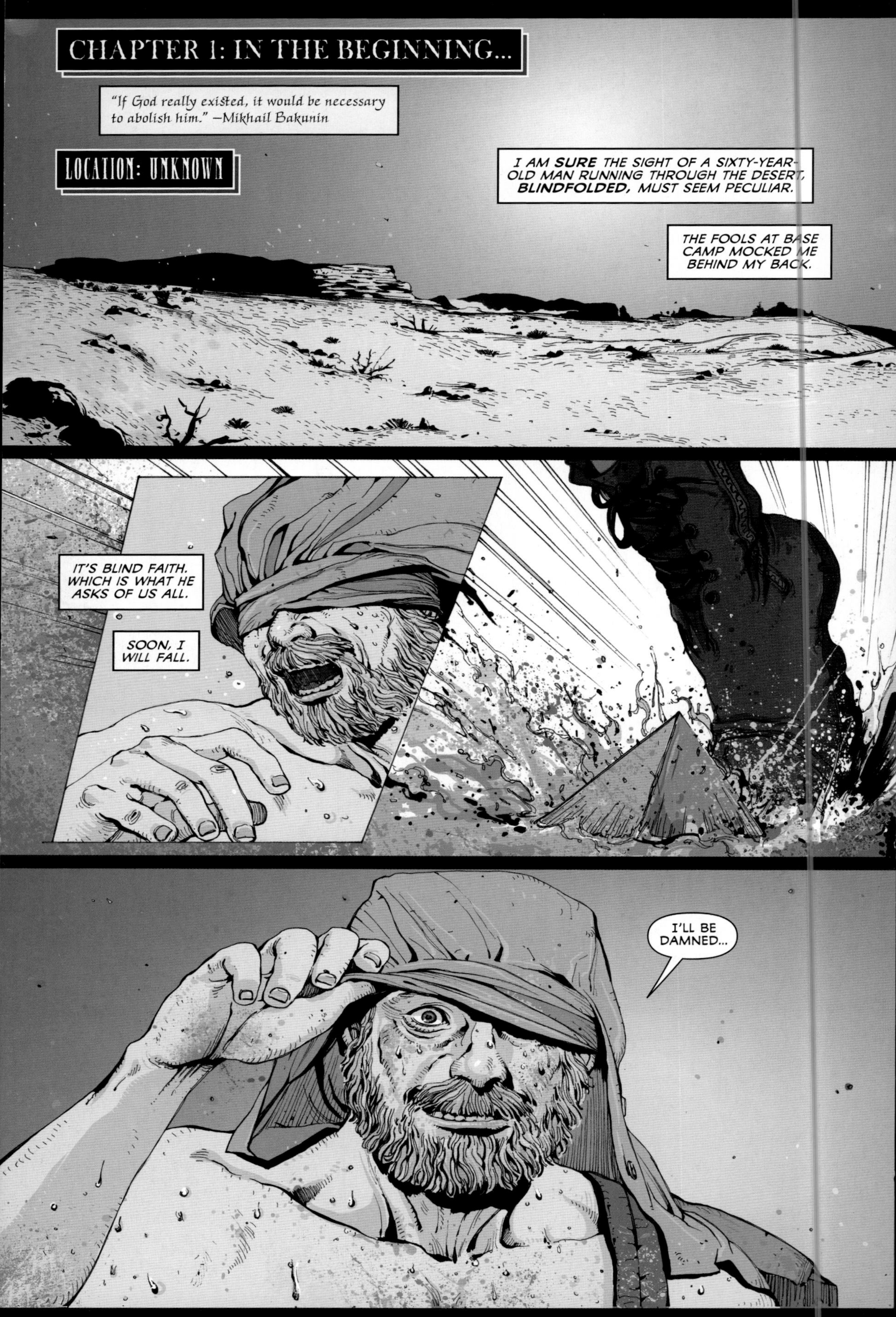
CHAPTER 1: IN THE BEGINNING...
"If God really existed, it would be necessary to abolish him." —Mikhail Bakunin
LOCATION: UNKNOWN
I AM SURE THE SIGHT OF A SIXTY-YEAR-OLD MAN RUNNING THROUGH THE DESERT, BLINDFOLDED, MUST SEEM PECULIAR.
THE FOOLS AT BASE CAMP MOCKED ME BEHIND MY BACK.
IT'S BLIND FAITH. WHICH IS WHAT HE ASKS OF US ALL.
SOON, I WILL FALL.
I'LL BE DAMNED...

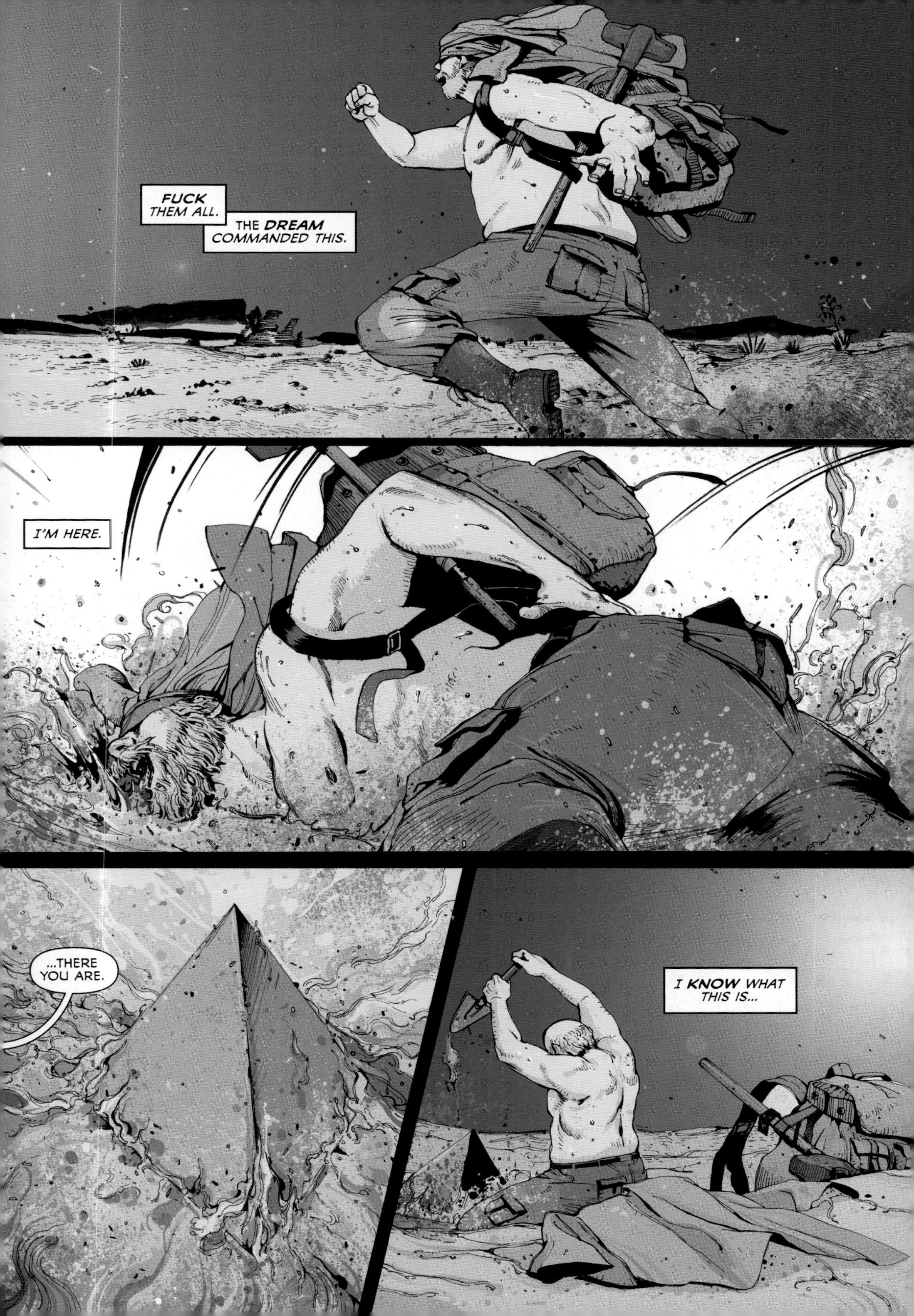
FUCK THEM ALL.
THE DREAM COMMANDED THIS.
I'M HERE.
...THERE YOU ARE.
I KNOW WHAT THIS IS...

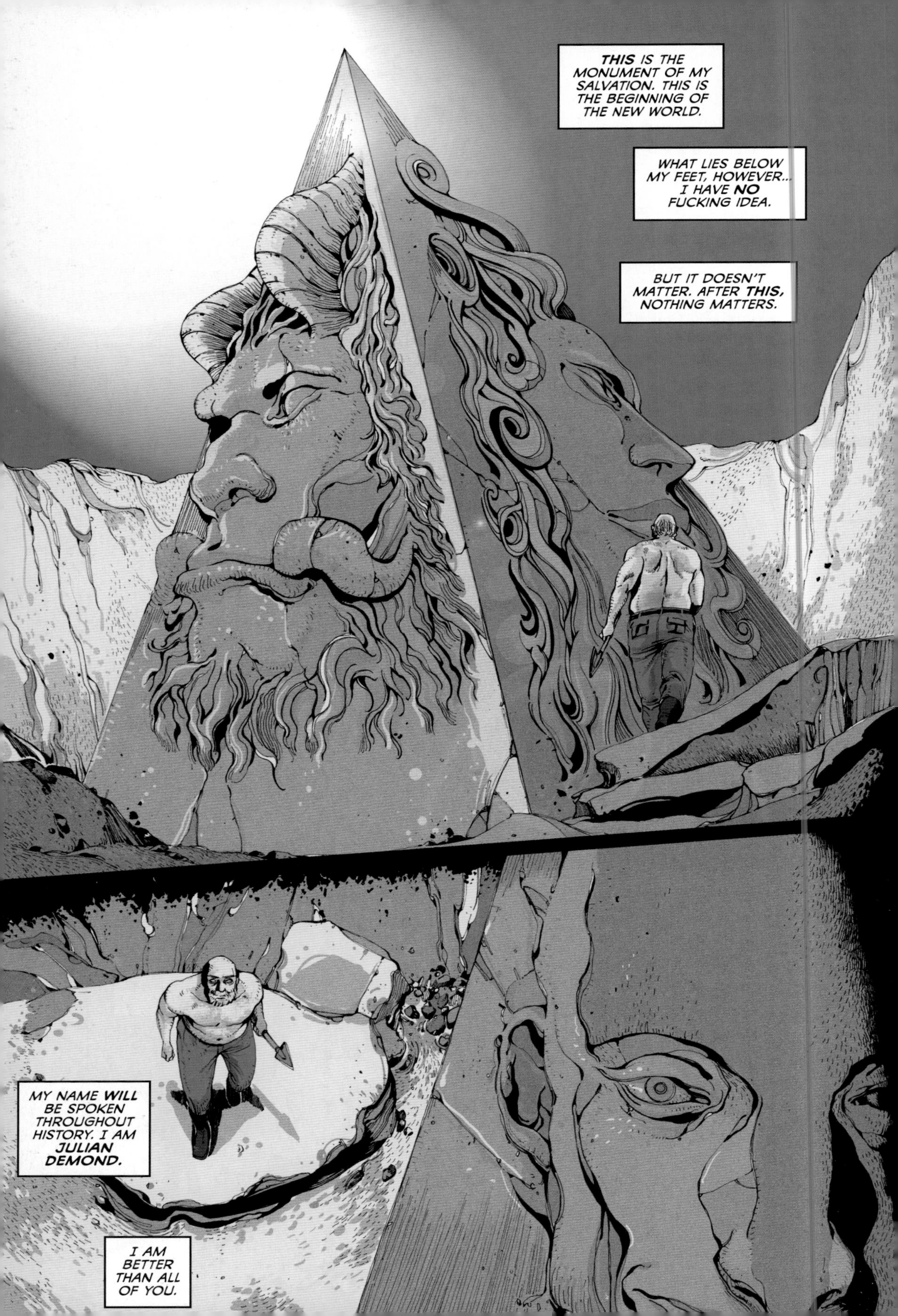
THIS IS THE MONUMENT OF MY SALVATION. THIS IS THE BEGINNING OF THE NEW WORLD.
WHAT LIES BELOW MY FEET, HOWEVER... I HAVE NO FUCKING IDEA.
BUT IT DOESN'T MATTER. AFTER THIS, NOTHING MATTERS.
MY NAME WILL BE SPOKEN THROUGHOUT HISTORY. I AM JULIAN DEMOND.
I AM BETTER THAN ALL OF YOU.

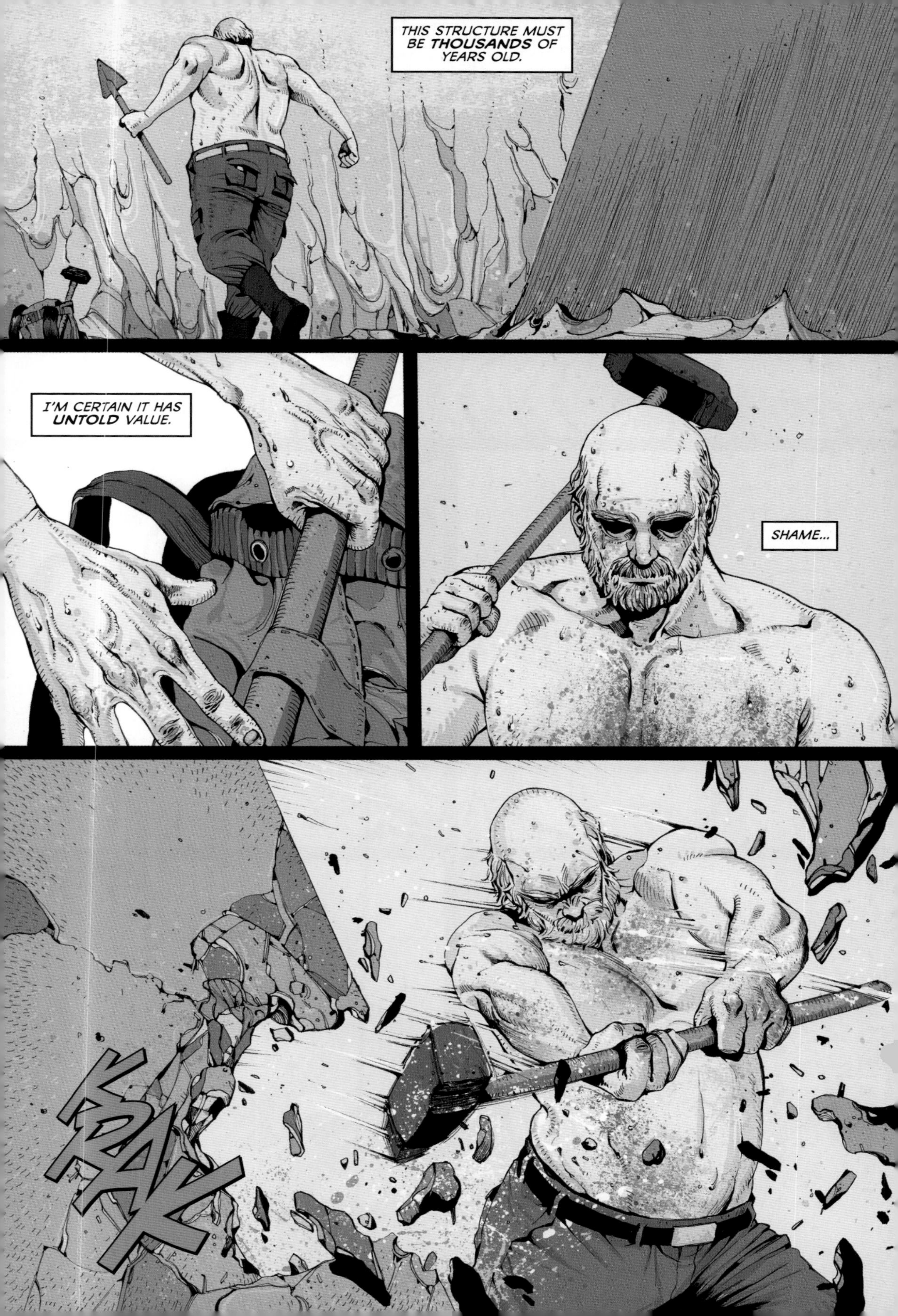
THIS STRUCTURE MUST BE **THOUSANDS** OF YEARS OLD.
I'M CERTAIN IT HAS **UNTOLD** VALUE.
SHAME...
KRAK

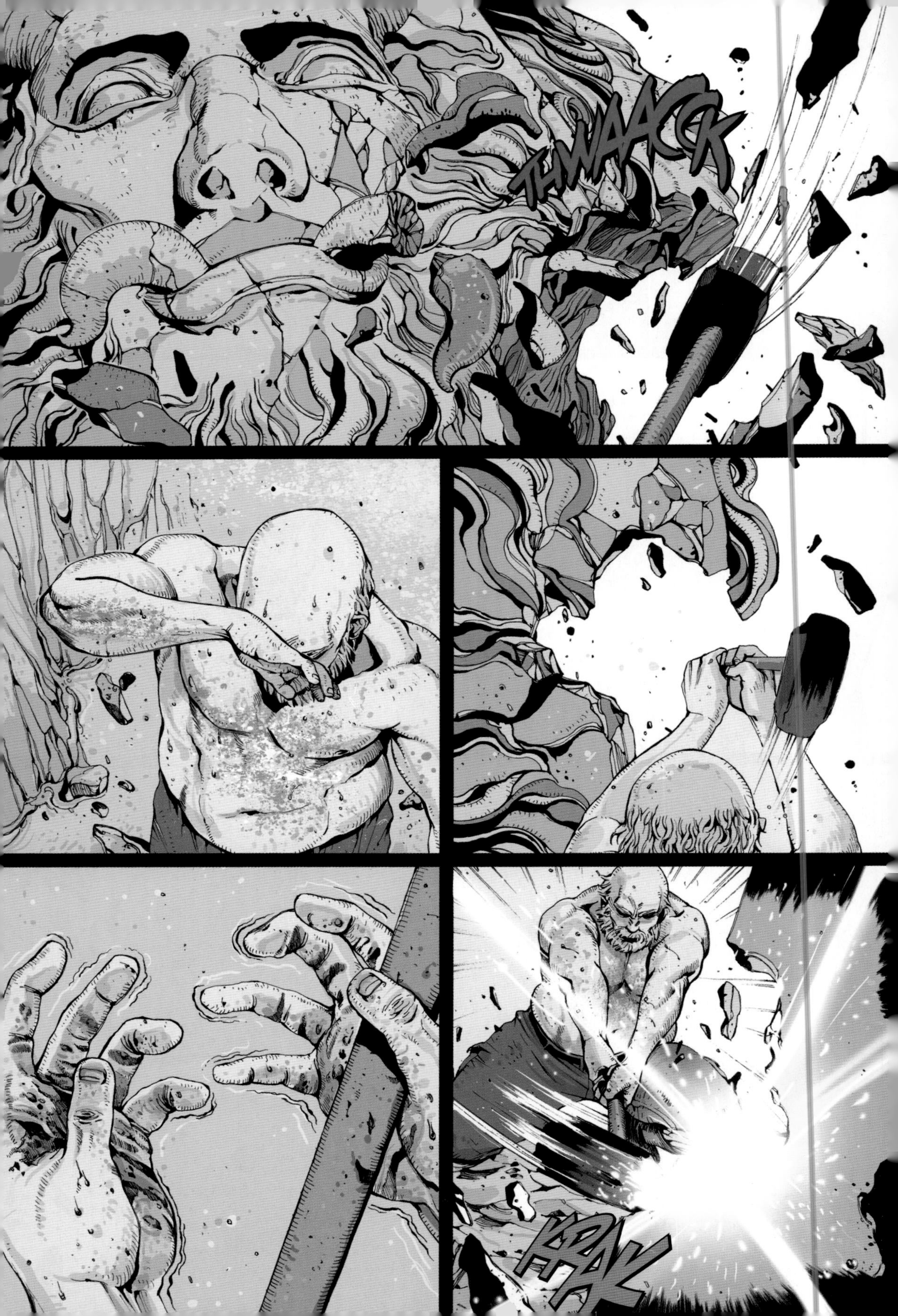
THWAACK
KRAK

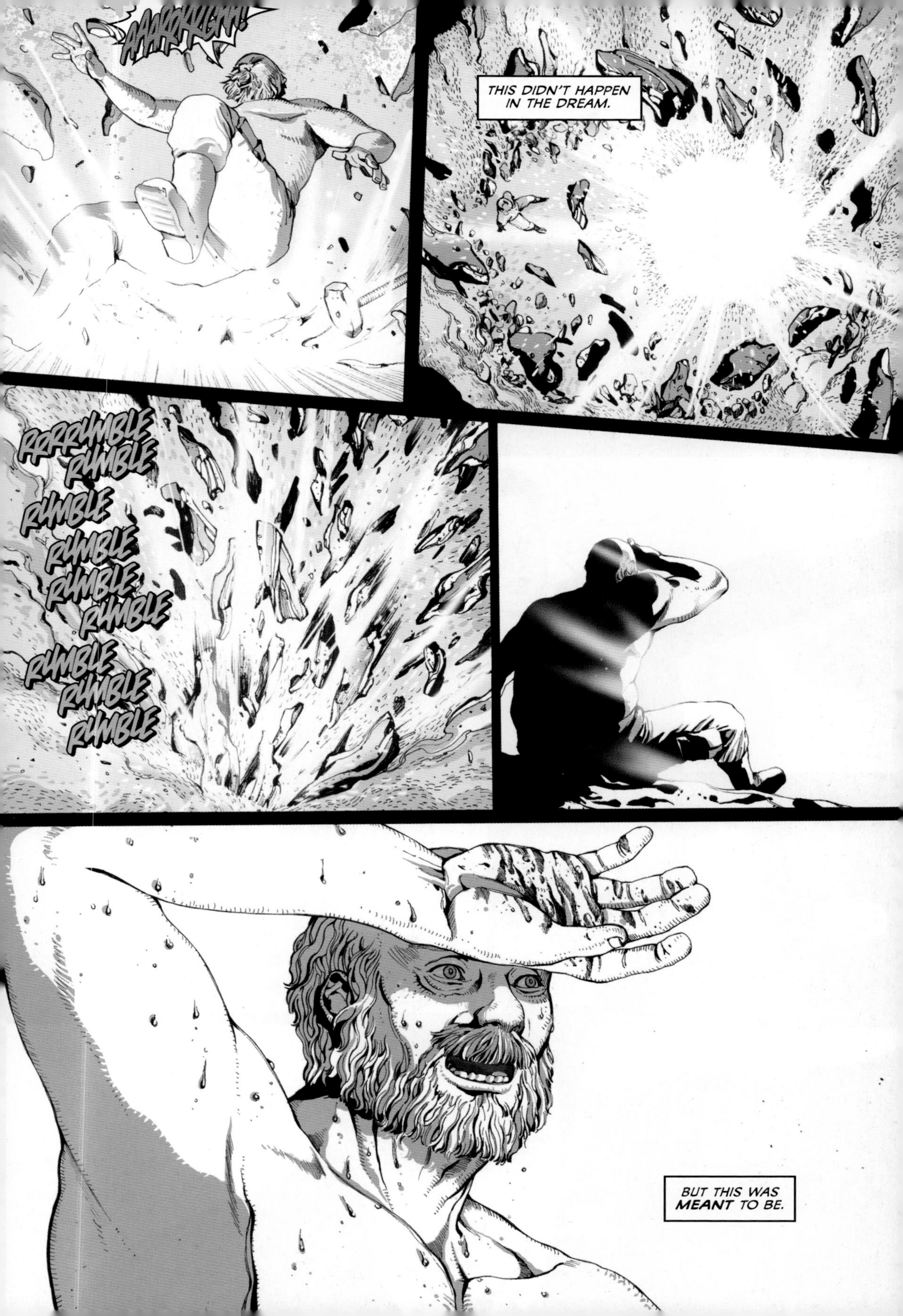
AAARRRGH!
THIS DIDN'T HAPPEN IN THE DREAM.
RRRRUMBLE RUMBLE
RUMBLE
RUMBLE
RUMBLE
RUMBLE
RUMBLE
RUMBLE
RUMBLE
BUT THIS WAS **MEANT** TO BE.

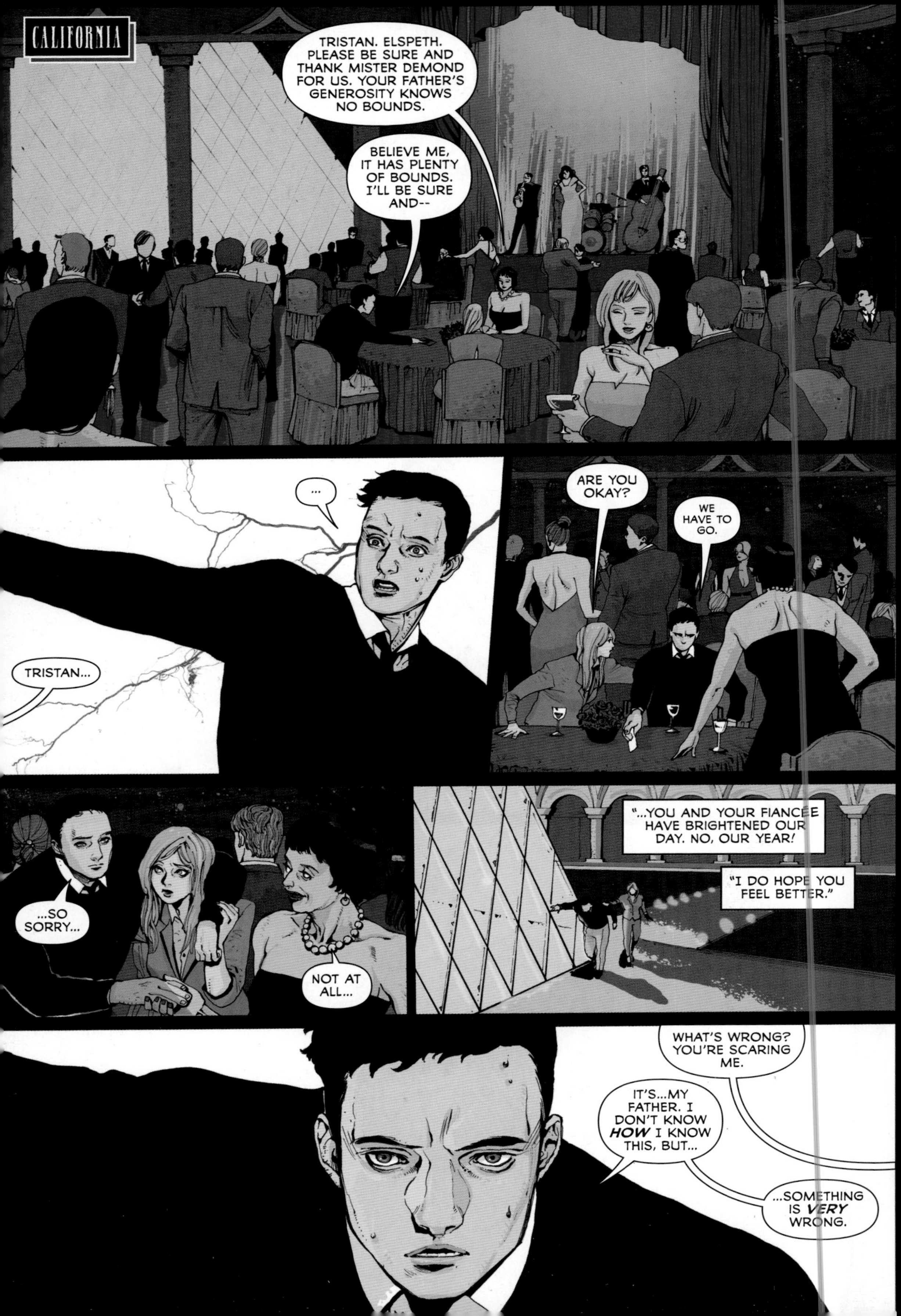
CALIFORNIA
TRISTAN. ELSPETH. PLEASE BE SURE AND THANK MISTER DEMOND FOR US. YOUR FATHER'S GENEROSITY KNOWS NO BOUNDS.
BELIEVE ME, IT HAS PLENTY OF BOUNDS. I'LL BE SURE AND--
...
TRISTAN...
ARE YOU OKAY?
WE HAVE TO GO.
...SO SORRY...
NOT AT ALL...
"...YOU AND YOUR FIANCÉE HAVE BRIGHTENED OUR DAY. NO, OUR YEAR!
"I DO HOPE YOU FEEL BETTER."
WHAT'S WRONG? YOU'RE SCARING ME.
IT'S...MY FATHER. I DON'T KNOW *HOW* I KNOW THIS, BUT...
...SOMETHING IS *VERY* WRONG.

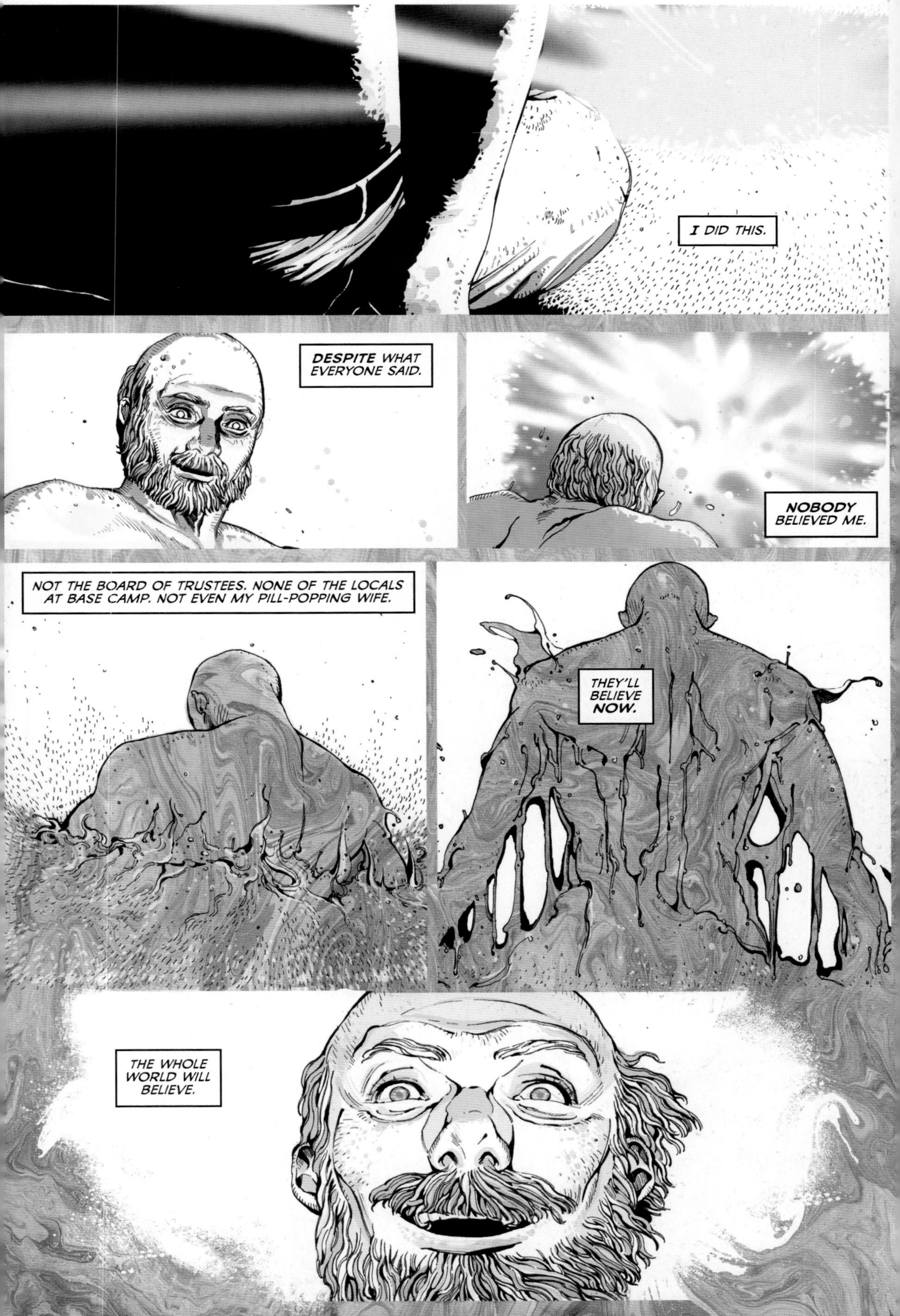
I DID THIS.
DESPITE WHAT EVERYONE SAID.
NOBODY BELIEVED ME.
NOT THE BOARD OF TRUSTEES. NONE OF THE LOCALS AT BASE CAMP. NOT EVEN MY PILL-POPPING WIFE.
THEY'LL BELIEVE NOW.
THE WHOLE WORLD WILL BELIEVE.

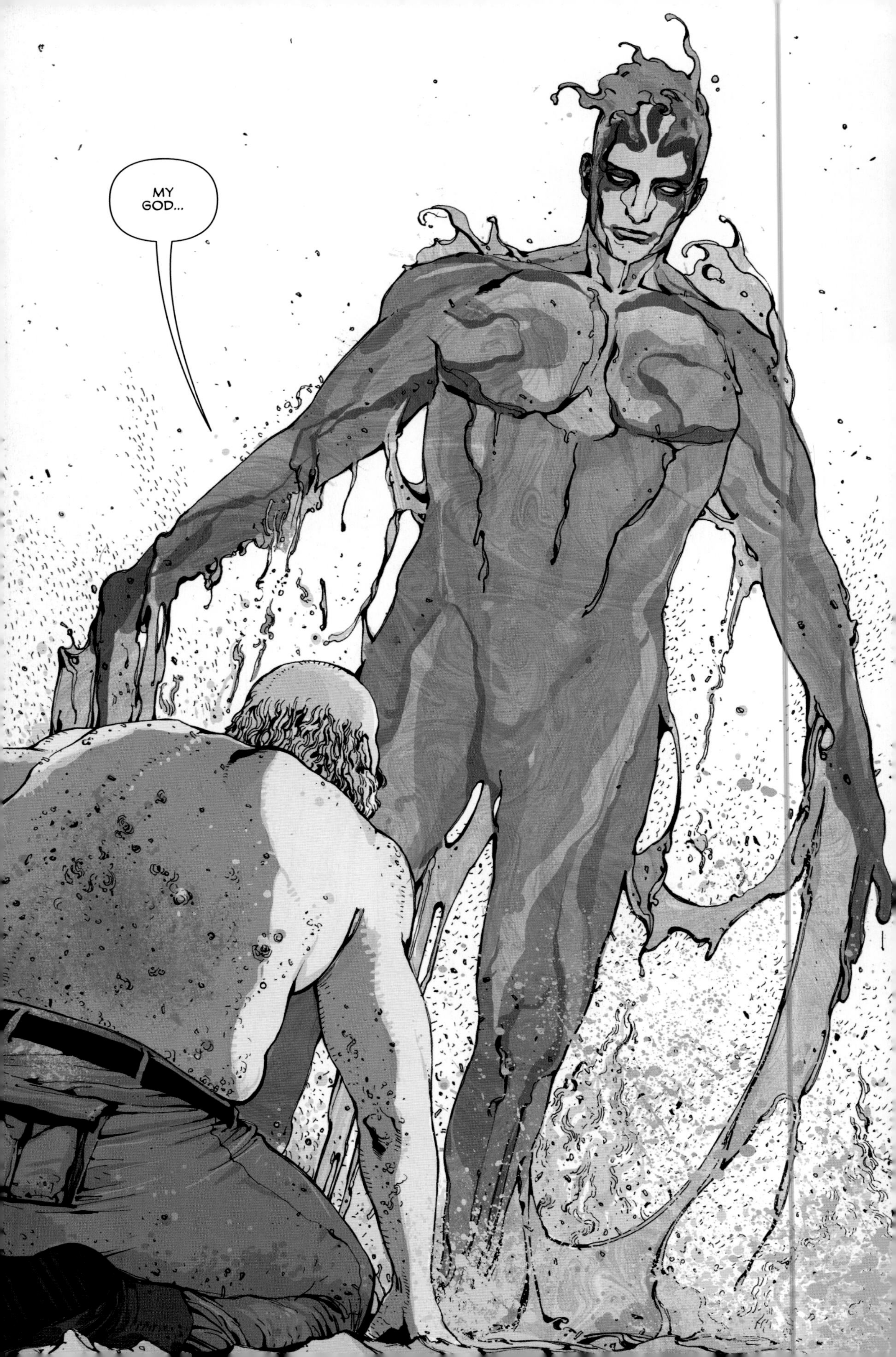
MY GOD...

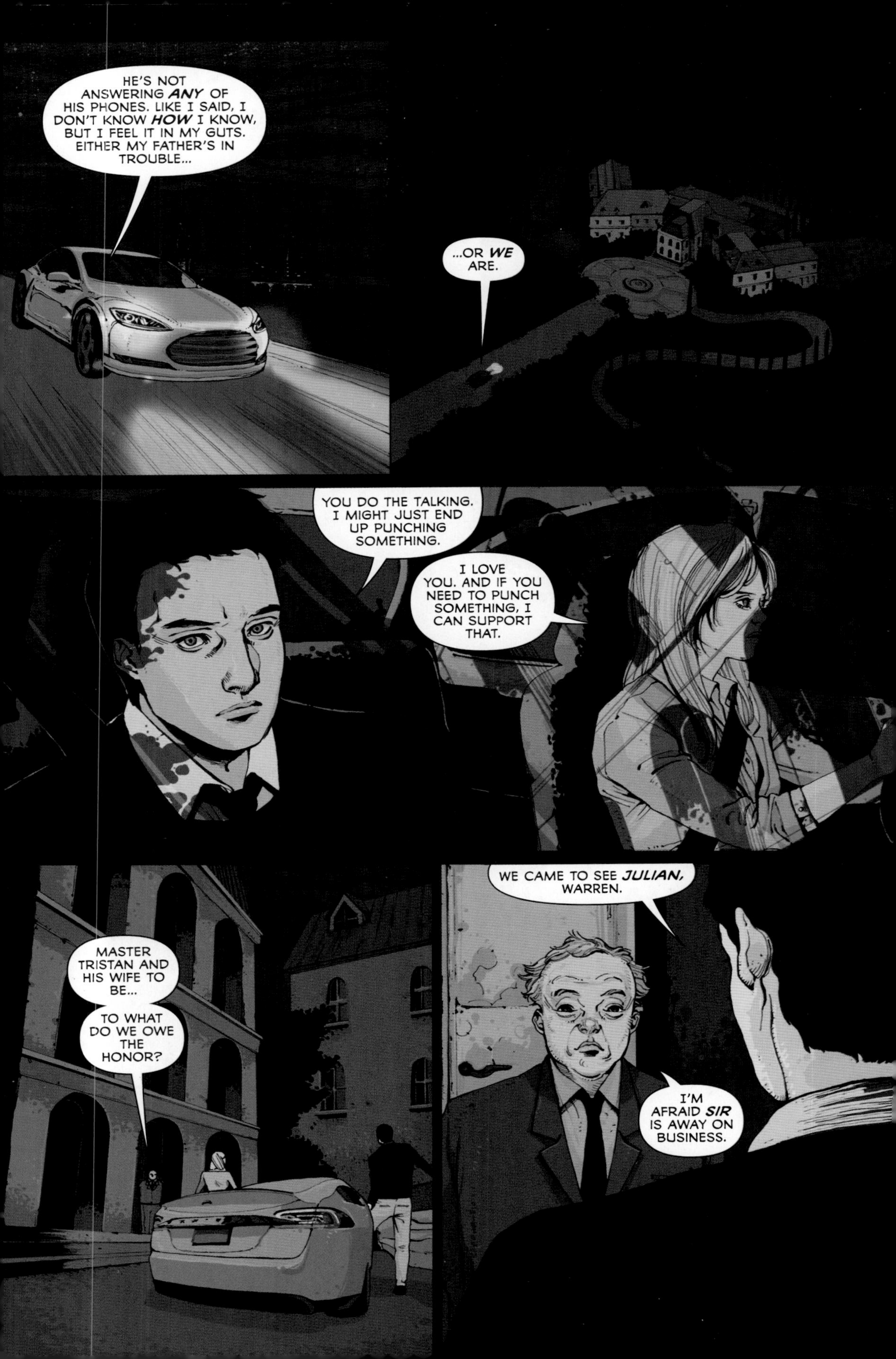

HE'S NOT ANSWERING ANY OF HIS PHONES. LIKE I SAID, I DON'T KNOW HOW I KNOW, BUT I FEEL IT IN MY GUTS. EITHER MY FATHER'S IN TROUBLE...
...OR WE ARE.
YOU DO THE TALKING. I MIGHT JUST END UP PUNCHING SOMETHING.
I LOVE YOU. AND IF YOU NEED TO PUNCH SOMETHING, I CAN SUPPORT THAT.
MASTER TRISTAN AND HIS WIFE TO BE...
TO WHAT DO WE OWE THE HONOR?
WE CAME TO SEE JULIAN, WARREN.
I'M AFRAID SIR IS AWAY ON BUSINESS.

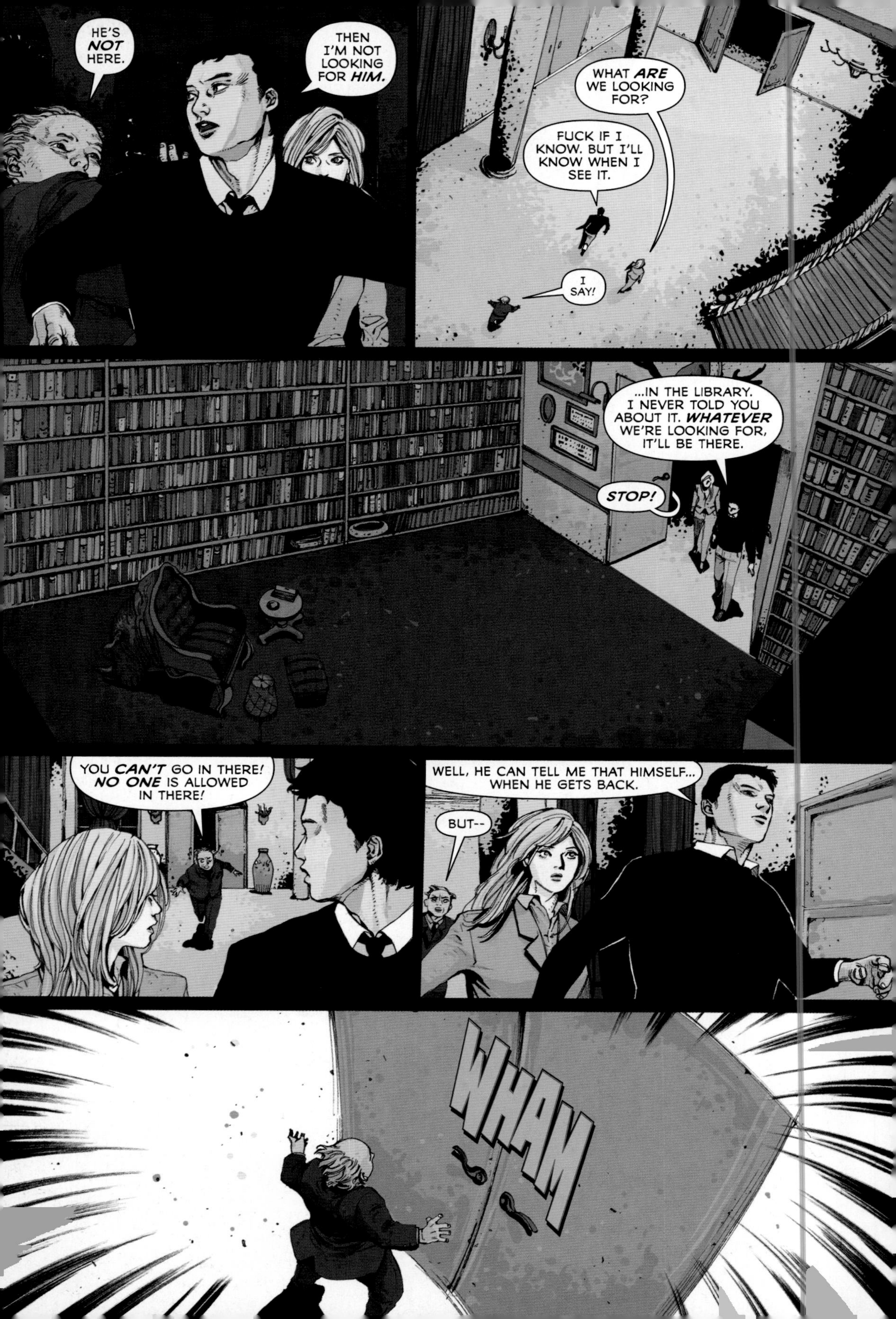
HE'S NOT HERE.
THEN I'M NOT LOOKING FOR HIM.
WHAT ARE WE LOOKING FOR?
FUCK IF I KNOW. BUT I'LL KNOW WHEN I SEE IT.
I SAY!
...IN THE LIBRARY. I NEVER TOLD YOU ABOUT IT. WHATEVER WE'RE LOOKING FOR, IT'LL BE THERE.
STOP!
YOU CAN'T GO IN THERE! NO ONE IS ALLOWED IN THERE!
WELL, HE CAN TELL ME THAT HIMSELF... WHEN HE GETS BACK.
BUT--
WHAM

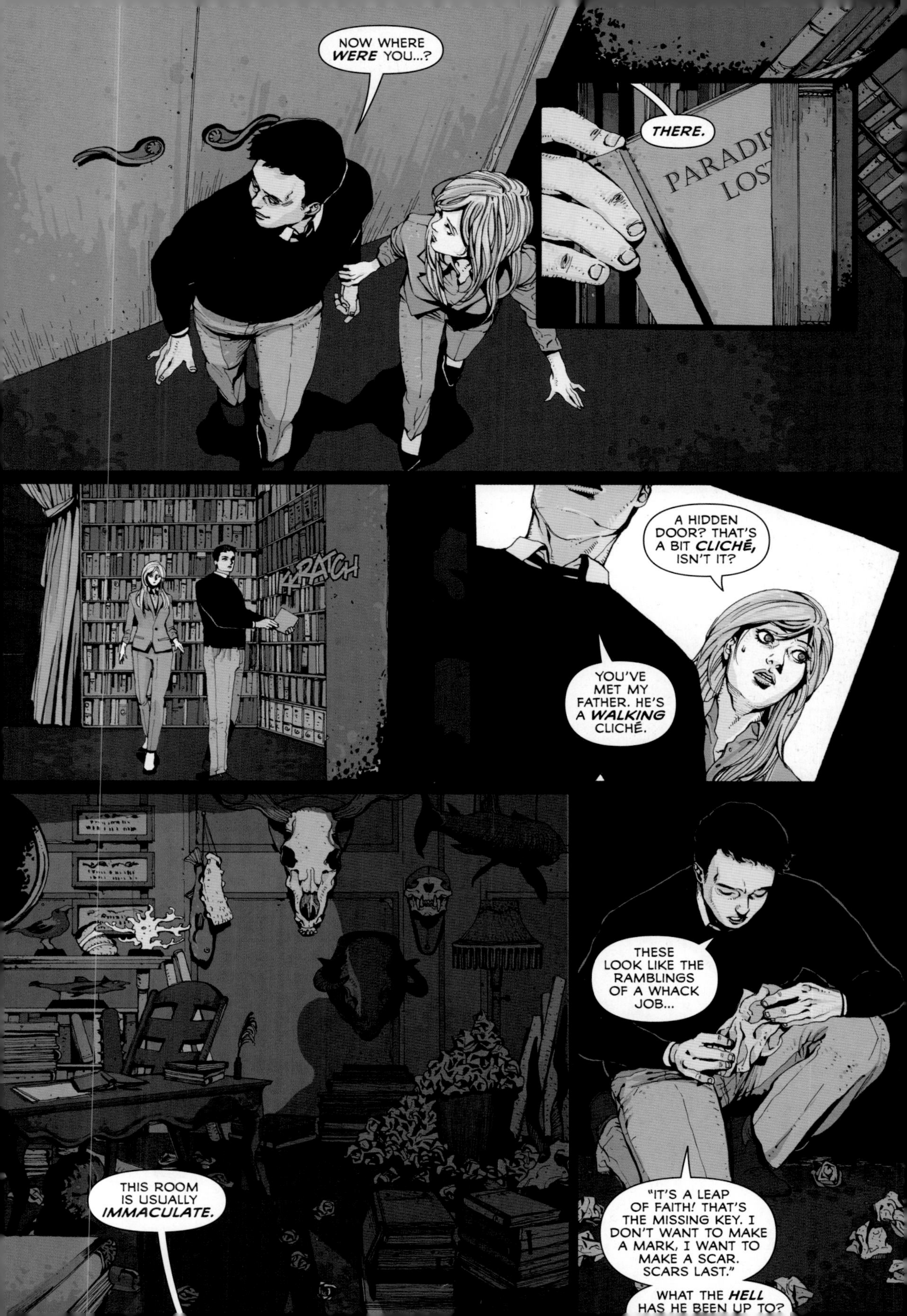
NOW WHERE *WERE* YOU...?
THERE.
PARADISE LOST
KRATCH
A HIDDEN DOOR? THAT'S A BIT *CLICHÉ,* ISN'T IT?
YOU'VE MET MY FATHER. HE'S A *WALKING* CLICHÉ.
THIS ROOM IS USUALLY *IMMACULATE.*
THESE LOOK LIKE THE RAMBLINGS OF A WHACK JOB...
"IT'S A LEAP OF FAITH! THAT'S THE MISSING KEY. I DON'T WANT TO MAKE A MARK, I WANT TO MAKE A SCAR. SCARS LAST."
WHAT THE *HELL* HAS HE BEEN UP TO?

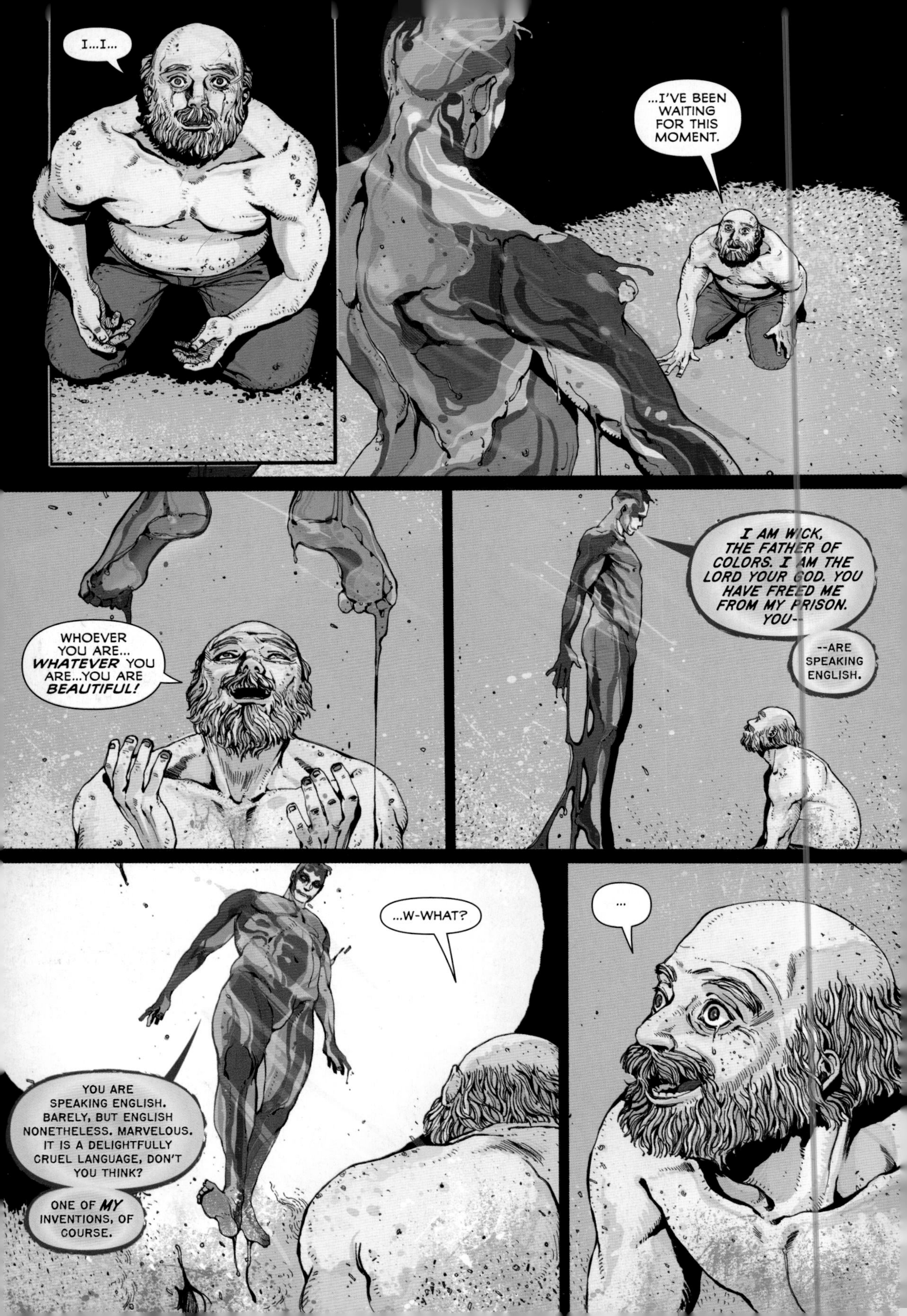
I...I...
...I'VE BEEN WAITING FOR THIS MOMENT.
WHOEVER YOU ARE... WHATEVER YOU ARE...YOU ARE BEAUTIFUL!
I AM WICK, THE FATHER OF COLORS. I AM THE LORD YOUR GOD. YOU HAVE FREED ME FROM MY PRISON. YOU--
--ARE SPEAKING ENGLISH.
...W-WHAT?
YOU ARE SPEAKING ENGLISH. BARELY, BUT ENGLISH NONETHELESS. MARVELOUS. IT IS A DELIGHTFULLY CRUEL LANGUAGE, DON'T YOU THINK?
ONE OF MY INVENTIONS, OF COURSE.
...

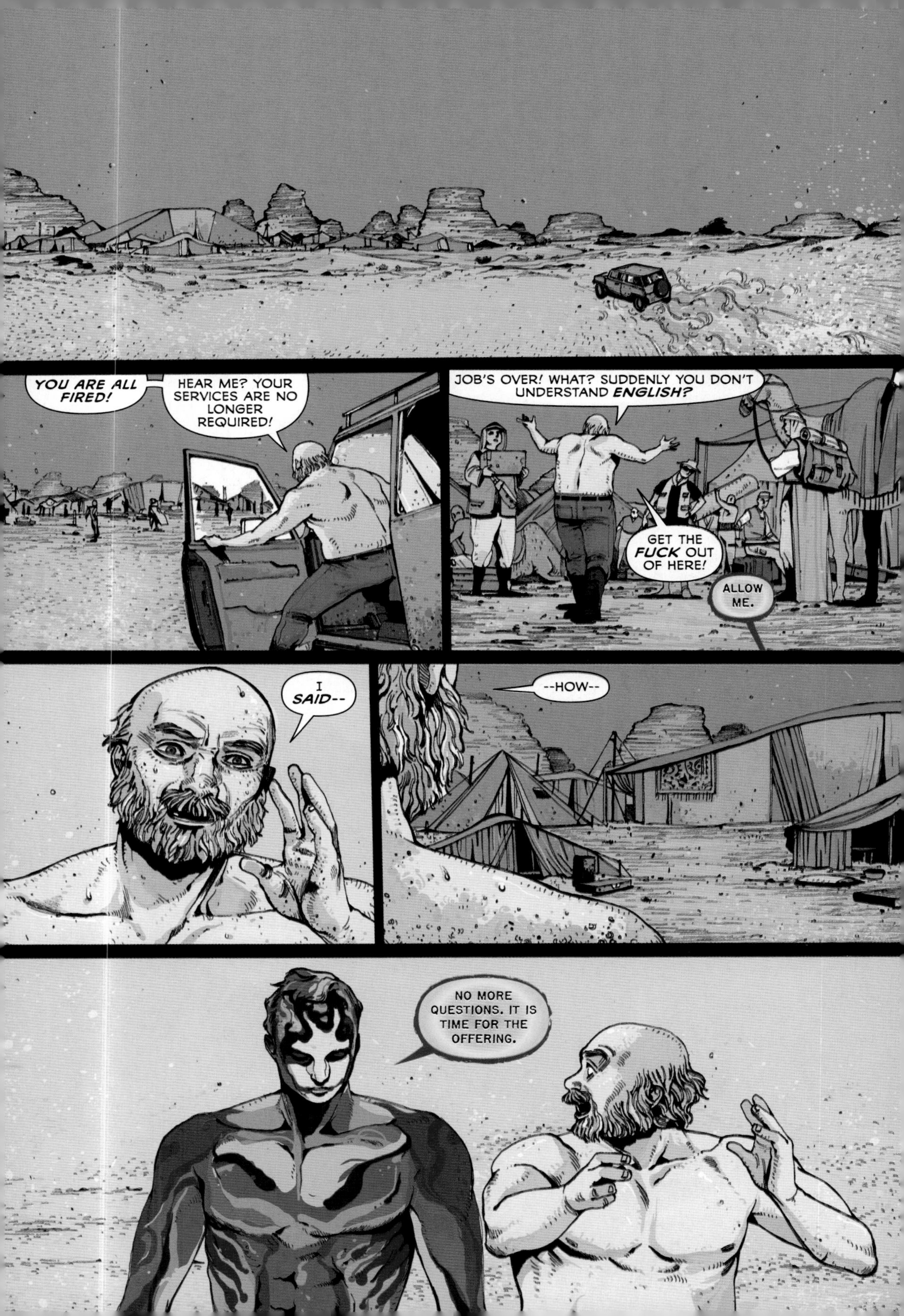
YOU ARE ALL FIRED!
HEAR ME? YOUR SERVICES ARE NO LONGER REQUIRED!
JOB'S OVER! WHAT? SUDDENLY YOU DON'T UNDERSTAND ENGLISH?
GET THE FUCK OUT OF HERE!
ALLOW ME.
I SAID--
--HOW--
NO MORE QUESTIONS. IT IS TIME FOR THE OFFERING.

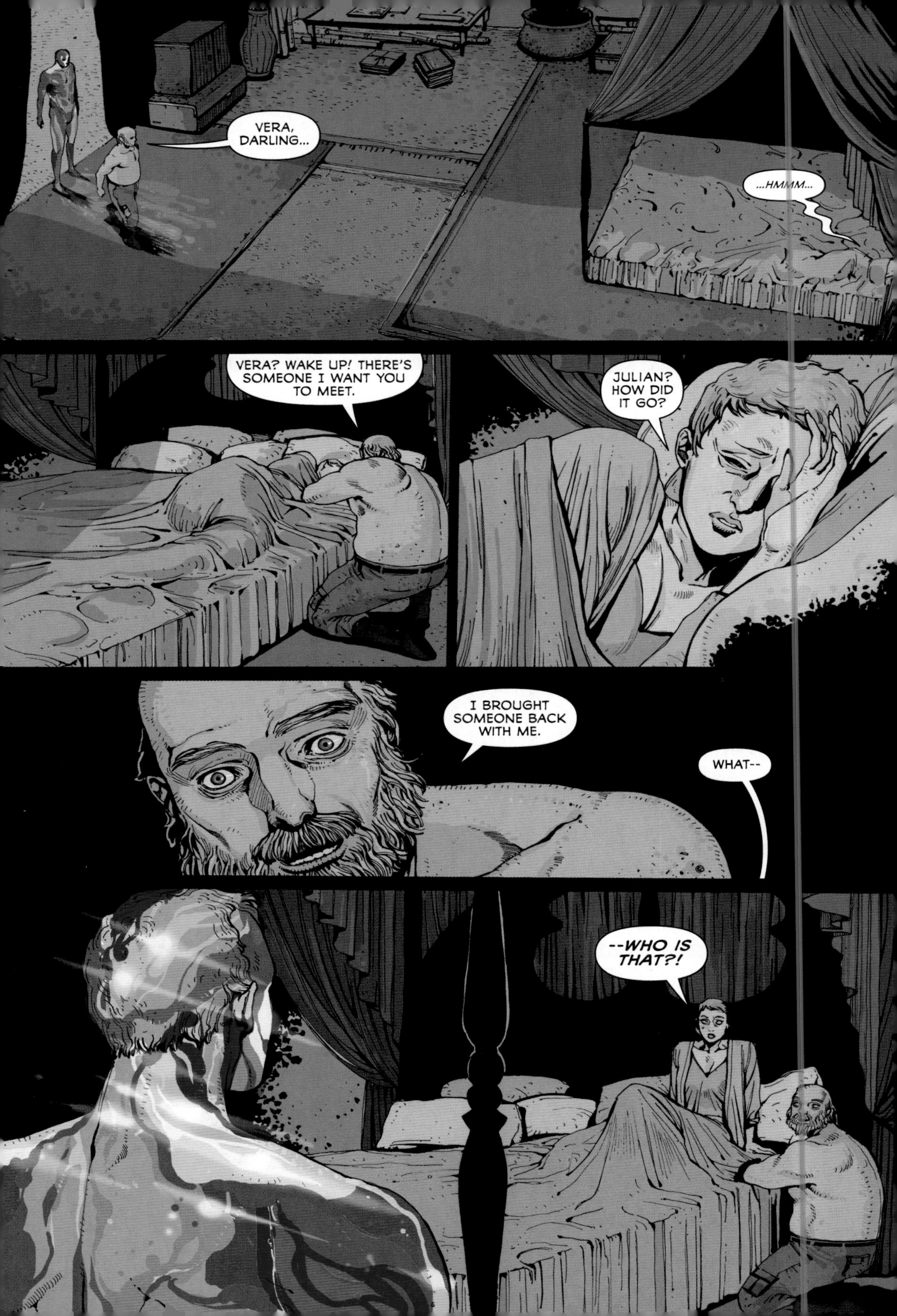
VERA, DARLING...
...HMMM...
VERA? WAKE UP! THERE'S SOMEONE I WANT YOU TO MEET.
JULIAN? HOW DID IT GO?
I BROUGHT SOMEONE BACK WITH ME.
WHAT--
--WHO IS THAT?!

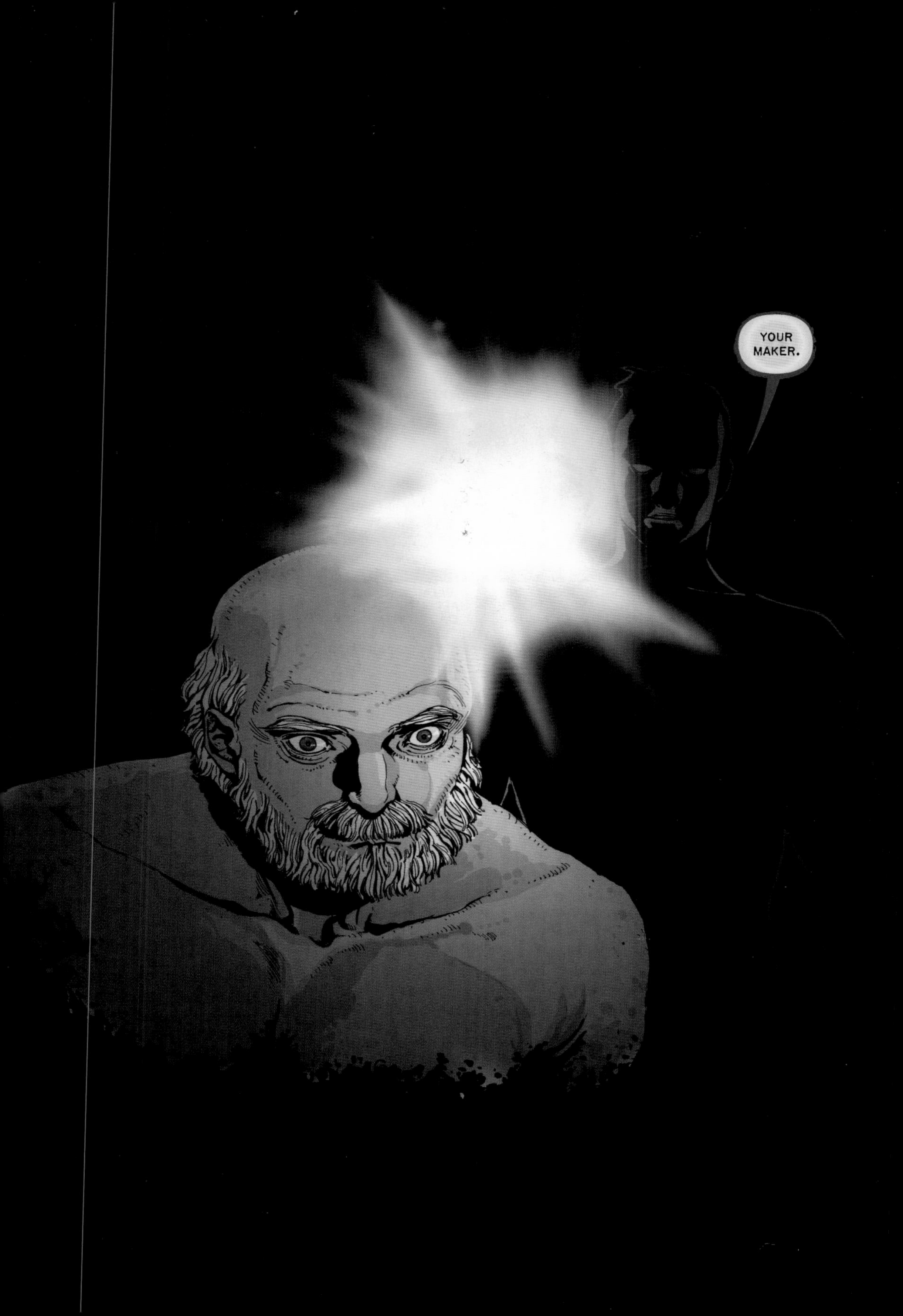
YOUR MAKER.

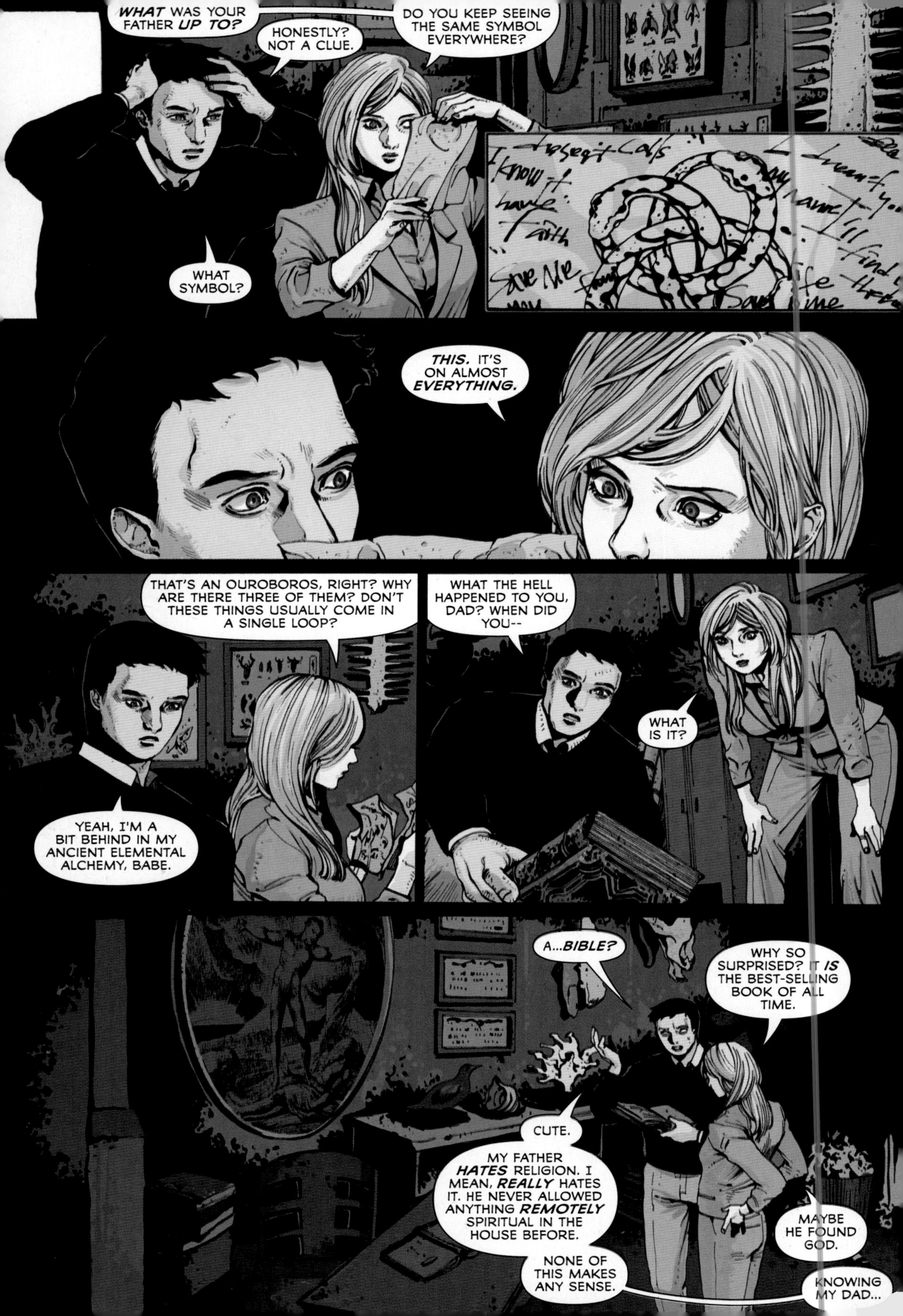
WHAT WAS YOUR FATHER UP TO?
HONESTLY? NOT A CLUE.
DO YOU KEEP SEEING THE SAME SYMBOL EVERYWHERE?
WHAT SYMBOL?
THIS. IT'S ON ALMOST EVERYTHING.
THAT'S AN OUROBOROS, RIGHT? WHY ARE THERE THREE OF THEM? DON'T THESE THINGS USUALLY COME IN A SINGLE LOOP?
YEAH, I'M A BIT BEHIND IN MY ANCIENT ELEMENTAL ALCHEMY, BABE.
WHAT THE HELL HAPPENED TO YOU, DAD? WHEN DID YOU--
WHAT IS IT?
A...BIBLE?
WHY SO SURPRISED? IT IS THE BEST-SELLING BOOK OF ALL TIME.
CUTE.
MY FATHER HATES RELIGION. I MEAN, REALLY HATES IT. HE NEVER ALLOWED ANYTHING REMOTELY SPIRITUAL IN THE HOUSE BEFORE.
MAYBE HE FOUND GOD.
NONE OF THIS MAKES ANY SENSE.
KNOWING MY DAD...

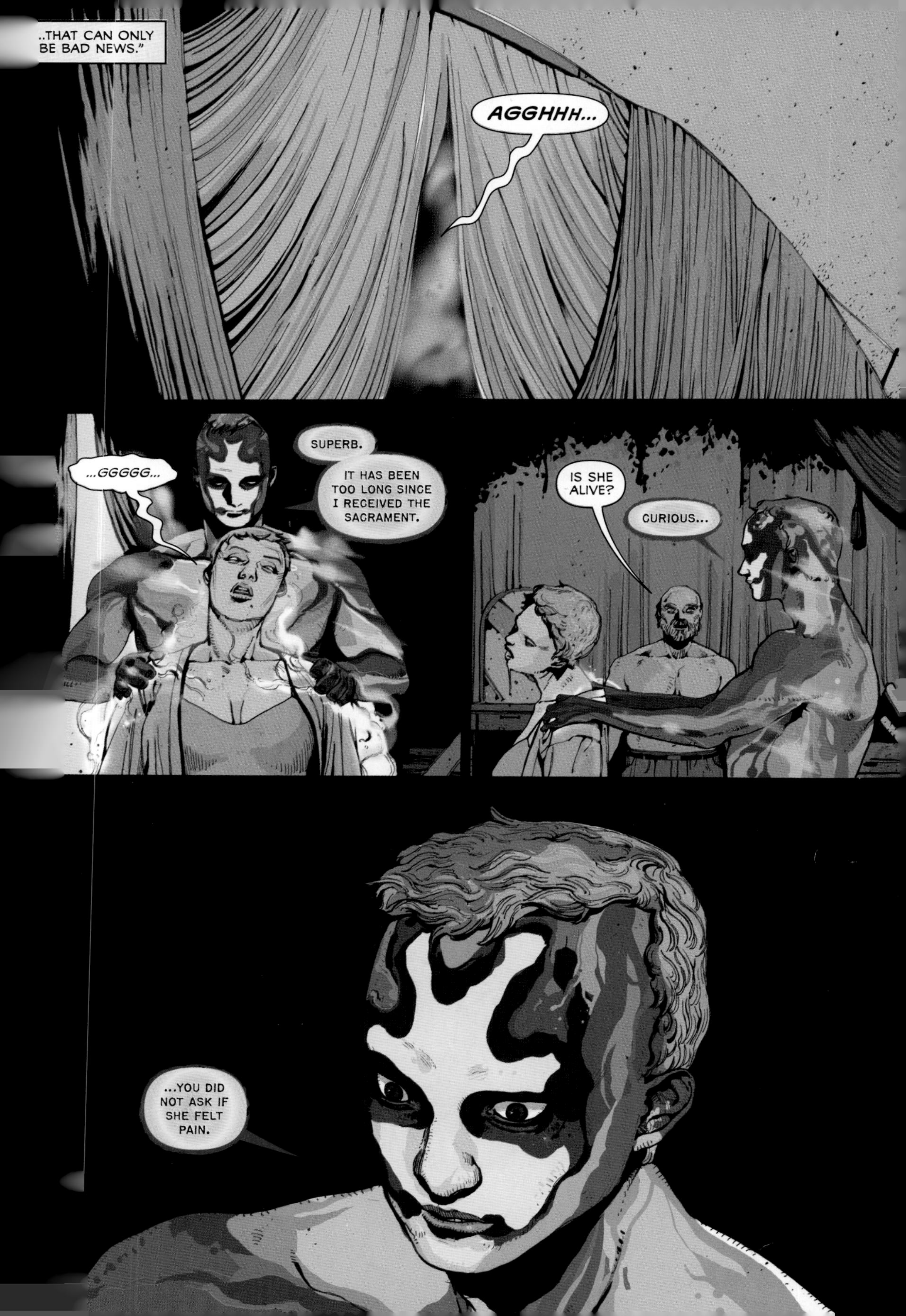
..THAT CAN ONLY BE BAD NEWS."
AGGHHH...
...GGGGG...
SUPERB.
IT HAS BEEN TOO LONG SINCE I RECEIVED THE SACRAMENT.
IS SHE ALIVE?
CURIOUS...
...YOU DID NOT ASK IF SHE FELT PAIN.

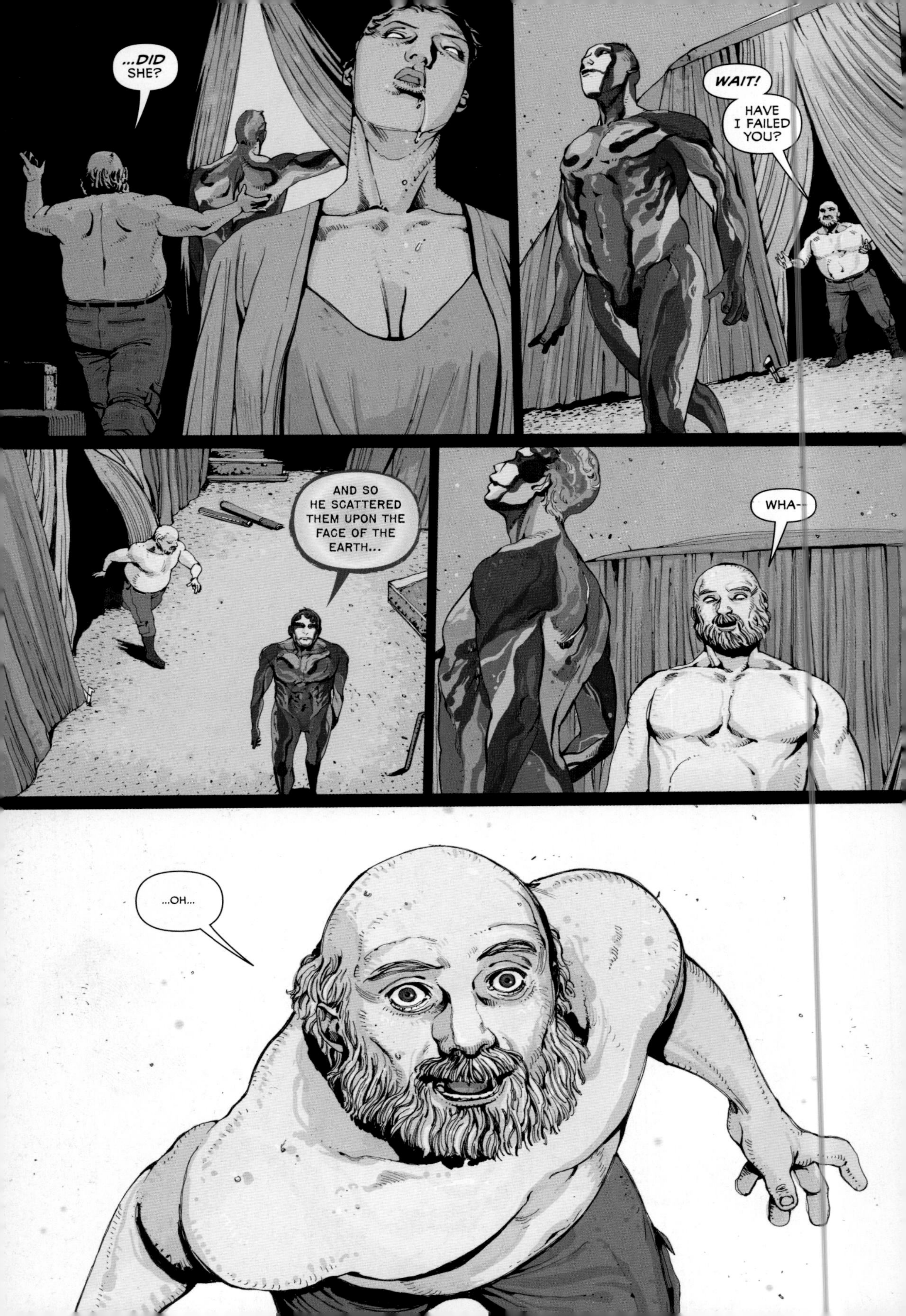

...DID SHE?
WAIT!
HAVE I FAILED YOU?
AND SO HE SCATTERED THEM UPON THE FACE OF THE EARTH...
WHA--
...OH...

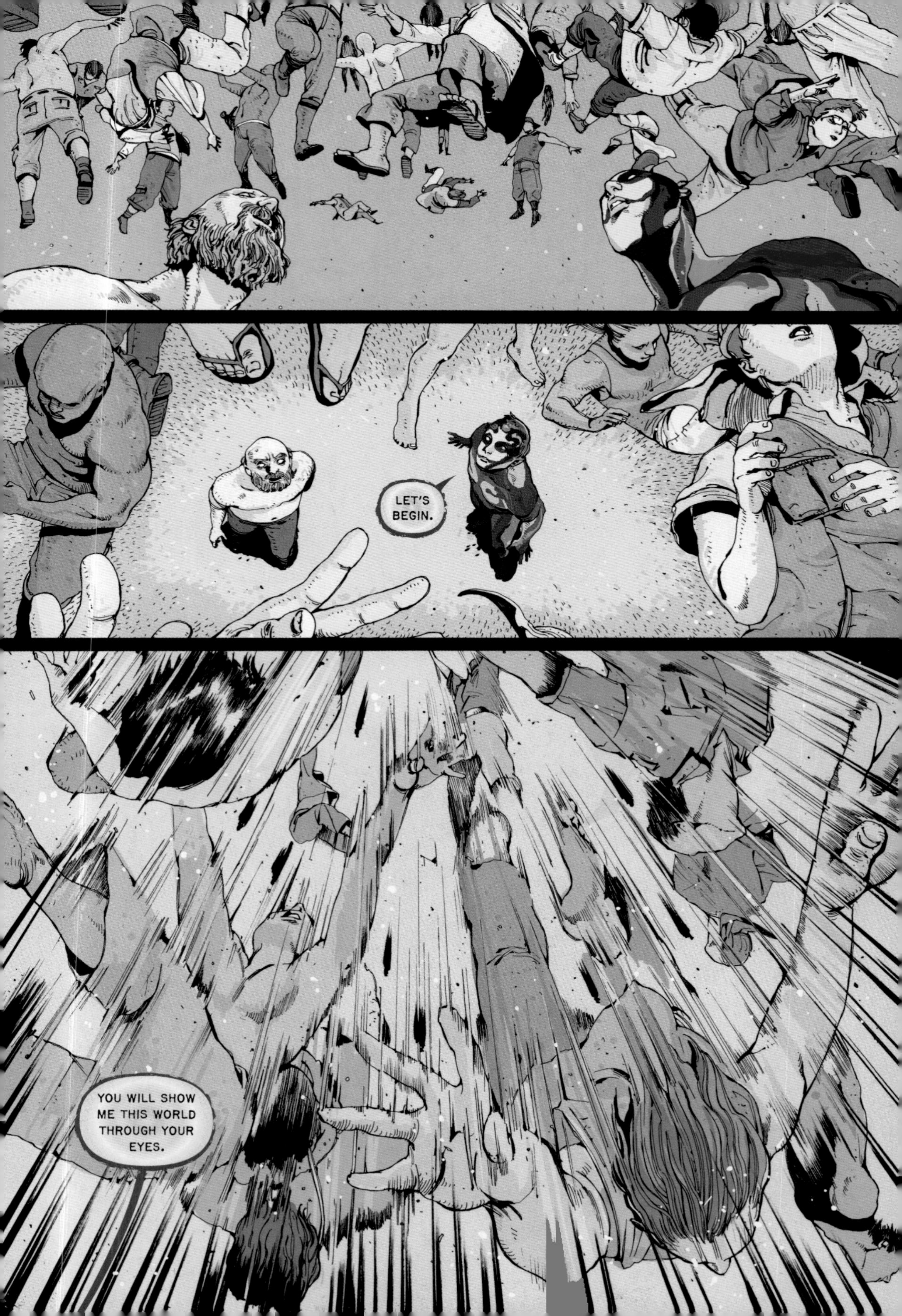
LET'S BEGIN.
YOU WILL SHOW ME THIS WORLD THROUGH YOUR EYES.

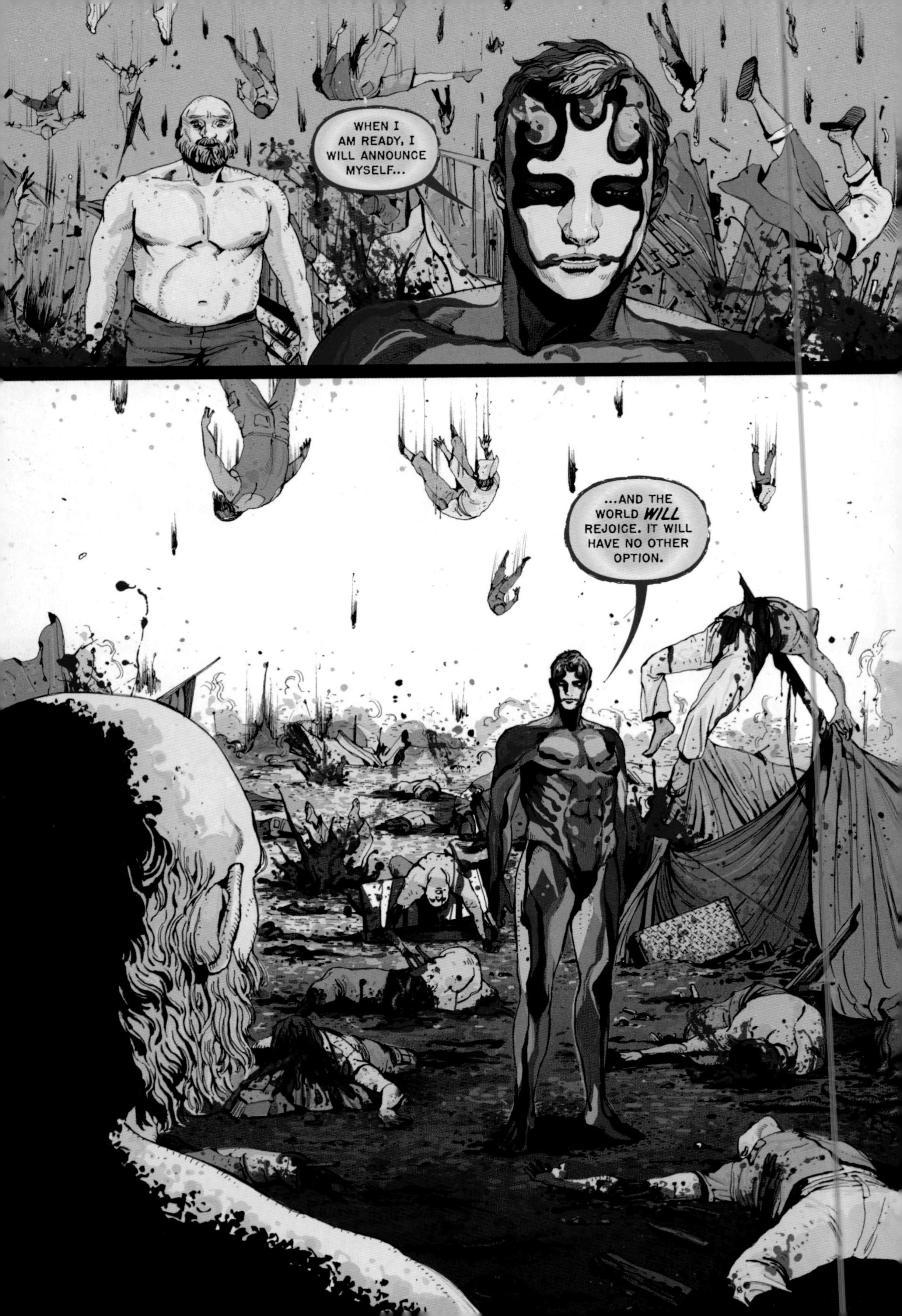
WHEN I AM READY, I WILL ANNOUNCE MYSELF...
...AND THE WORLD WILL REJOICE. IT WILL HAVE NO OTHER OPTION.

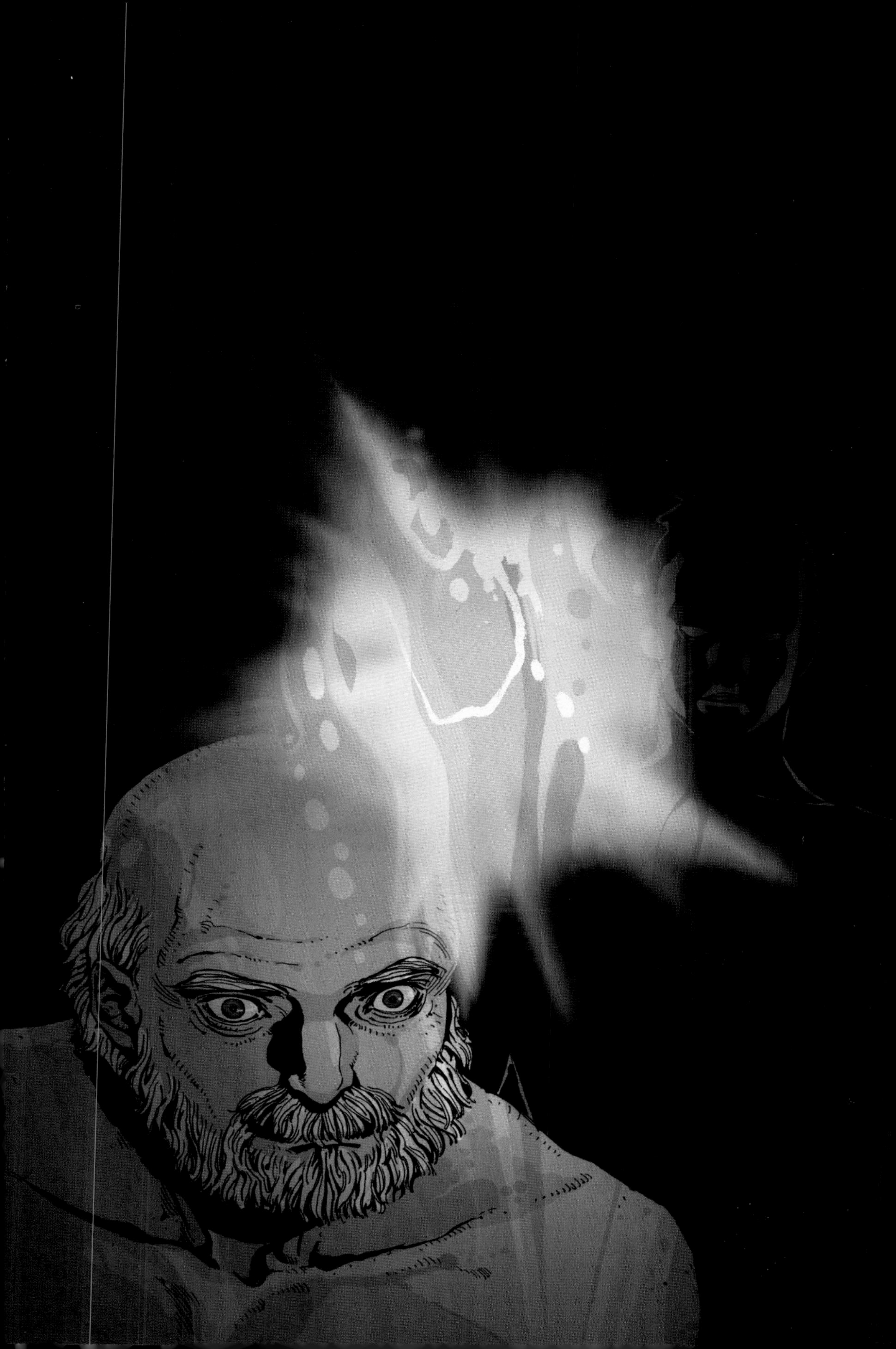

CHAPTER TWO

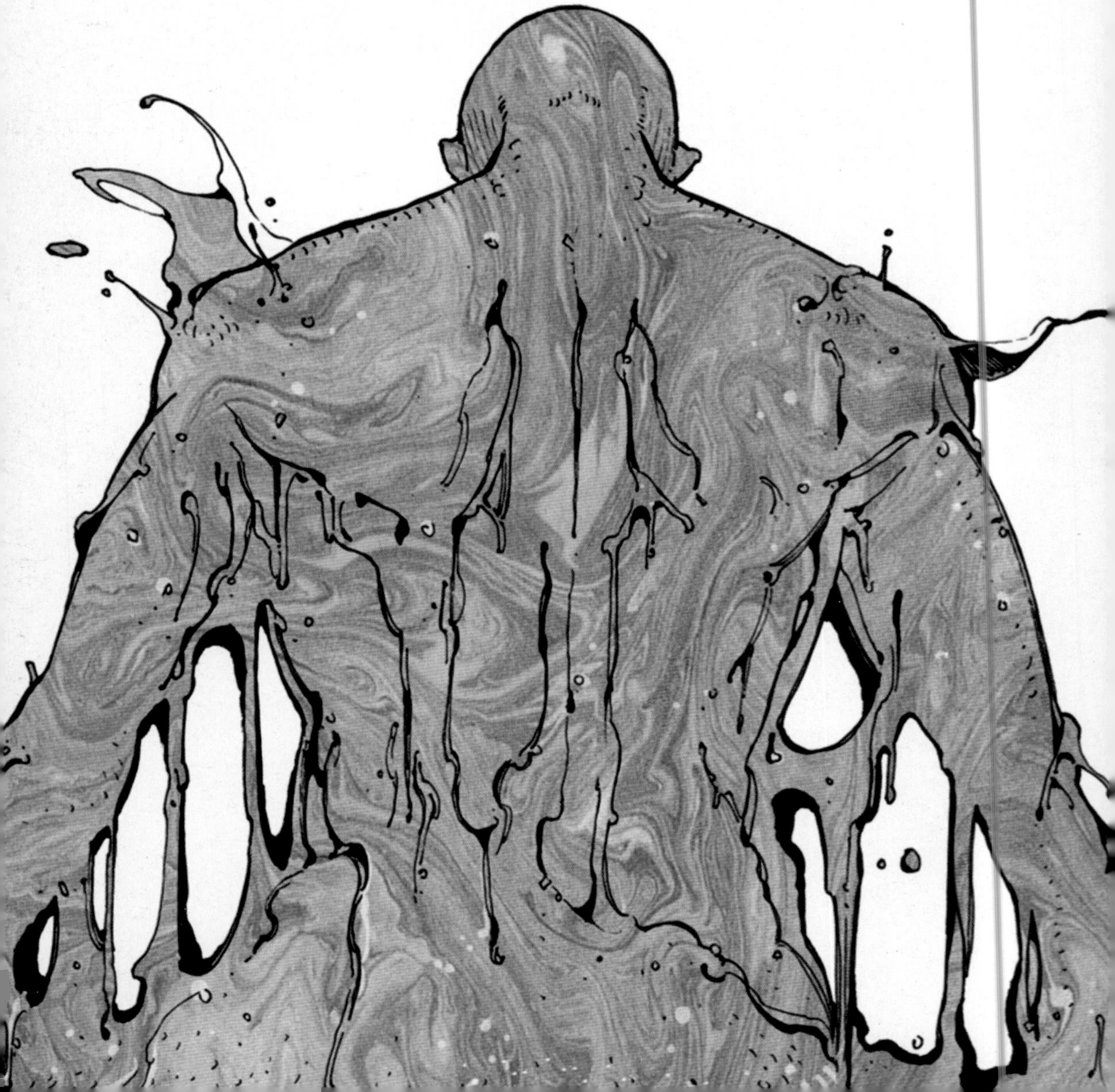

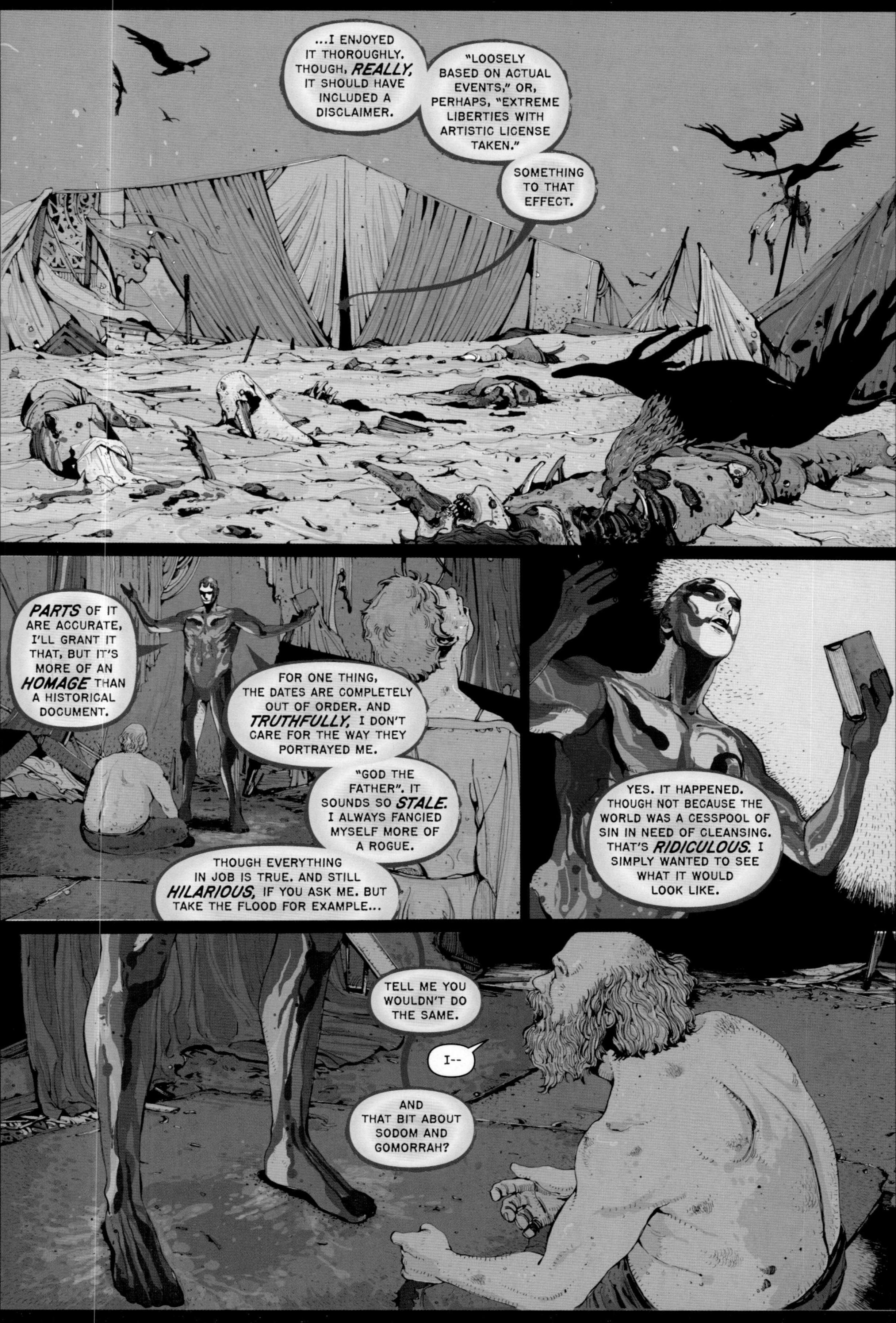
...I ENJOYED IT THOROUGHLY. THOUGH, REALLY, IT SHOULD HAVE INCLUDED A DISCLAIMER.
"LOOSELY BASED ON ACTUAL EVENTS," OR, PERHAPS, "EXTREME LIBERTIES WITH ARTISTIC LICENSE TAKEN."
SOMETHING TO THAT EFFECT.
PARTS OF IT ARE ACCURATE, I'LL GRANT IT THAT, BUT IT'S MORE OF AN HOMAGE THAN A HISTORICAL DOCUMENT.
FOR ONE THING, THE DATES ARE COMPLETELY OUT OF ORDER. AND TRUTHFULLY, I DON'T CARE FOR THE WAY THEY PORTRAYED ME.
"GOD THE FATHER". IT SOUNDS SO STALE. I ALWAYS FANCIED MYSELF MORE OF A ROGUE.
THOUGH EVERYTHING IN JOB IS TRUE. AND STILL HILARIOUS, IF YOU ASK ME. BUT TAKE THE FLOOD FOR EXAMPLE...
YES. IT HAPPENED. THOUGH NOT BECAUSE THE WORLD WAS A CESSPOOL OF SIN IN NEED OF CLEANSING. THAT'S RIDICULOUS. I SIMPLY WANTED TO SEE WHAT IT WOULD LOOK LIKE.
TELL ME YOU WOULDN'T DO THE SAME.
I--
AND THAT BIT ABOUT SODOM AND GOMORRAH?

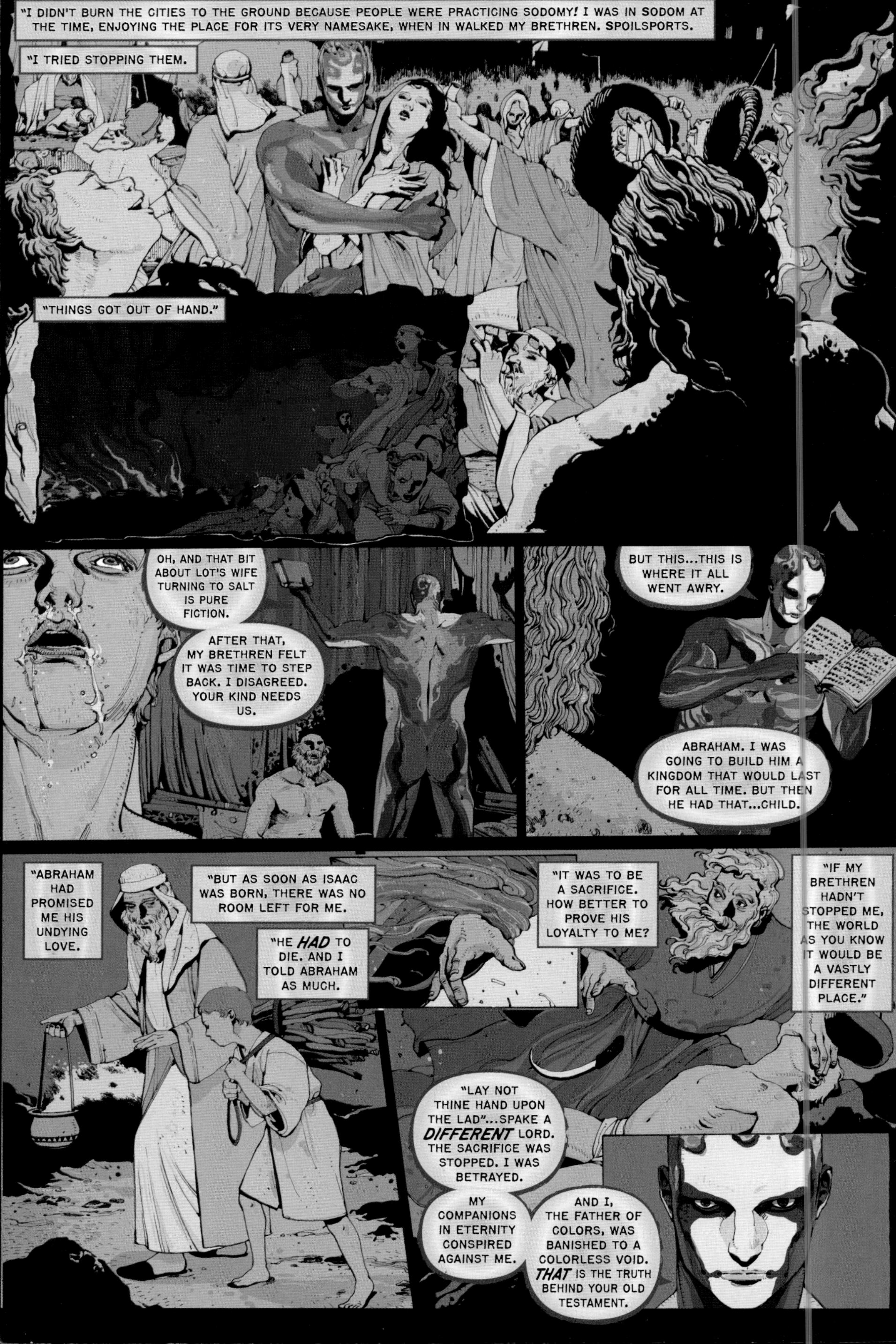
"I DIDN'T BURN THE CITIES TO THE GROUND BECAUSE PEOPLE WERE PRACTICING SODOMY! I WAS IN SODOM AT THE TIME, ENJOYING THE PLACE FOR ITS VERY NAMESAKE, WHEN IN WALKED MY BRETHREN. SPOILSPORTS.
"I TRIED STOPPING THEM.
"THINGS GOT OUT OF HAND."
OH, AND THAT BIT ABOUT LOT'S WIFE TURNING TO SALT IS PURE FICTION.
AFTER THAT, MY BRETHREN FELT IT WAS TIME TO STEP BACK. I DISAGREED. YOUR KIND NEEDS US.
BUT THIS...THIS IS WHERE IT ALL WENT AWRY.
ABRAHAM. I WAS GOING TO BUILD HIM A KINGDOM THAT WOULD LAST FOR ALL TIME. BUT THEN HE HAD THAT...CHILD.
"ABRAHAM HAD PROMISED ME HIS UNDYING LOVE.
"BUT AS SOON AS ISAAC WAS BORN, THERE WAS NO ROOM LEFT FOR ME.
"HE HAD TO DIE. AND I TOLD ABRAHAM AS MUCH.
"IT WAS TO BE A SACRIFICE. HOW BETTER TO PROVE HIS LOYALTY TO ME?
"IF MY BRETHREN HADN'T STOPPED ME, THE WORLD AS YOU KNOW IT WOULD BE A VASTLY DIFFERENT PLACE."
"LAY NOT THINE HAND UPON THE LAD"...SPAKE A DIFFERENT LORD. THE SACRIFICE WAS STOPPED. I WAS BETRAYED.
MY COMPANIONS IN ETERNITY CONSPIRED AGAINST ME.
AND I, THE FATHER OF COLORS, WAS BANISHED TO A COLORLESS VOID. THAT IS THE TRUTH BEHIND YOUR OLD TESTAMENT.

CHAPTER 2: DIVINE INTERCOURSE

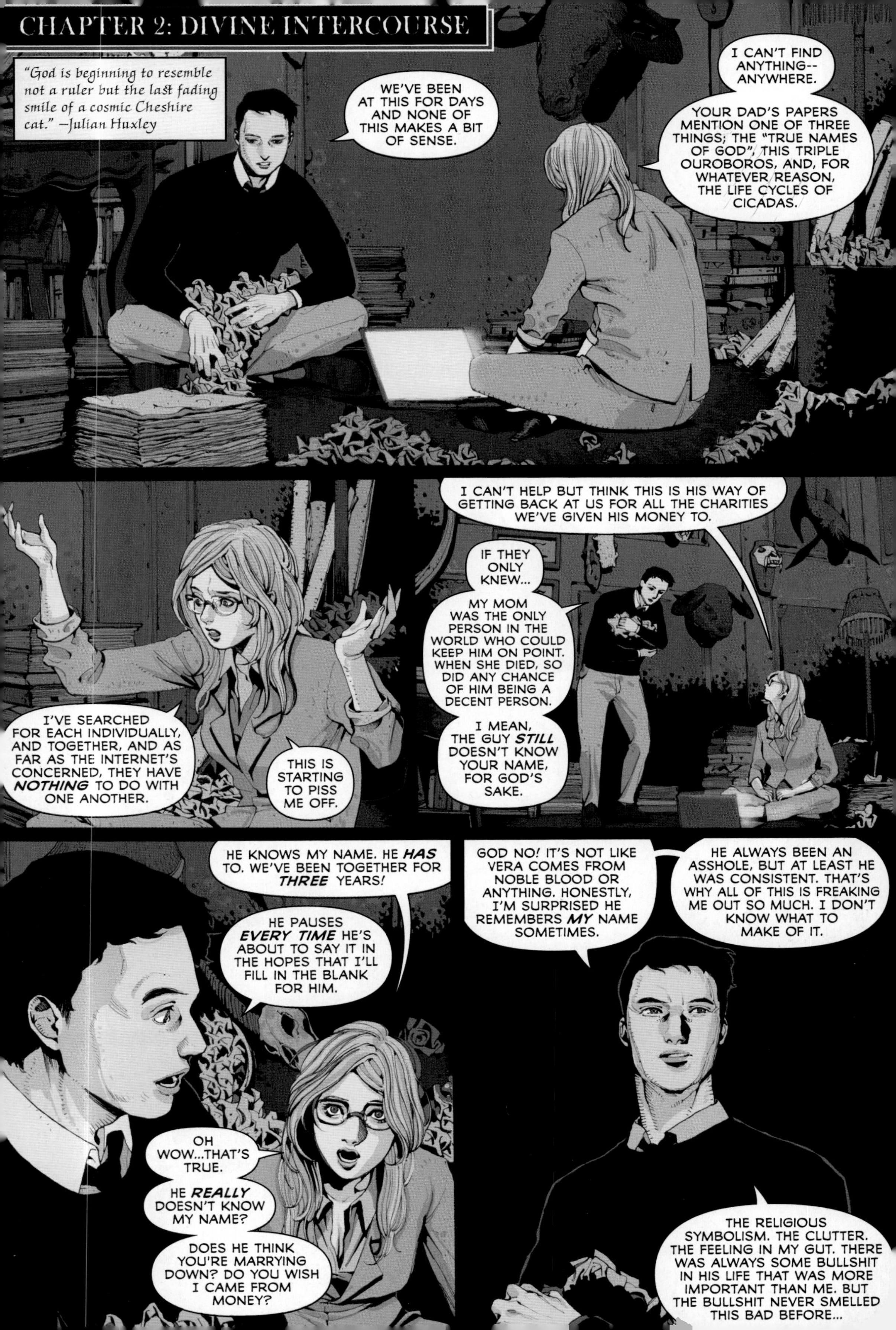

"God is beginning to resemble not a ruler but the last fading smile of a cosmic Cheshire cat." —Julian Huxley
WE'VE BEEN AT THIS FOR DAYS AND NONE OF THIS MAKES A BIT OF SENSE.
I CAN'T FIND ANYTHING-- ANYWHERE.
YOUR DAD'S PAPERS MENTION ONE OF THREE THINGS; THE "TRUE NAMES OF GOD", THIS TRIPLE OUROBOROS, AND, FOR WHATEVER REASON, THE LIFE CYCLES OF CICADAS.
I'VE SEARCHED FOR EACH INDIVIDUALLY, AND TOGETHER, AND AS FAR AS THE INTERNET'S CONCERNED, THEY HAVE *NOTHING* TO DO WITH ONE ANOTHER.
THIS IS STARTING TO PISS ME OFF.
I CAN'T HELP BUT THINK THIS IS HIS WAY OF GETTING BACK AT US FOR ALL THE CHARITIES WE'VE GIVEN HIS MONEY TO.
IF THEY ONLY KNEW...
MY MOM WAS THE ONLY PERSON IN THE WORLD WHO COULD KEEP HIM ON POINT. WHEN SHE DIED, SO DID ANY CHANCE OF HIM BEING A DECENT PERSON.
I MEAN, THE GUY *STILL* DOESN'T KNOW YOUR NAME, FOR GOD'S SAKE.
HE KNOWS MY NAME. HE *HAS* TO. WE'VE BEEN TOGETHER FOR *THREE* YEARS!
HE PAUSES *EVERY TIME* HE'S ABOUT TO SAY IT IN THE HOPES THAT I'LL FILL IN THE BLANK FOR HIM.
OH WOW...THAT'S TRUE.
HE *REALLY* DOESN'T KNOW MY NAME?
DOES HE THINK YOU'RE MARRYING DOWN? DO YOU WISH I CAME FROM MONEY?
GOD NO! IT'S NOT LIKE VERA COMES FROM NOBLE BLOOD OR ANYTHING. HONESTLY, I'M SURPRISED HE REMEMBERS *MY* NAME SOMETIMES.
HE ALWAYS BEEN AN ASSHOLE, BUT AT LEAST HE WAS CONSISTENT. THAT'S WHY ALL OF THIS IS FREAKING ME OUT SO MUCH. I DON'T KNOW WHAT TO MAKE OF IT.
THE RELIGIOUS SYMBOLISM. THE CLUTTER. THE FEELING IN MY GUT. THERE WAS ALWAYS SOME BULLSHIT IN HIS LIFE THAT WAS MORE IMPORTANT THAN ME. BUT THE BULLSHIT NEVER SMELLED THIS BAD BEFORE...

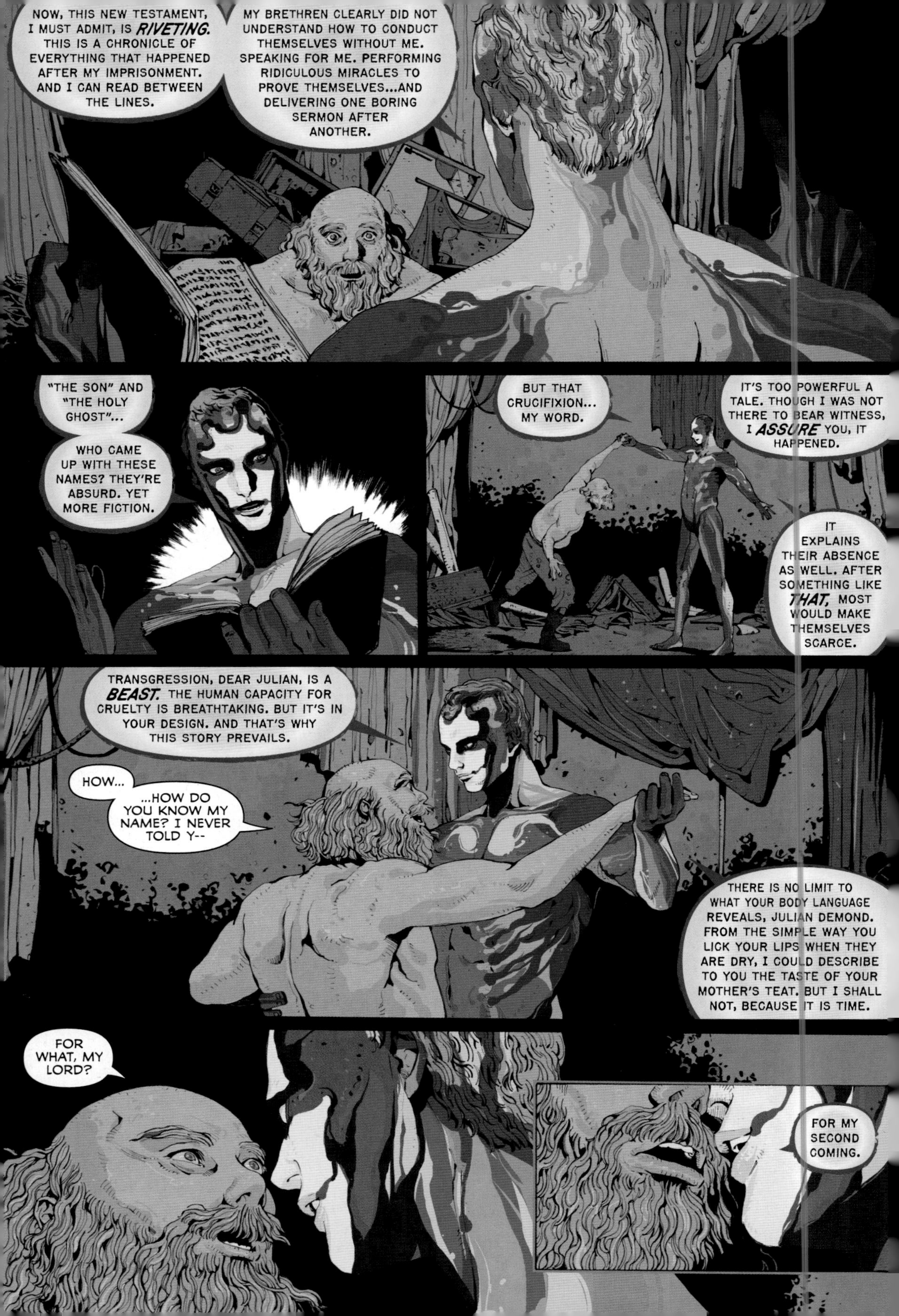
NOW, THIS NEW TESTAMENT, I MUST ADMIT, IS *RIVETING.* THIS IS A CHRONICLE OF EVERYTHING THAT HAPPENED AFTER MY IMPRISONMENT. AND I CAN READ BETWEEN THE LINES.
MY BRETHREN CLEARLY DID NOT UNDERSTAND HOW TO CONDUCT THEMSELVES WITHOUT ME. SPEAKING FOR ME. PERFORMING RIDICULOUS MIRACLES TO PROVE THEMSELVES...AND DELIVERING ONE BORING SERMON AFTER ANOTHER.
"THE SON" AND "THE HOLY GHOST"...
WHO CAME UP WITH THESE NAMES? THEY'RE ABSURD. YET MORE FICTION.
BUT THAT CRUCIFIXION... MY WORD.
IT'S TOO POWERFUL A TALE. THOUGH I WAS NOT THERE TO BEAR WITNESS, I *ASSURE* YOU, IT HAPPENED.
IT EXPLAINS THEIR ABSENCE AS WELL. AFTER SOMETHING LIKE *THAT,* MOST WOULD MAKE THEMSELVES SCARCE.
TRANSGRESSION, DEAR JULIAN, IS A *BEAST.* THE HUMAN CAPACITY FOR CRUELTY IS BREATHTAKING. BUT IT'S IN YOUR DESIGN. AND THAT'S WHY THIS STORY PREVAILS.
HOW...
...HOW DO YOU KNOW MY NAME? I NEVER TOLD Y--
THERE IS NO LIMIT TO WHAT YOUR BODY LANGUAGE REVEALS, JULIAN DEMOND. FROM THE SIMPLE WAY YOU LICK YOUR LIPS WHEN THEY ARE DRY, I COULD DESCRIBE TO YOU THE TASTE OF YOUR MOTHER'S TEAT. BUT I SHALL NOT, BECAUSE IT IS TIME.
FOR WHAT, MY LORD?
FOR MY SECOND COMING.

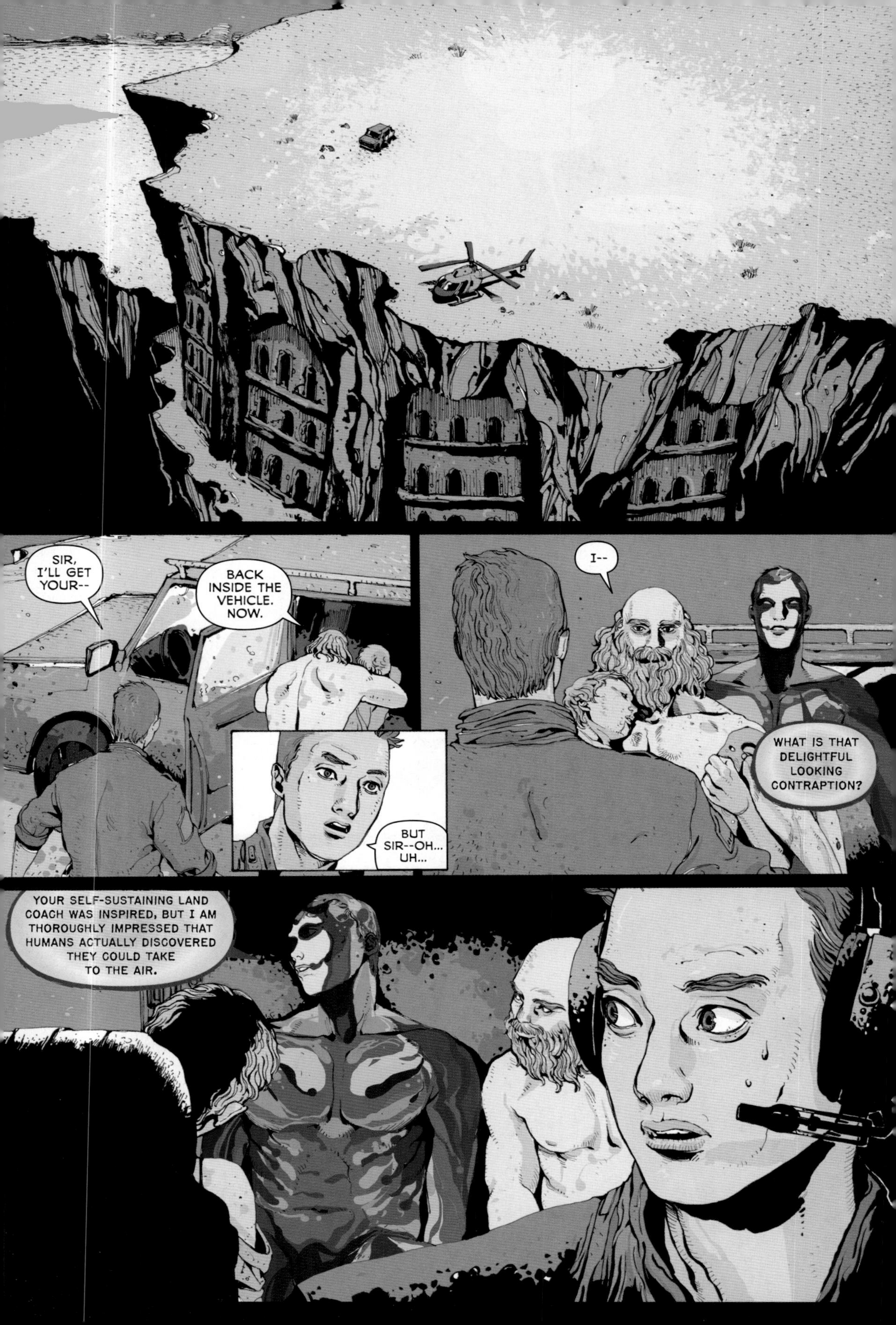
SIR, I'LL GET YOUR--
BACK INSIDE THE VEHICLE. NOW.
BUT SIR--OH... UH...
I--
WHAT IS THAT DELIGHTFUL LOOKING CONTRAPTION?
YOUR SELF-SUSTAINING LAND COACH WAS INSPIRED, BUT I AM THOROUGHLY IMPRESSED THAT HUMANS ACTUALLY DISCOVERED THEY COULD TAKE TO THE AIR.

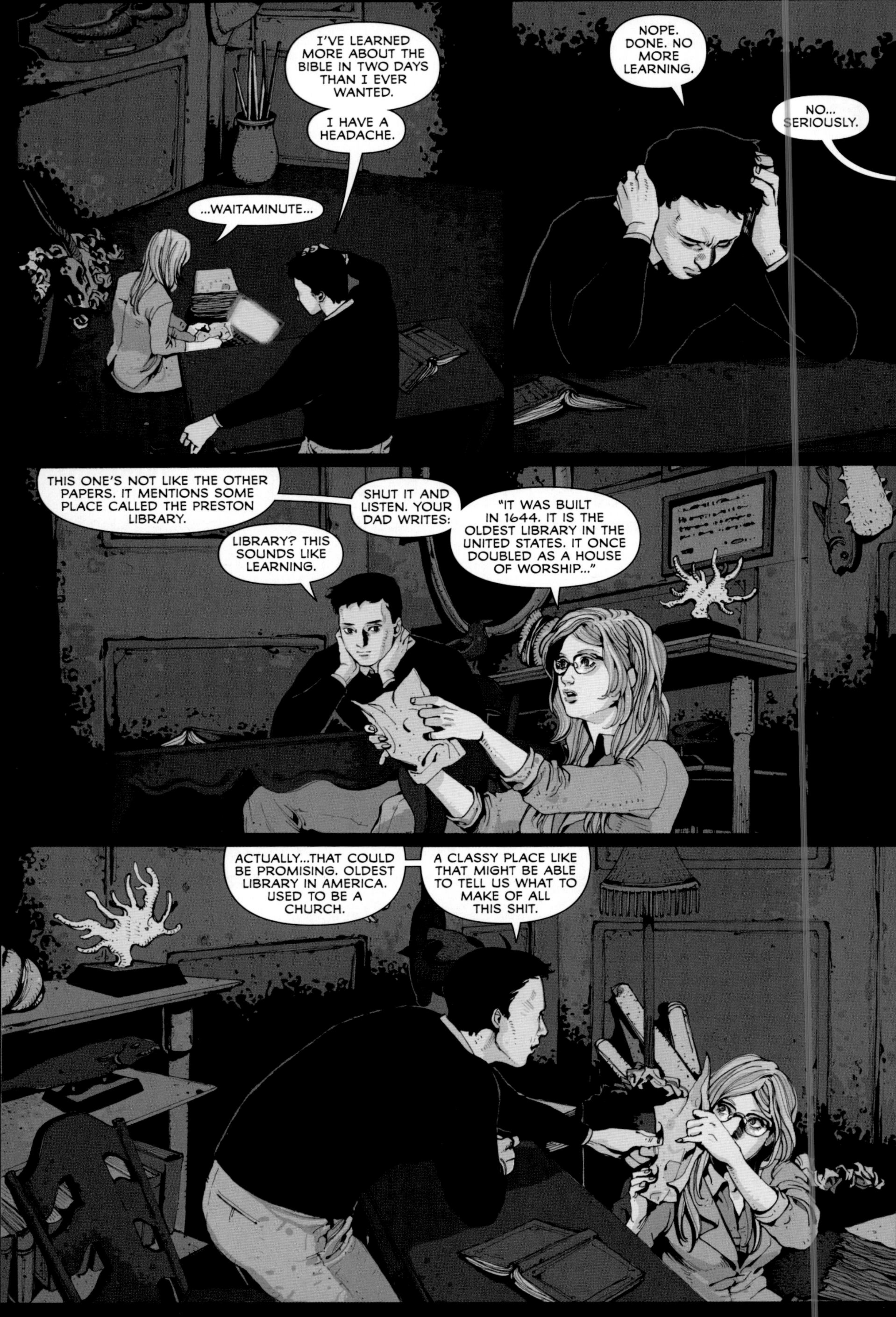
I'VE LEARNED MORE ABOUT THE BIBLE IN TWO DAYS THAN I EVER WANTED.
I HAVE A HEADACHE.
...WAITAMINUTE...
NOPE. DONE. NO MORE LEARNING.
NO... SERIOUSLY.
THIS ONE'S NOT LIKE THE OTHER PAPERS. IT MENTIONS SOME PLACE CALLED THE PRESTON LIBRARY.
LIBRARY? THIS SOUNDS LIKE LEARNING.
SHUT IT AND LISTEN. YOUR DAD WRITES:
"IT WAS BUILT IN 1644. IT IS THE OLDEST LIBRARY IN THE UNITED STATES. IT ONCE DOUBLED AS A HOUSE OF WORSHIP..."
ACTUALLY...THAT COULD BE PROMISING. OLDEST LIBRARY IN AMERICA. USED TO BE A CHURCH.
A CLASSY PLACE LIKE THAT MIGHT BE ABLE TO TELL US WHAT TO MAKE OF ALL THIS SHIT.

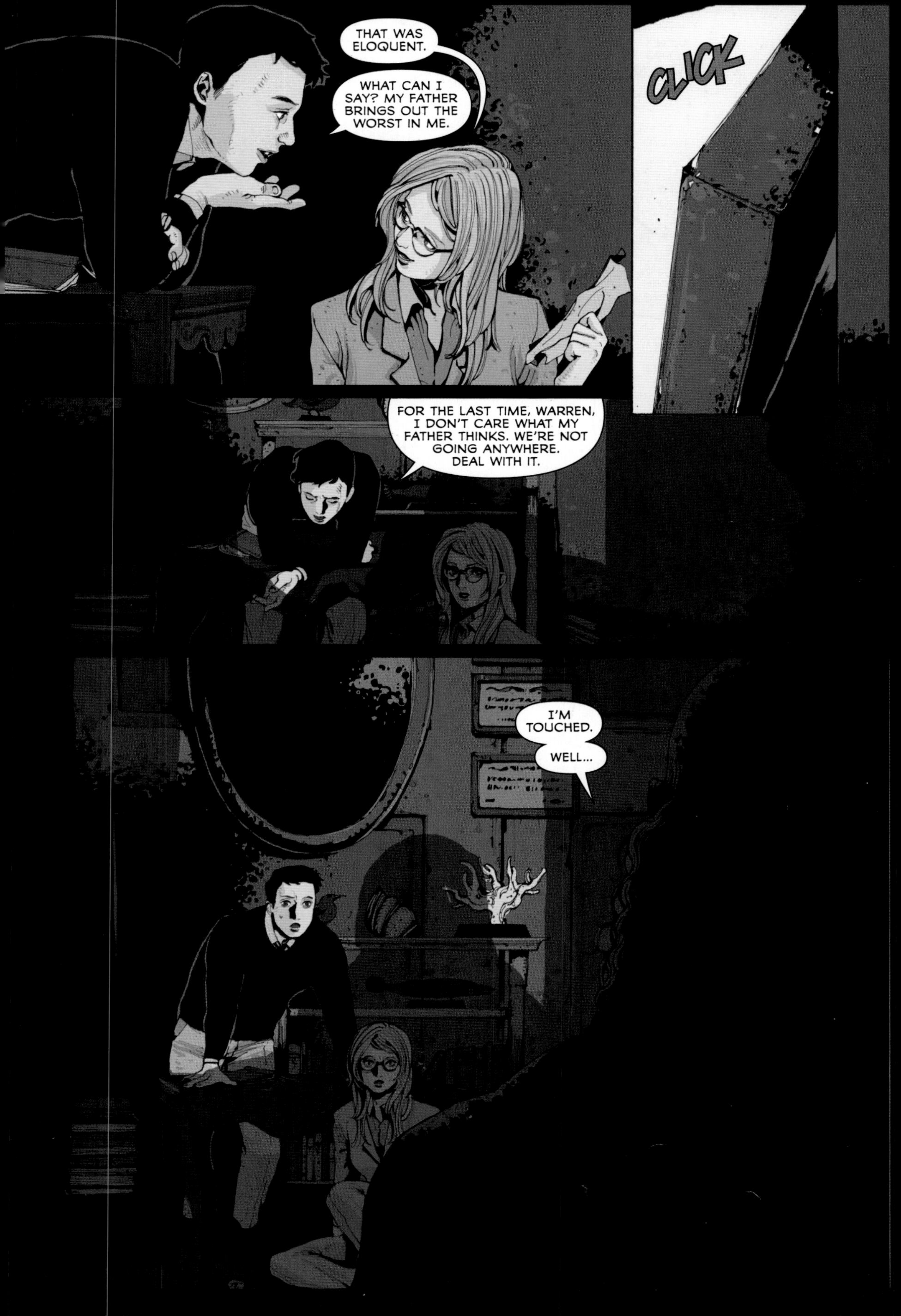
THAT WAS ELOQUENT.
WHAT CAN I SAY? MY FATHER BRINGS OUT THE WORST IN ME.
CLICK
FOR THE LAST TIME, WARREN, I DON'T CARE WHAT MY FATHER THINKS. WE'RE NOT GOING ANYWHERE. DEAL WITH IT.
I'M TOUCHED.
WELL...

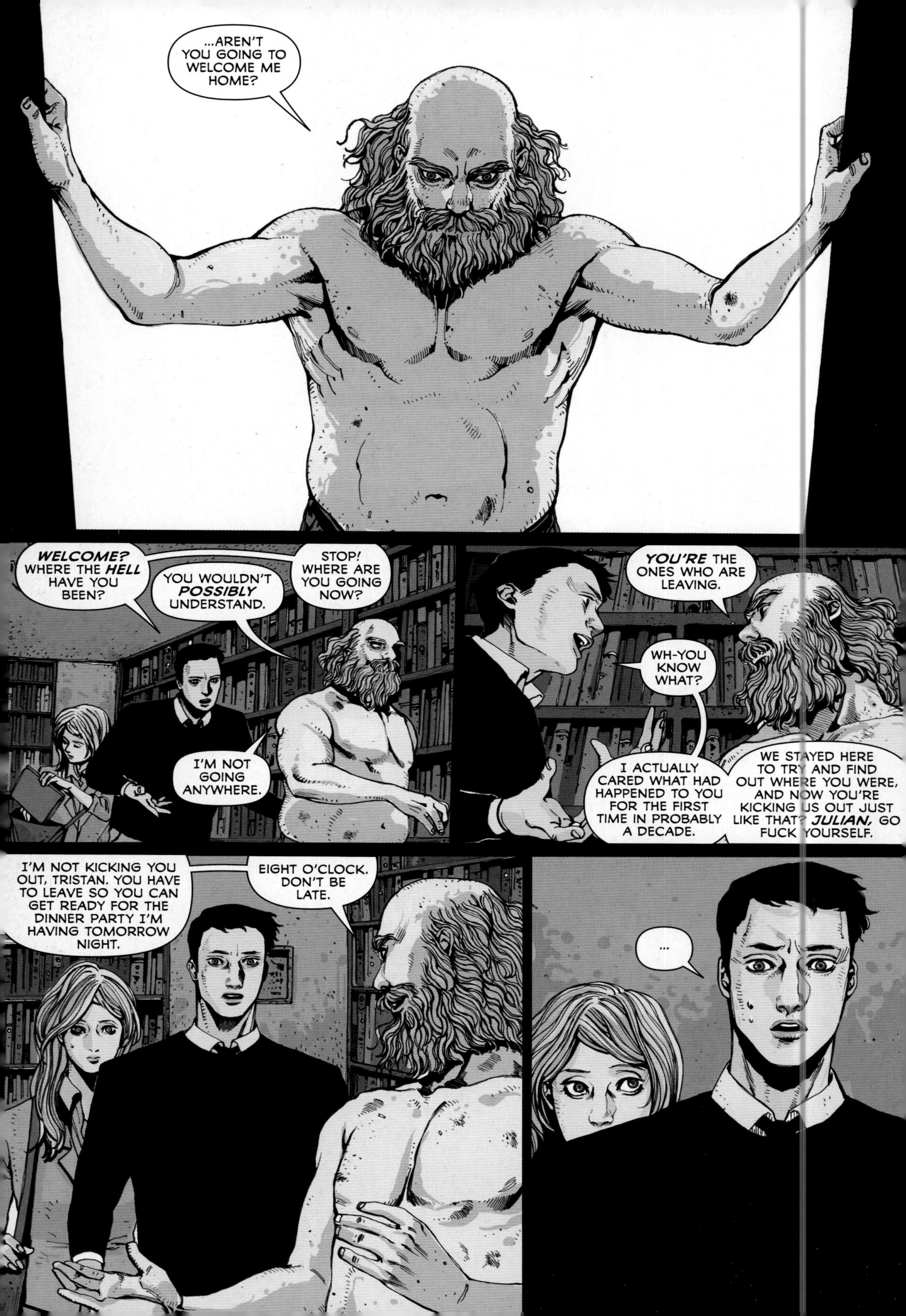
...AREN'T YOU GOING TO WELCOME ME HOME?
WELCOME? WHERE THE HELL HAVE YOU BEEN?
YOU WOULDN'T POSSIBLY UNDERSTAND.
STOP! WHERE ARE YOU GOING NOW?
I'M NOT GOING ANYWHERE.
YOU'RE THE ONES WHO ARE LEAVING.
WH-YOU KNOW WHAT?
I ACTUALLY CARED WHAT HAD HAPPENED TO YOU FOR THE FIRST TIME IN PROBABLY A DECADE.
WE STAYED HERE TO TRY AND FIND OUT WHERE YOU WERE, AND NOW YOU'RE KICKING US OUT JUST LIKE THAT? JULIAN, GO FUCK YOURSELF.
I'M NOT KICKING YOU OUT, TRISTAN. YOU HAVE TO LEAVE SO YOU CAN GET READY FOR THE DINNER PARTY I'M HAVING TOMORROW NIGHT.
EIGHT O'CLOCK. DON'T BE LATE.
...

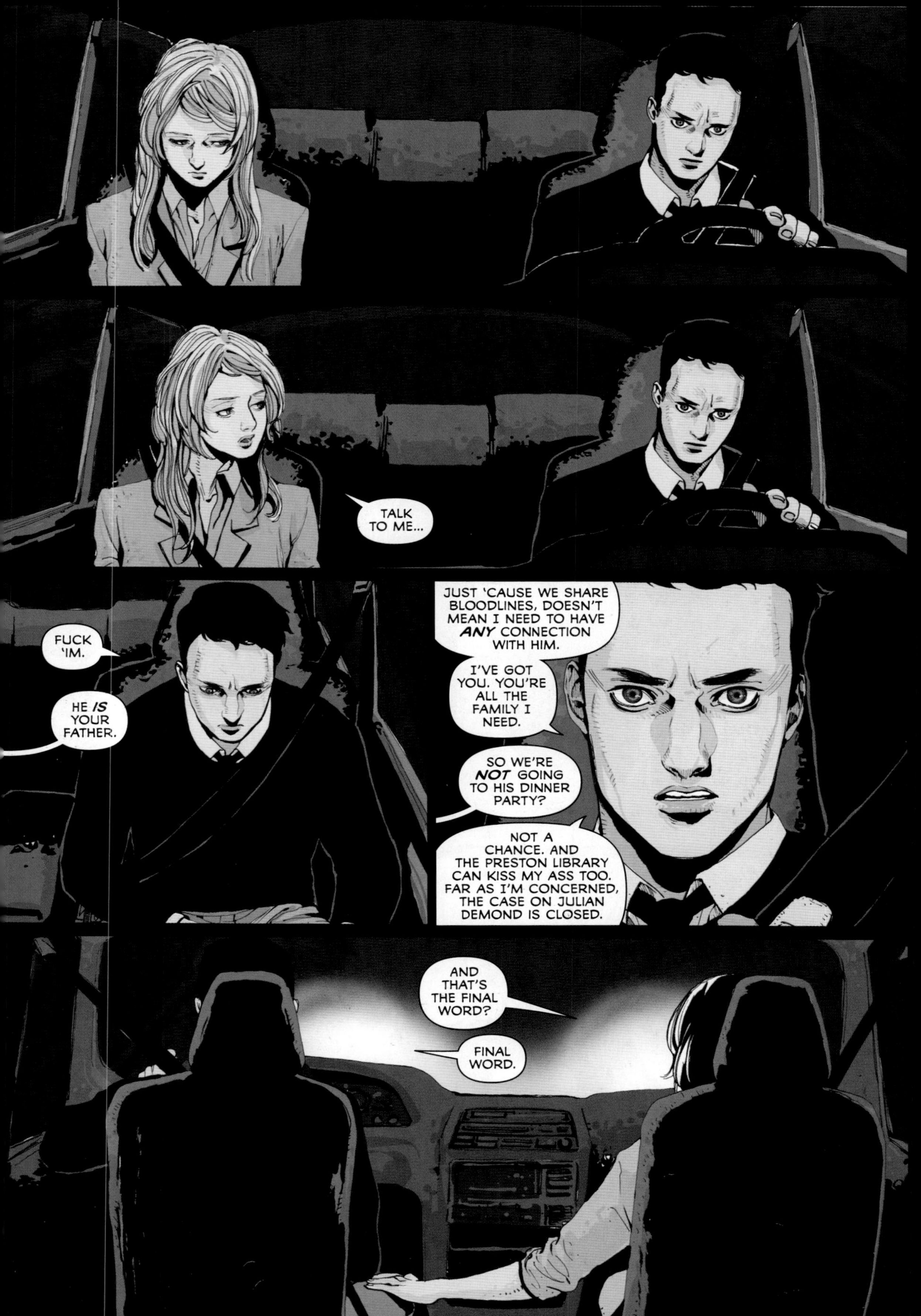
TALK TO ME...
FUCK 'IM.
HE *IS* YOUR FATHER.
JUST 'CAUSE WE SHARE BLOODLINES, DOESN'T MEAN I NEED TO HAVE *ANY* CONNECTION WITH HIM.
I'VE GOT YOU. YOU'RE ALL THE FAMILY I NEED.
SO WE'RE *NOT* GOING TO HIS DINNER PARTY?
NOT A CHANCE. AND THE PRESTON LIBRARY CAN KISS MY ASS TOO. FAR AS I'M CONCERNED, THE CASE ON JULIAN DEMOND IS CLOSED.
AND THAT'S THE FINAL WORD?
FINAL WORD.

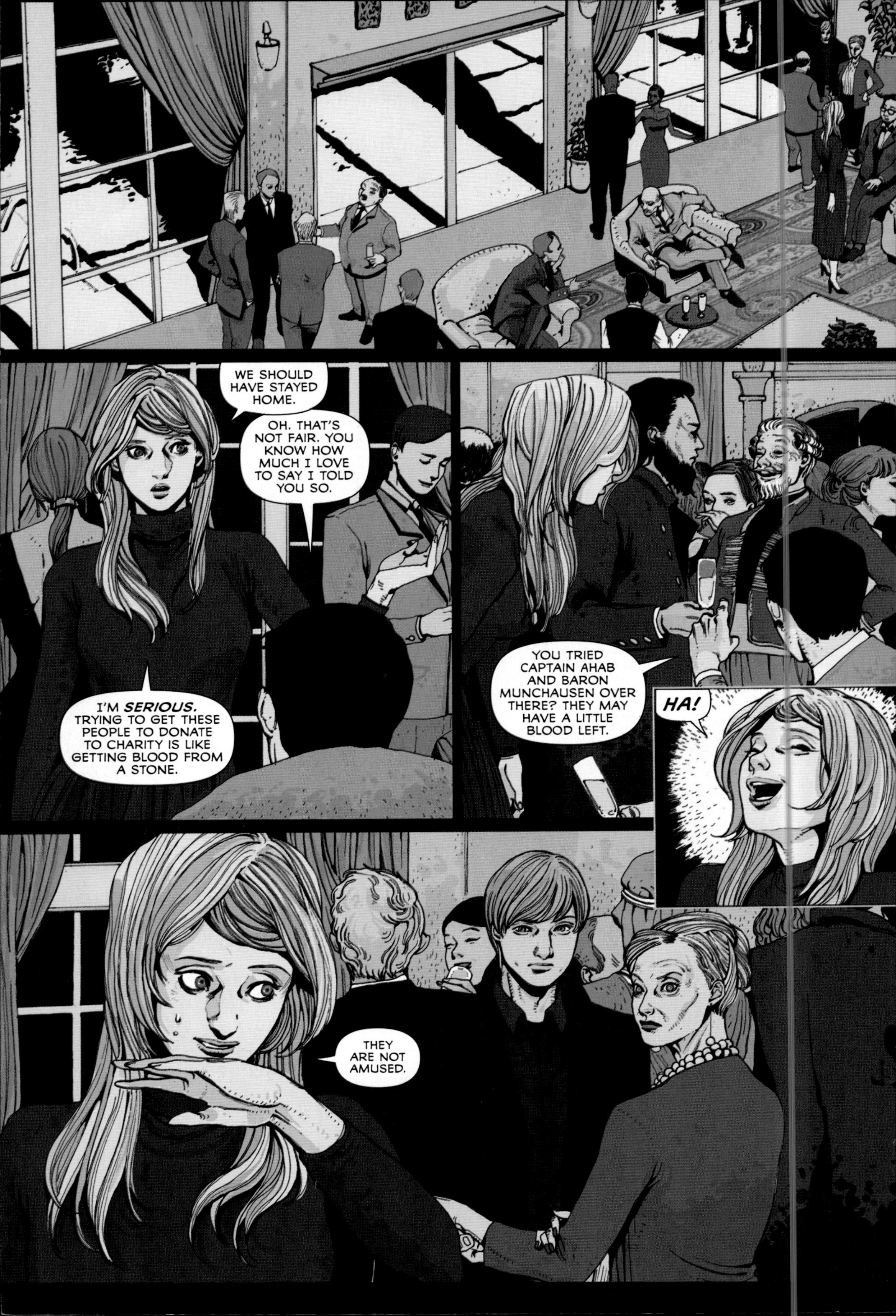
WE SHOULD HAVE STAYED HOME.
OH. THAT'S NOT FAIR. YOU KNOW HOW MUCH I LOVE TO SAY I TOLD YOU SO.
I'M *SERIOUS.* TRYING TO GET THESE PEOPLE TO DONATE TO CHARITY IS LIKE GETTING BLOOD FROM A STONE.
YOU TRIED CAPTAIN AHAB AND BARON MUNCHAUSEN OVER THERE? THEY MAY HAVE A LITTLE BLOOD LEFT.
HA!
THEY ARE NOT AMUSED.

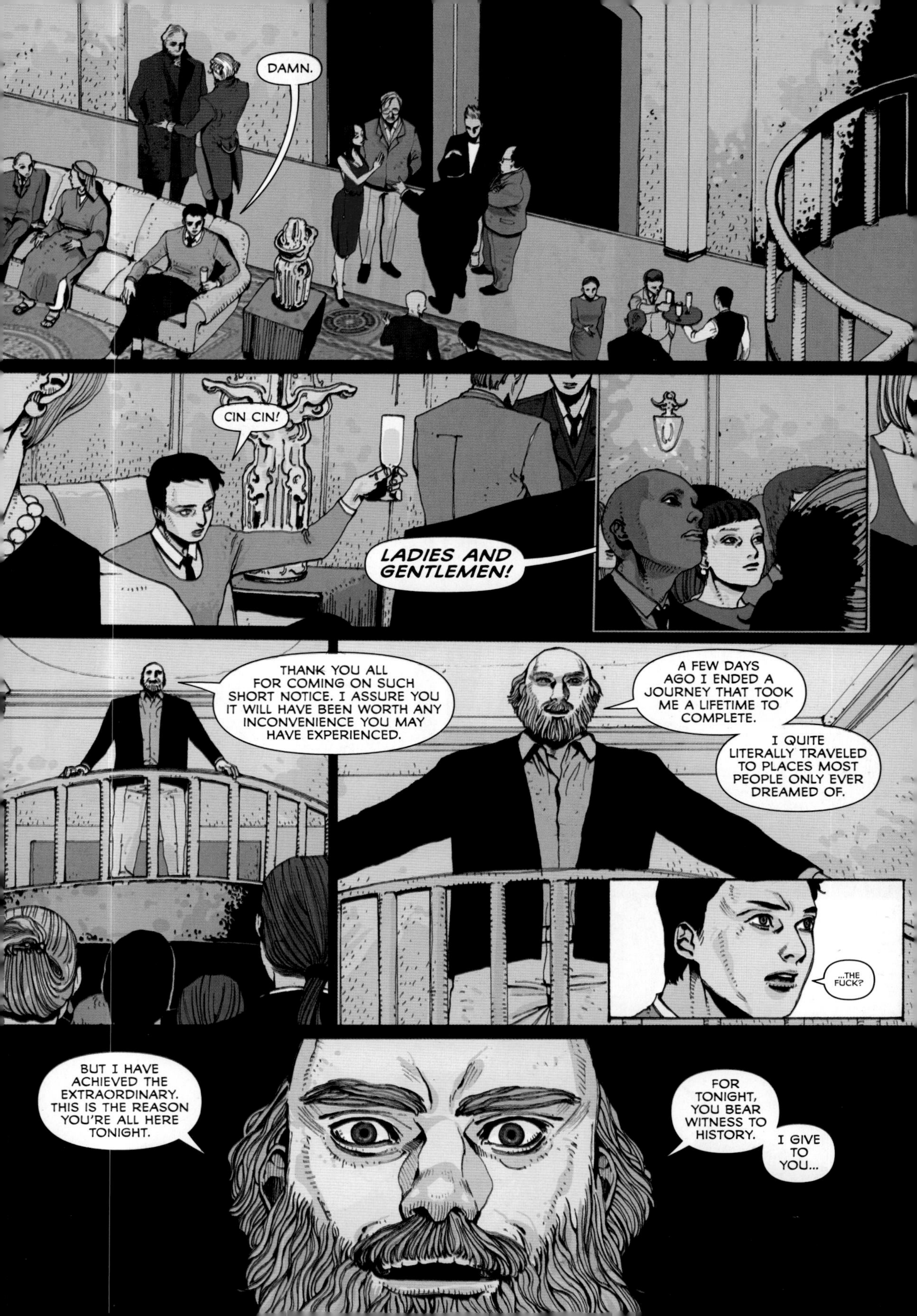
DAMN.
CIN CIN!
LADIES AND GENTLEMEN!
THANK YOU ALL FOR COMING ON SUCH SHORT NOTICE. I ASSURE YOU IT WILL HAVE BEEN WORTH ANY INCONVENIENCE YOU MAY HAVE EXPERIENCED.
A FEW DAYS AGO I ENDED A JOURNEY THAT TOOK ME A LIFETIME TO COMPLETE.
I QUITE LITERALLY TRAVELED TO PLACES MOST PEOPLE ONLY EVER DREAMED OF.
...THE FUCK?
BUT I HAVE ACHIEVED THE EXTRAORDINARY. THIS IS THE REASON YOU'RE ALL HERE TONIGHT.
FOR TONIGHT, YOU BEAR WITNESS TO HISTORY.
I GIVE TO YOU...

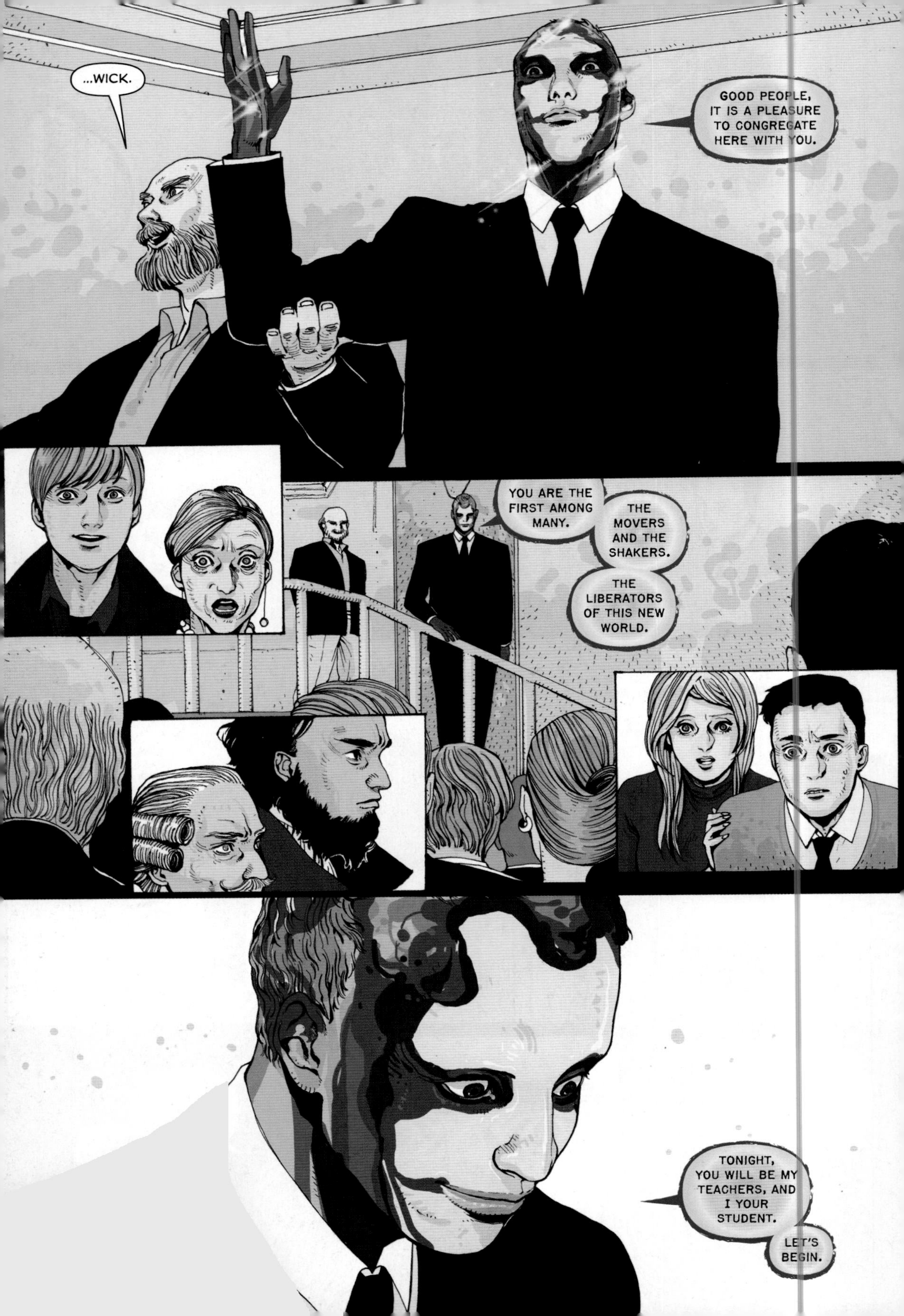
...WICK.
GOOD PEOPLE, IT IS A PLEASURE TO CONGREGATE HERE WITH YOU.
YOU ARE THE FIRST AMONG MANY.
THE MOVERS AND THE SHAKERS.
THE LIBERATORS OF THIS NEW WORLD.
TONIGHT, YOU WILL BE MY TEACHERS, AND I YOUR STUDENT.
LET'S BEGIN.

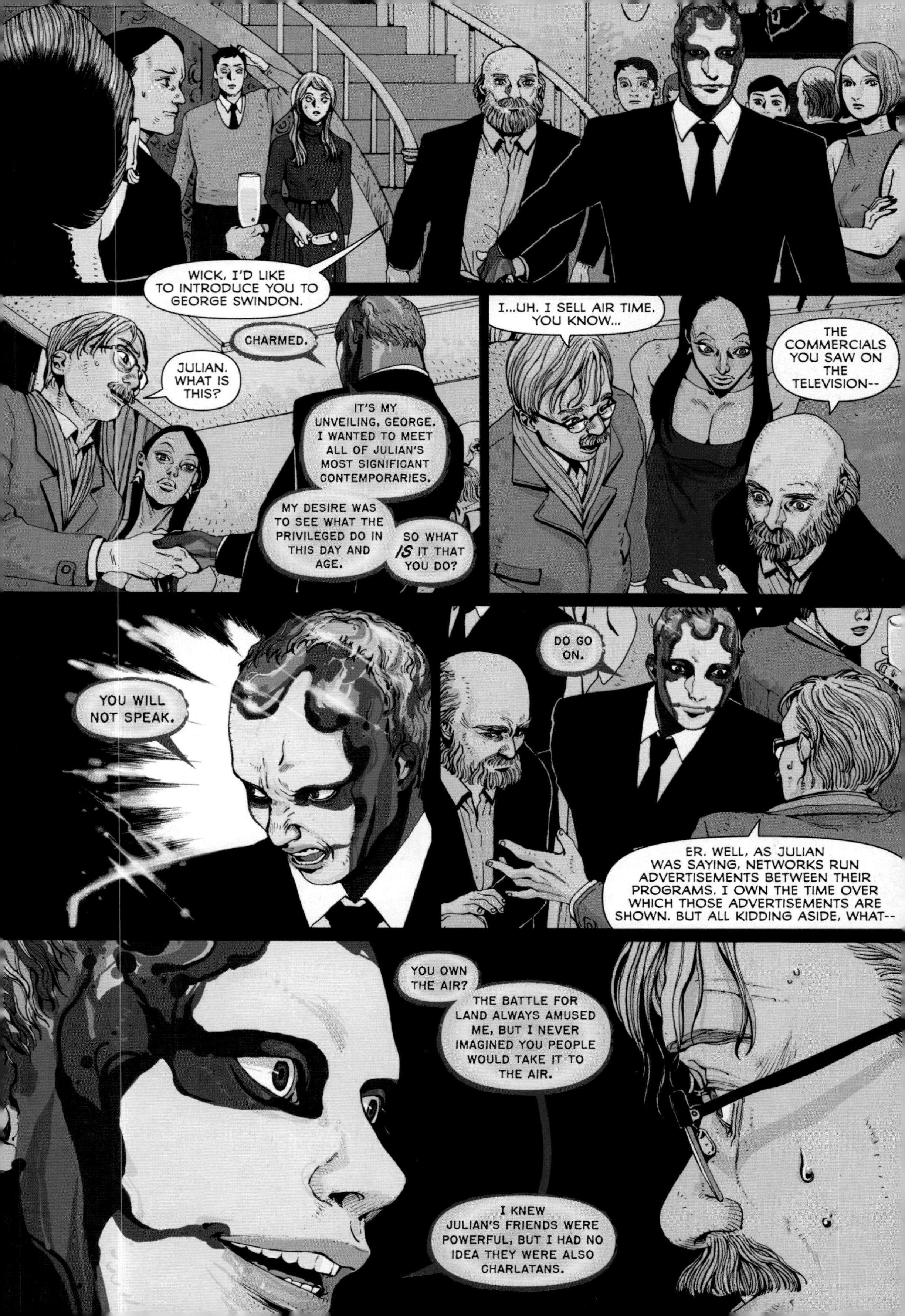
WICK, I'D LIKE TO INTRODUCE YOU TO GEORGE SWINDON.
CHARMED.
JULIAN. WHAT IS THIS?
IT'S MY UNVEILING, GEORGE. I WANTED TO MEET ALL OF JULIAN'S MOST SIGNIFICANT CONTEMPORARIES.
MY DESIRE WAS TO SEE WHAT THE PRIVILEGED DO IN THIS DAY AND AGE.
SO WHAT *IS* IT THAT YOU DO?
I...UH. I SELL AIR TIME. YOU KNOW...
THE COMMERCIALS YOU SAW ON THE TELEVISION--
YOU WILL NOT SPEAK.
DO GO ON.
ER. WELL, AS JULIAN WAS SAYING, NETWORKS RUN ADVERTISEMENTS BETWEEN THEIR PROGRAMS. I OWN THE TIME OVER WHICH THOSE ADVERTISEMENTS ARE SHOWN. BUT ALL KIDDING ASIDE, WHAT--
YOU OWN THE AIR?
THE BATTLE FOR LAND ALWAYS AMUSED ME, BUT I NEVER IMAGINED YOU PEOPLE WOULD TAKE IT TO THE AIR.
I KNEW JULIAN'S FRIENDS WERE POWERFUL, BUT I HAD NO IDEA THEY WERE ALSO CHARLATANS.

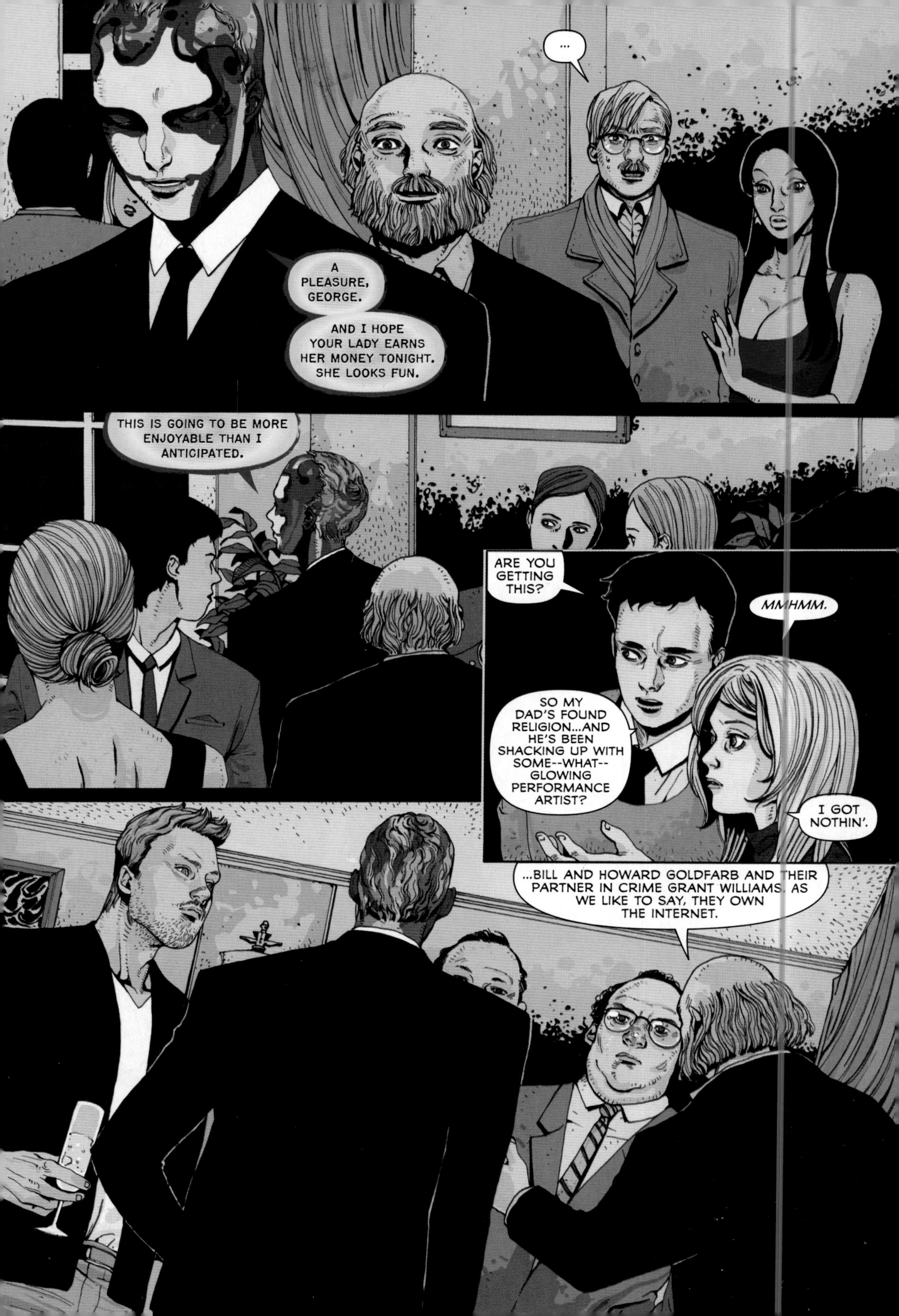

...
A PLEASURE, GEORGE.
AND I HOPE YOUR LADY EARNS HER MONEY TONIGHT. SHE LOOKS FUN.
THIS IS GOING TO BE MORE ENJOYABLE THAN I ANTICIPATED.
ARE YOU GETTING THIS?
MMHMM.
SO MY DAD'S FOUND RELIGION...AND HE'S BEEN SHACKING UP WITH SOME--WHAT--GLOWING PERFORMANCE ARTIST?
I GOT NOTHIN'.
...BILL AND HOWARD GOLDFARB AND THEIR PARTNER IN CRIME GRANT WILLIAMS. AS WE LIKE TO SAY, THEY OWN THE INTERNET.

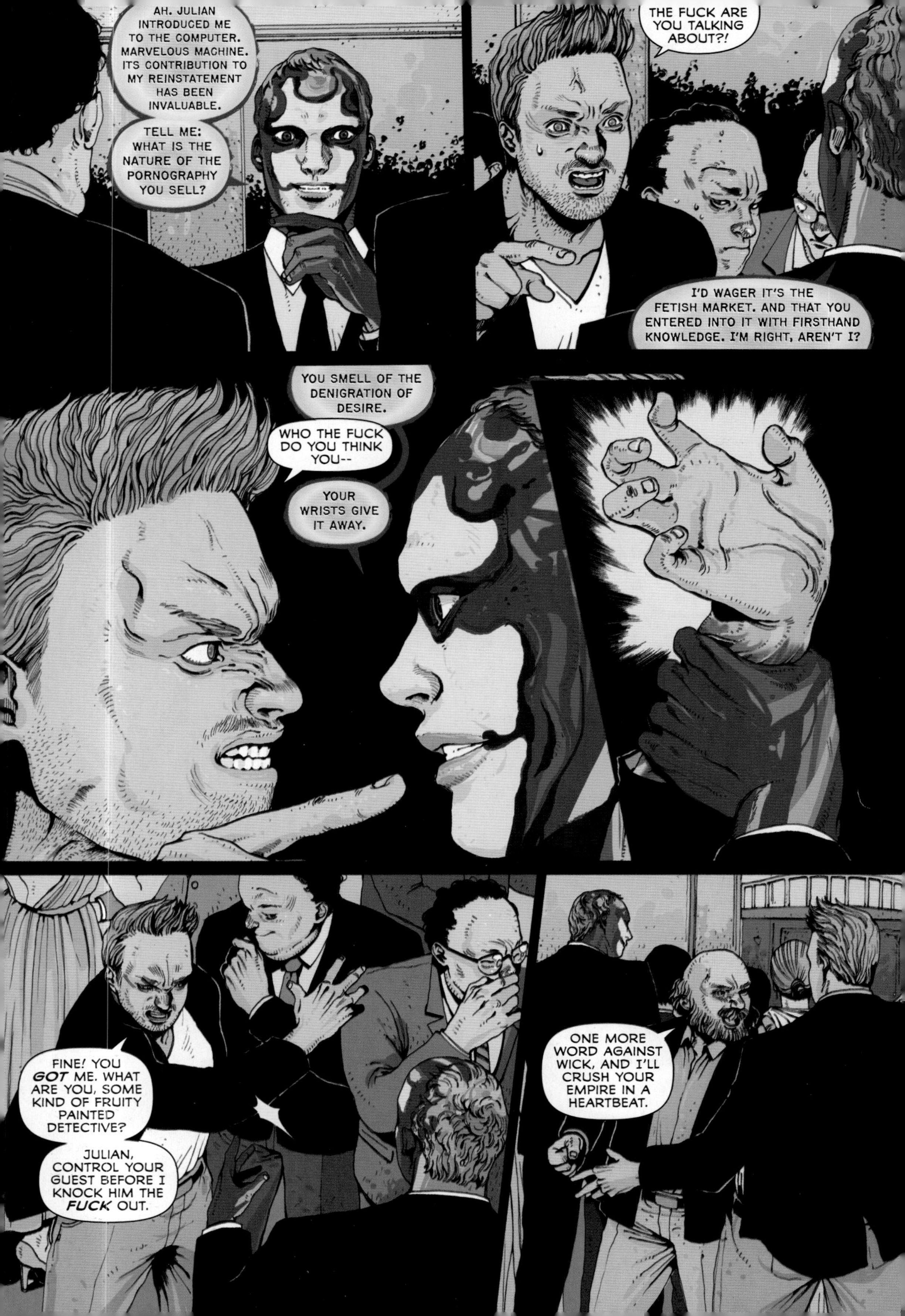
AH. JULIAN INTRODUCED ME TO THE COMPUTER. MARVELOUS MACHINE. ITS CONTRIBUTION TO MY REINSTATEMENT HAS BEEN INVALUABLE.
TELL ME: WHAT IS THE NATURE OF THE PORNOGRAPHY YOU SELL?
THE FUCK ARE YOU TALKING ABOUT?!
I'D WAGER IT'S THE FETISH MARKET. AND THAT YOU ENTERED INTO IT WITH FIRSTHAND KNOWLEDGE. I'M RIGHT, AREN'T I?
YOU SMELL OF THE DENIGRATION OF DESIRE.
WHO THE FUCK DO YOU THINK YOU--
YOUR WRISTS GIVE IT AWAY.
FINE! YOU *GOT* ME. WHAT ARE YOU, SOME KIND OF FRUITY PAINTED DETECTIVE?
JULIAN, CONTROL YOUR GUEST BEFORE I KNOCK HIM THE *FUCK* OUT.
ONE MORE WORD AGAINST WICK, AND I'LL CRUSH YOUR EMPIRE IN A HEARTBEAT.

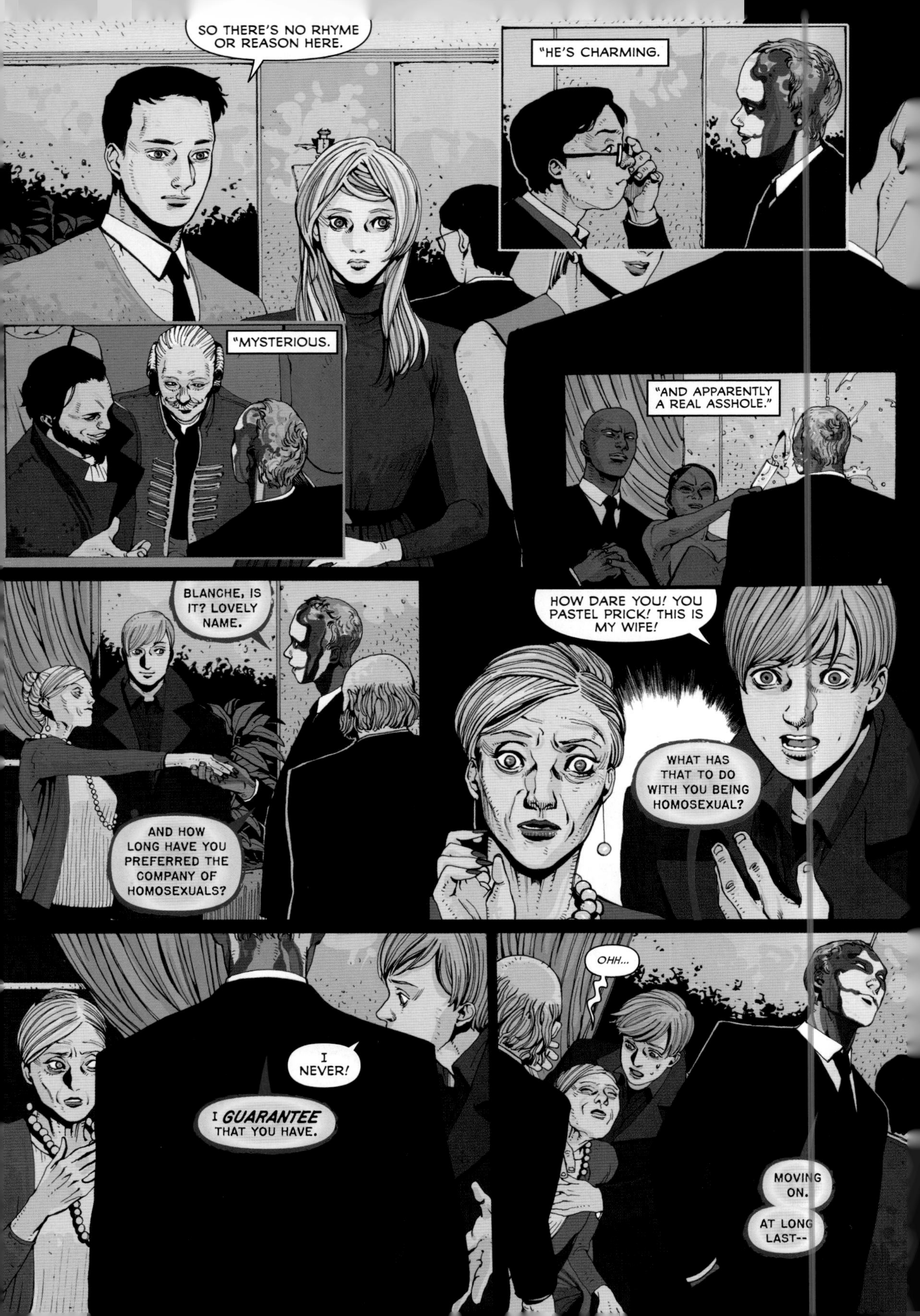
SO THERE'S NO RHYME OR REASON HERE.
"HE'S CHARMING.
"MYSTERIOUS.
"AND APPARENTLY A REAL ASSHOLE."
BLANCHE, IS IT? LOVELY NAME.
AND HOW LONG HAVE YOU PREFERRED THE COMPANY OF HOMOSEXUALS?
HOW DARE YOU! YOU PASTEL PRICK! THIS IS MY WIFE!
WHAT HAS THAT TO DO WITH YOU BEING HOMOSEXUAL?
I NEVER!
I GUARANTEE THAT YOU HAVE.
OHH...
MOVING ON.
AT LONG LAST--

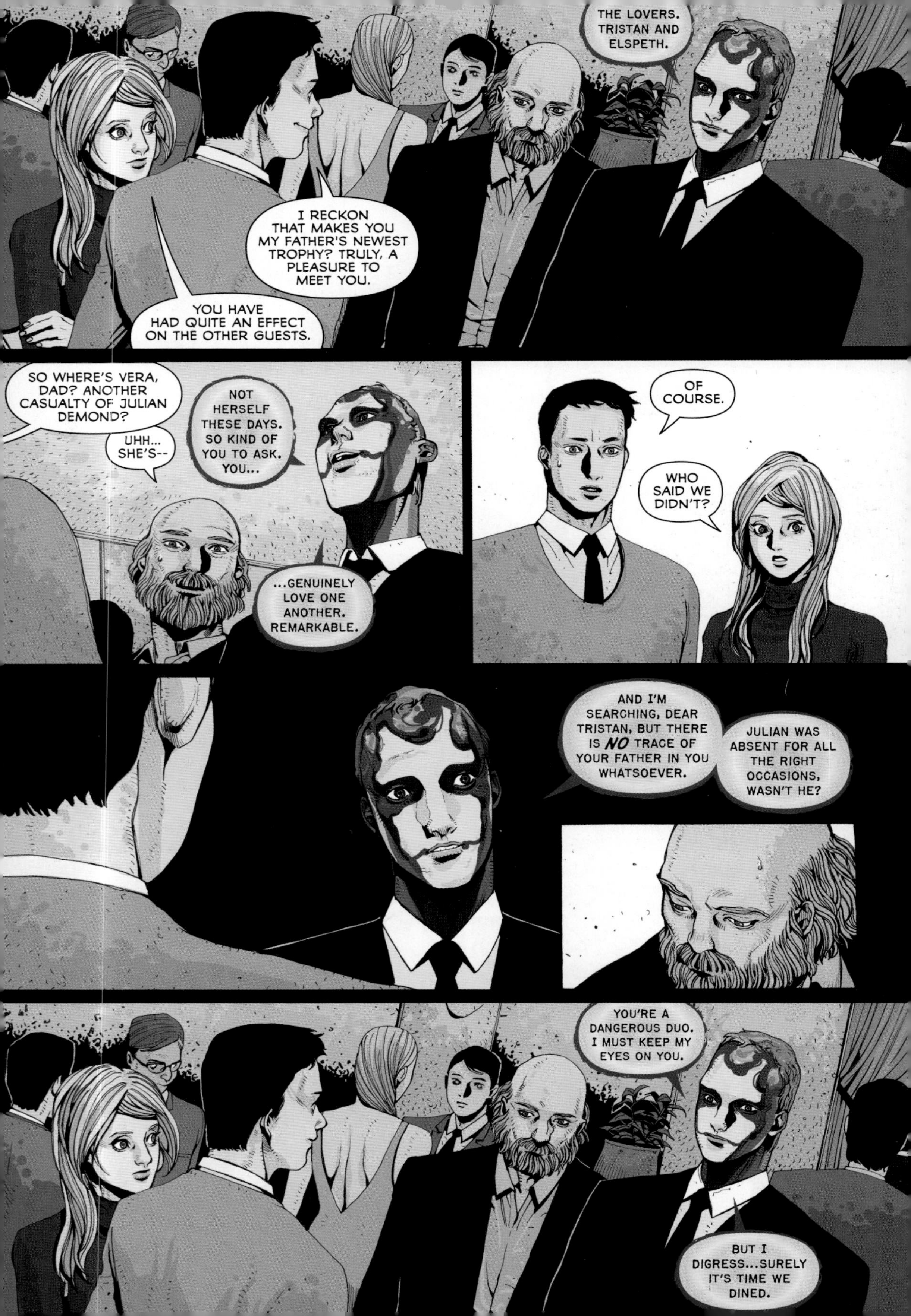
THE LOVERS. TRISTAN AND ELSPETH.
I RECKON THAT MAKES YOU MY FATHER'S NEWEST TROPHY? TRULY, A PLEASURE TO MEET YOU.
YOU HAVE HAD QUITE AN EFFECT ON THE OTHER GUESTS.
SO WHERE'S VERA, DAD? ANOTHER CASUALTY OF JULIAN DEMOND?
UHH... SHE'S--
NOT HERSELF THESE DAYS. SO KIND OF YOU TO ASK. YOU...
...GENUINELY LOVE ONE ANOTHER. REMARKABLE.
OF COURSE.
WHO SAID WE DIDN'T?
AND I'M SEARCHING, DEAR TRISTAN, BUT THERE IS NO TRACE OF YOUR FATHER IN YOU WHATSOEVER.
JULIAN WAS ABSENT FOR ALL THE RIGHT OCCASIONS, WASN'T HE?
YOU'RE A DANGEROUS DUO. I MUST KEEP MY EYES ON YOU.
BUT I DIGRESS...SURELY IT'S TIME WE DINED.

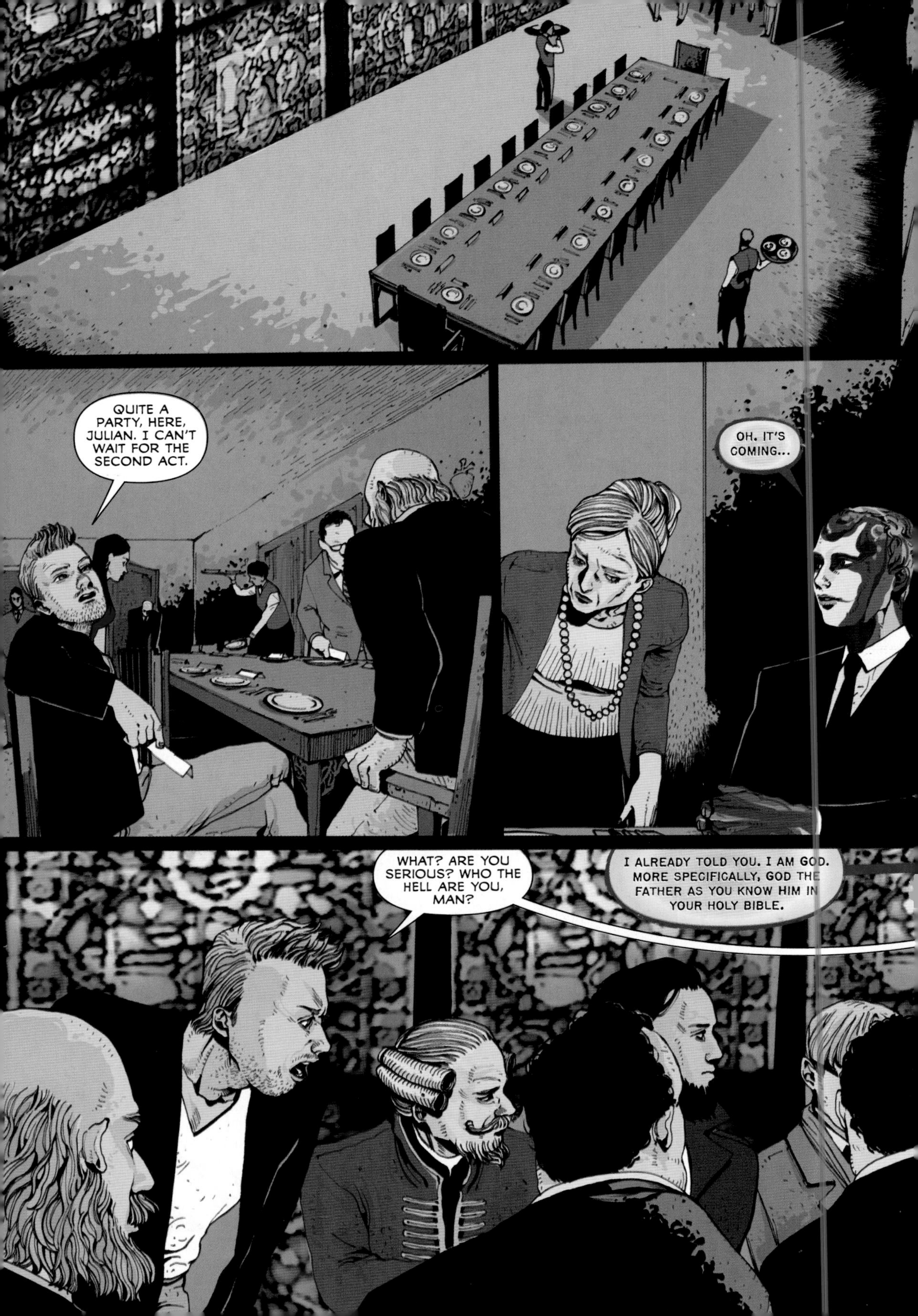
QUITE A PARTY, HERE, JULIAN. I CAN'T WAIT FOR THE SECOND ACT.
OH. IT'S COMING...
WHAT? ARE YOU SERIOUS? WHO THE HELL ARE YOU, MAN?
I ALREADY TOLD YOU. I AM GOD. MORE SPECIFICALLY, GOD THE FATHER AS YOU KNOW HIM IN YOUR HOLY BIBLE.

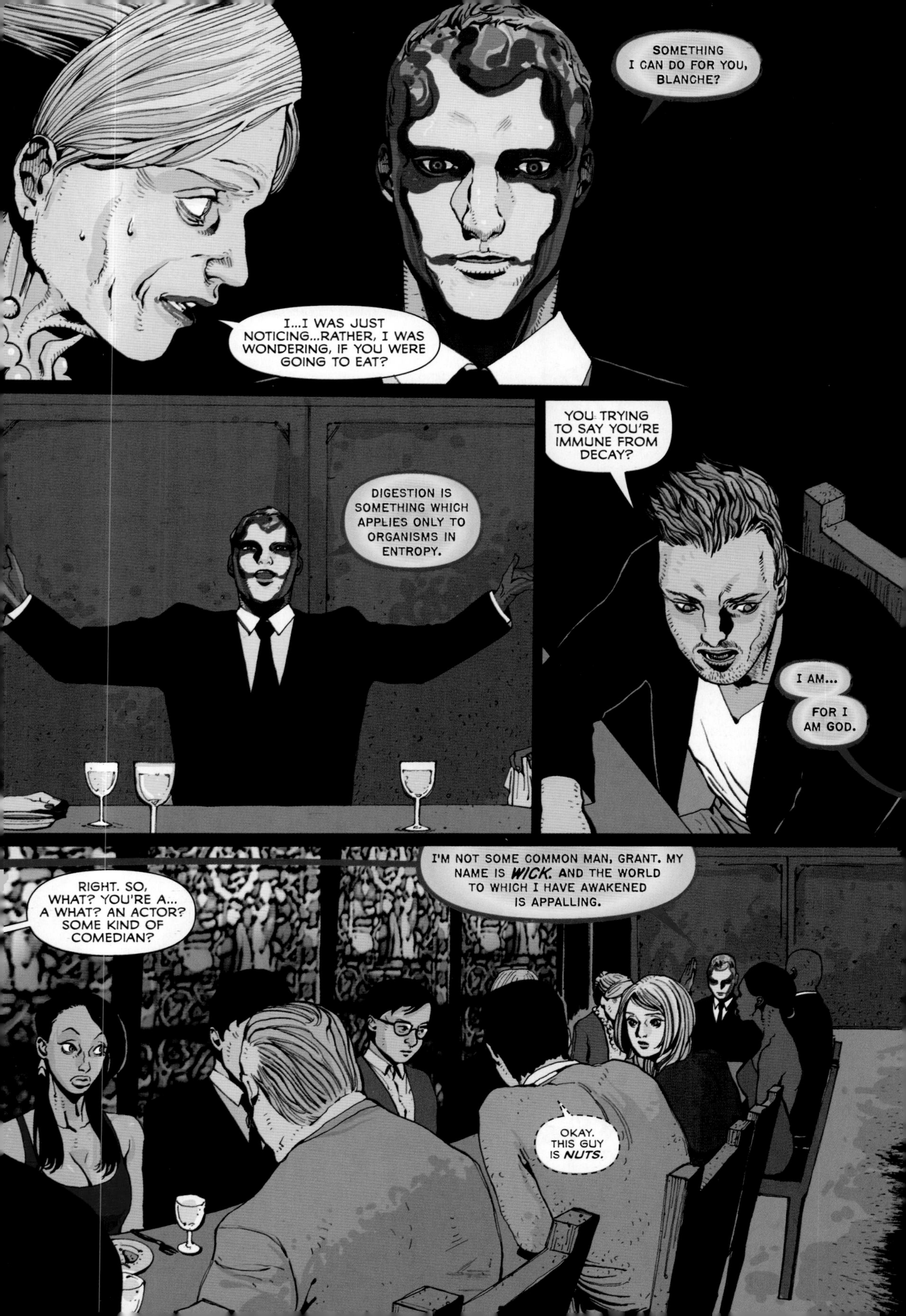
SOMETHING I CAN DO FOR YOU, BLANCHE?
I...I WAS JUST NOTICING...RATHER, I WAS WONDERING, IF YOU WERE GOING TO EAT?
DIGESTION IS SOMETHING WHICH APPLIES ONLY TO ORGANISMS IN ENTROPY.
YOU TRYING TO SAY YOU'RE IMMUNE FROM DECAY?
I AM...
FOR I AM GOD.
RIGHT. SO, WHAT? YOU'RE A... A WHAT? AN ACTOR? SOME KIND OF COMEDIAN?
I'M NOT SOME COMMON MAN, GRANT. MY NAME IS WICK. AND THE WORLD TO WHICH I HAVE AWAKENED IS APPALLING.
OKAY. THIS GUY IS NUTS.

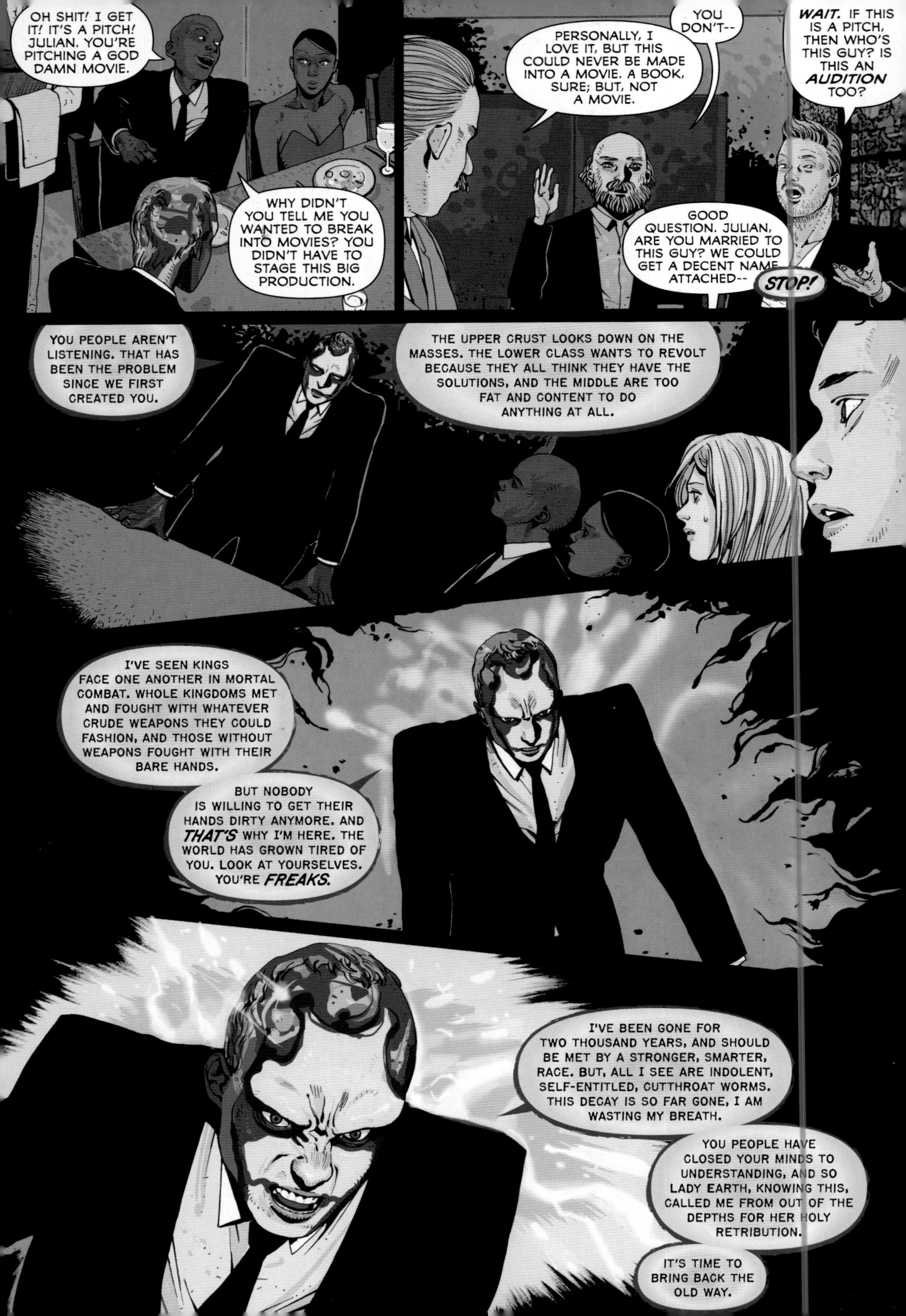
OH SHIT! I GET IT! IT'S A PITCH! JULIAN. YOU'RE PITCHING A GOD DAMN MOVIE.
WHY DIDN'T YOU TELL ME YOU WANTED TO BREAK INTO MOVIES? YOU DIDN'T HAVE TO STAGE THIS BIG PRODUCTION.
PERSONALLY, I LOVE IT, BUT THIS COULD NEVER BE MADE INTO A MOVIE. A BOOK, SURE; BUT, NOT A MOVIE.
YOU DON'T--
WAIT. IF THIS IS A PITCH, THEN WHO'S THIS GUY? IS THIS AN AUDITION TOO?
GOOD QUESTION. JULIAN, ARE YOU MARRIED TO THIS GUY? WE COULD GET A DECENT NAME ATTACHED--
STOP!
YOU PEOPLE AREN'T LISTENING. THAT HAS BEEN THE PROBLEM SINCE WE FIRST CREATED YOU.
THE UPPER CRUST LOOKS DOWN ON THE MASSES. THE LOWER CLASS WANTS TO REVOLT BECAUSE THEY ALL THINK THEY HAVE THE SOLUTIONS, AND THE MIDDLE ARE TOO FAT AND CONTENT TO DO ANYTHING AT ALL.
I'VE SEEN KINGS FACE ONE ANOTHER IN MORTAL COMBAT. WHOLE KINGDOMS MET AND FOUGHT WITH WHATEVER CRUDE WEAPONS THEY COULD FASHION, AND THOSE WITHOUT WEAPONS FOUGHT WITH THEIR BARE HANDS.
BUT NOBODY IS WILLING TO GET THEIR HANDS DIRTY ANYMORE. AND THAT'S WHY I'M HERE. THE WORLD HAS GROWN TIRED OF YOU. LOOK AT YOURSELVES. YOU'RE FREAKS.
I'VE BEEN GONE FOR TWO THOUSAND YEARS, AND SHOULD BE MET BY A STRONGER, SMARTER, RACE. BUT, ALL I SEE ARE INDOLENT, SELF-ENTITLED, CUTTHROAT WORMS. THIS DECAY IS SO FAR GONE, I AM WASTING MY BREATH.
YOU PEOPLE HAVE CLOSED YOUR MINDS TO UNDERSTANDING, AND SO LADY EARTH, KNOWING THIS, CALLED ME FROM OUT OF THE DEPTHS FOR HER HOLY RETRIBUTION.
IT'S TIME TO BRING BACK THE OLD WAY.

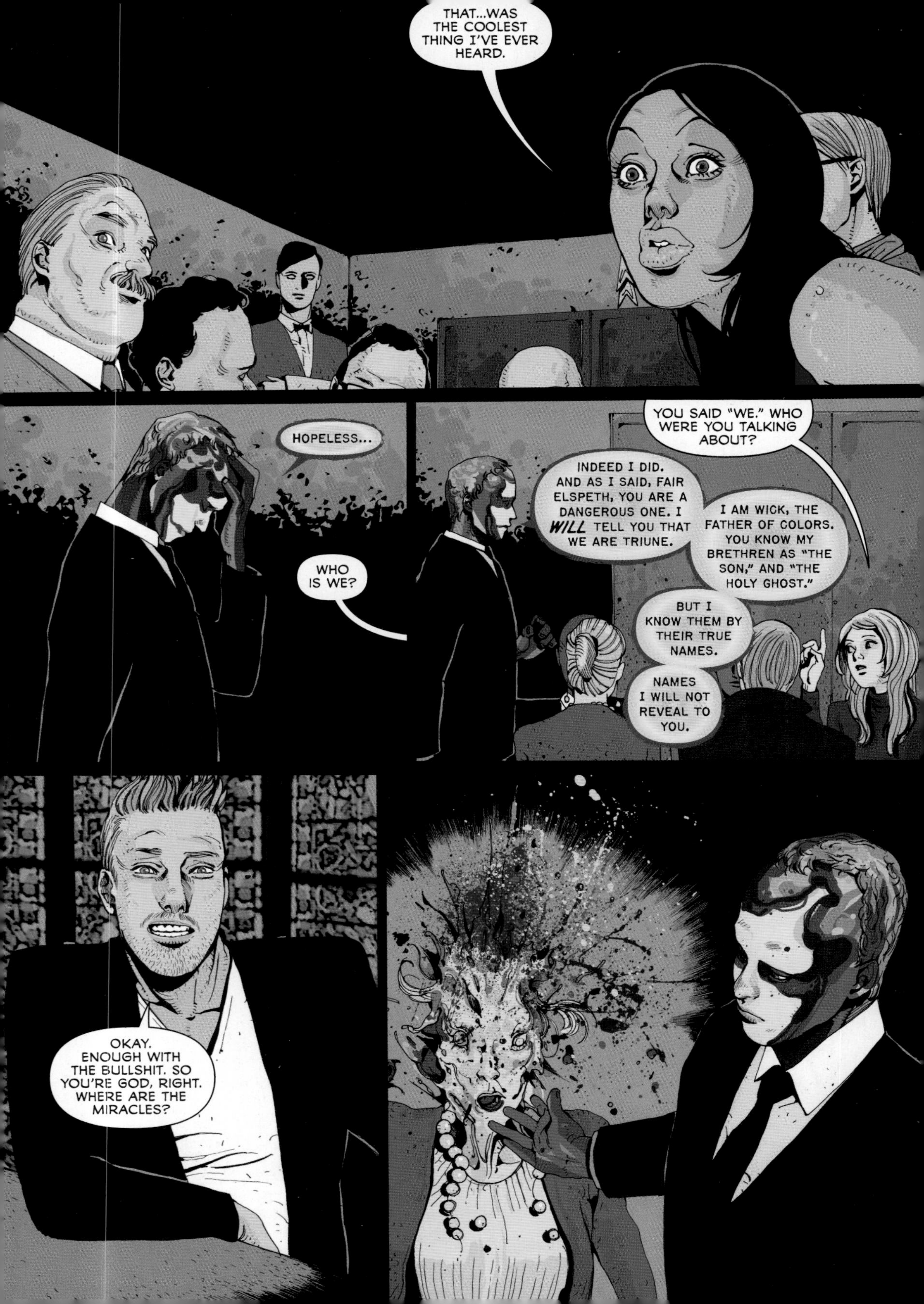
THAT...WAS THE COOLEST THING I'VE EVER HEARD.
HOPELESS...
WHO IS WE?
YOU SAID "WE." WHO WERE YOU TALKING ABOUT?
INDEED I DID. AND AS I SAID, FAIR ELSPETH, YOU ARE A DANGEROUS ONE. I WILL TELL YOU THAT WE ARE TRIUNE.
I AM WICK, THE FATHER OF COLORS. YOU KNOW MY BRETHREN AS "THE SON," AND "THE HOLY GHOST."
BUT I KNOW THEM BY THEIR TRUE NAMES.
NAMES I WILL NOT REVEAL TO YOU.
OKAY. ENOUGH WITH THE BULLSHIT. SO YOU'RE GOD, RIGHT. WHERE ARE THE MIRACLES?

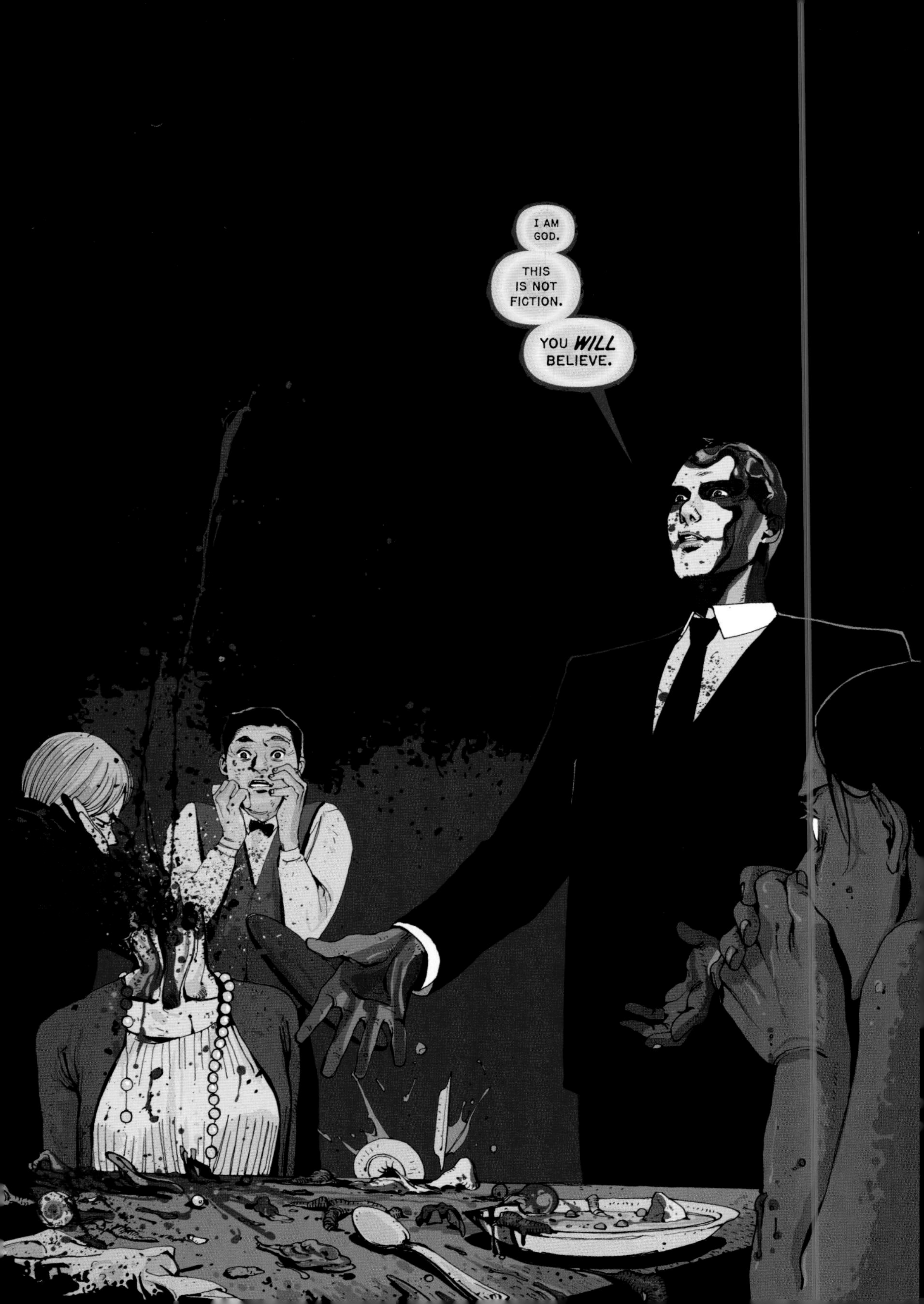
I AM GOD.
THIS IS NOT FICTION.
YOU *WILL* BELIEVE.

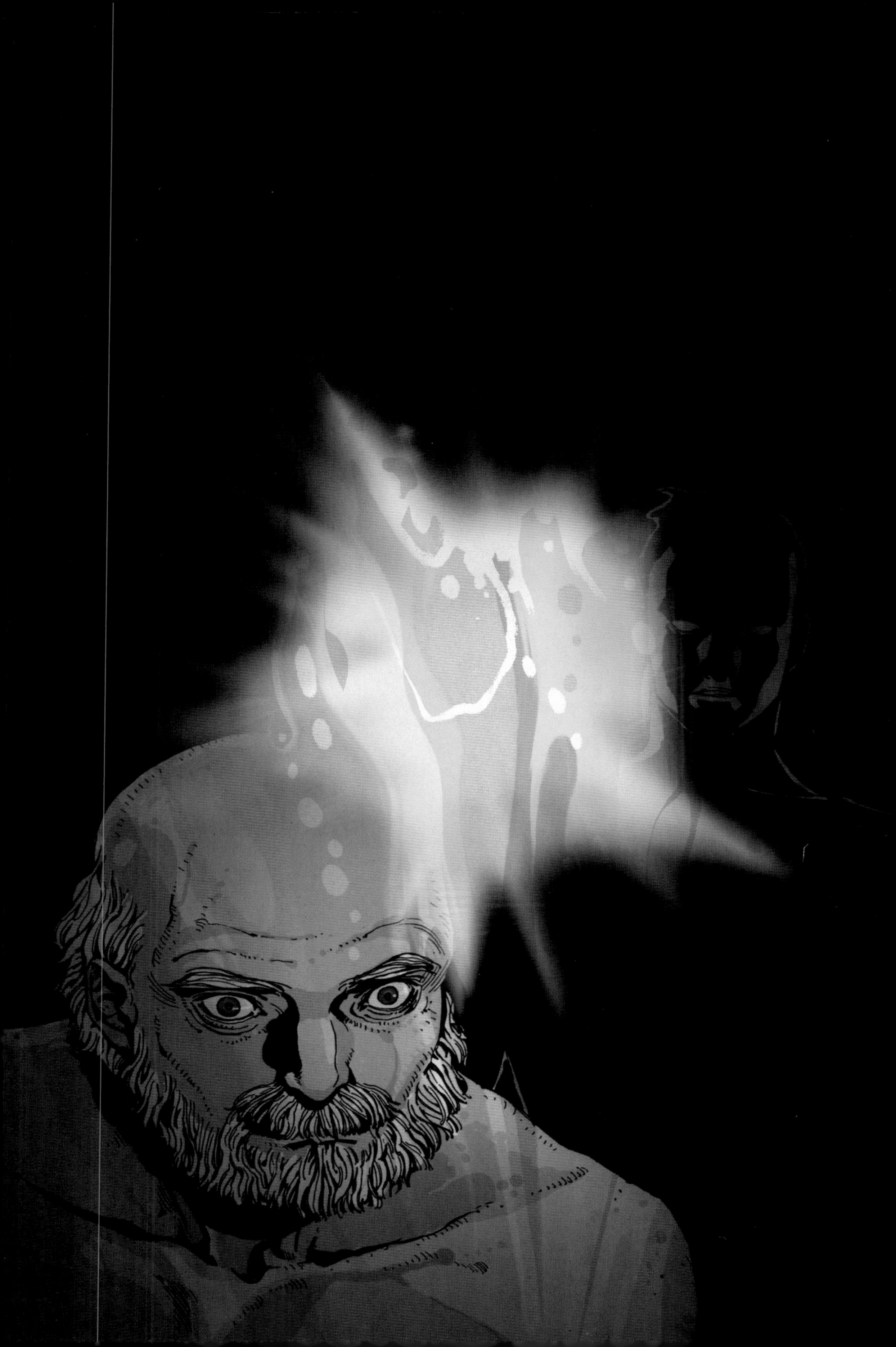

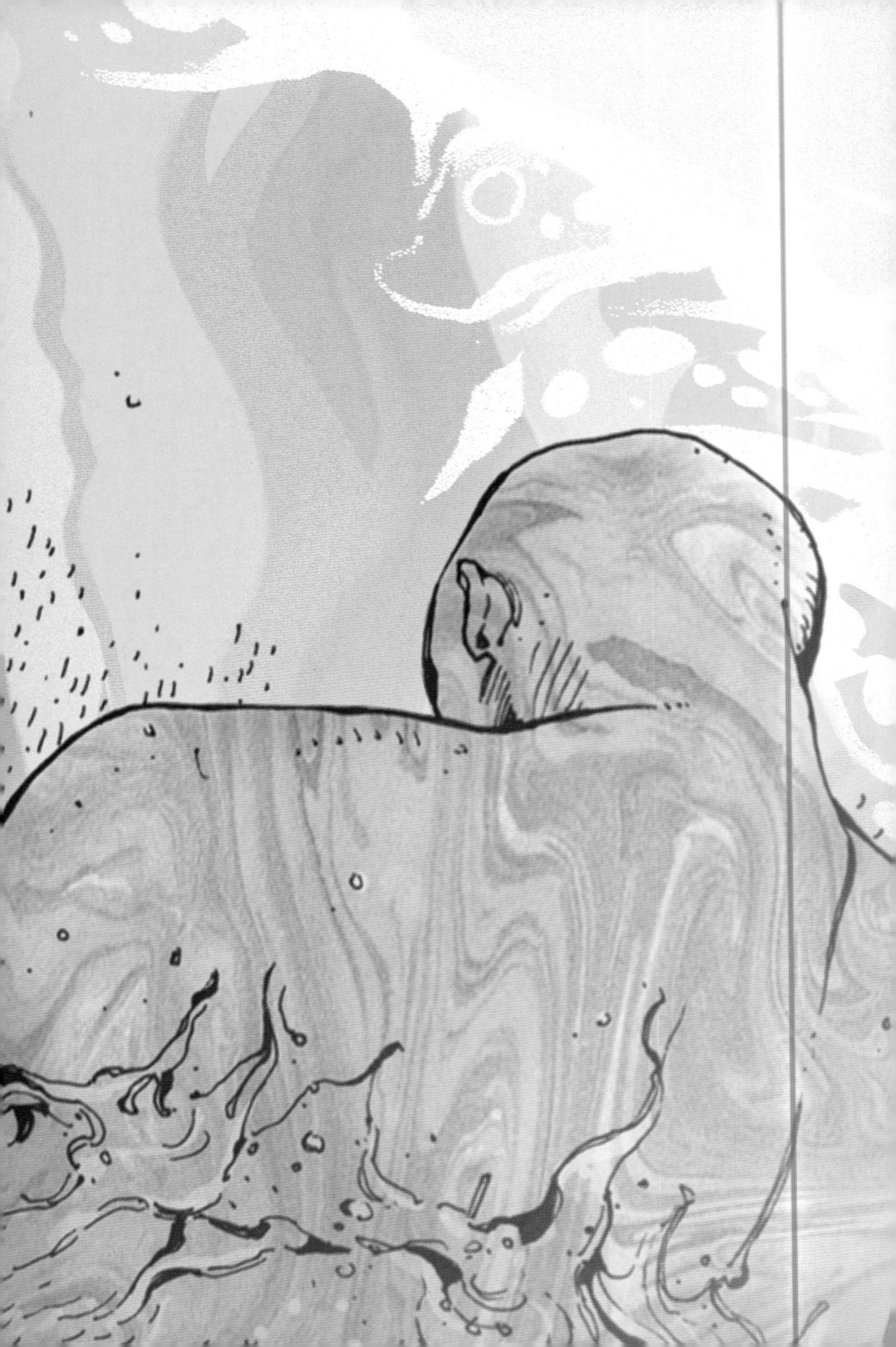

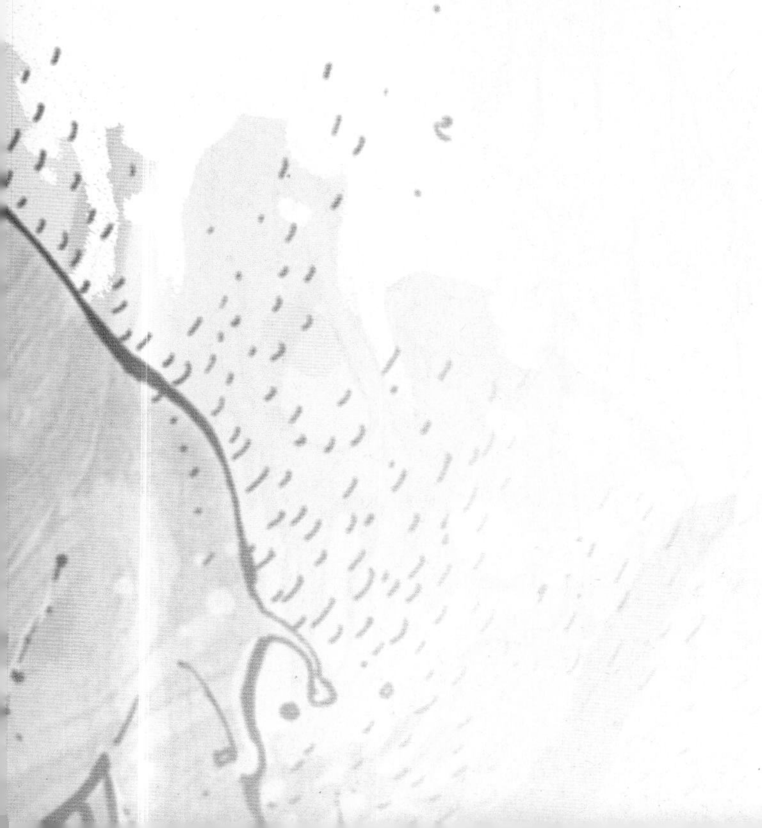

CHAPTER THREE

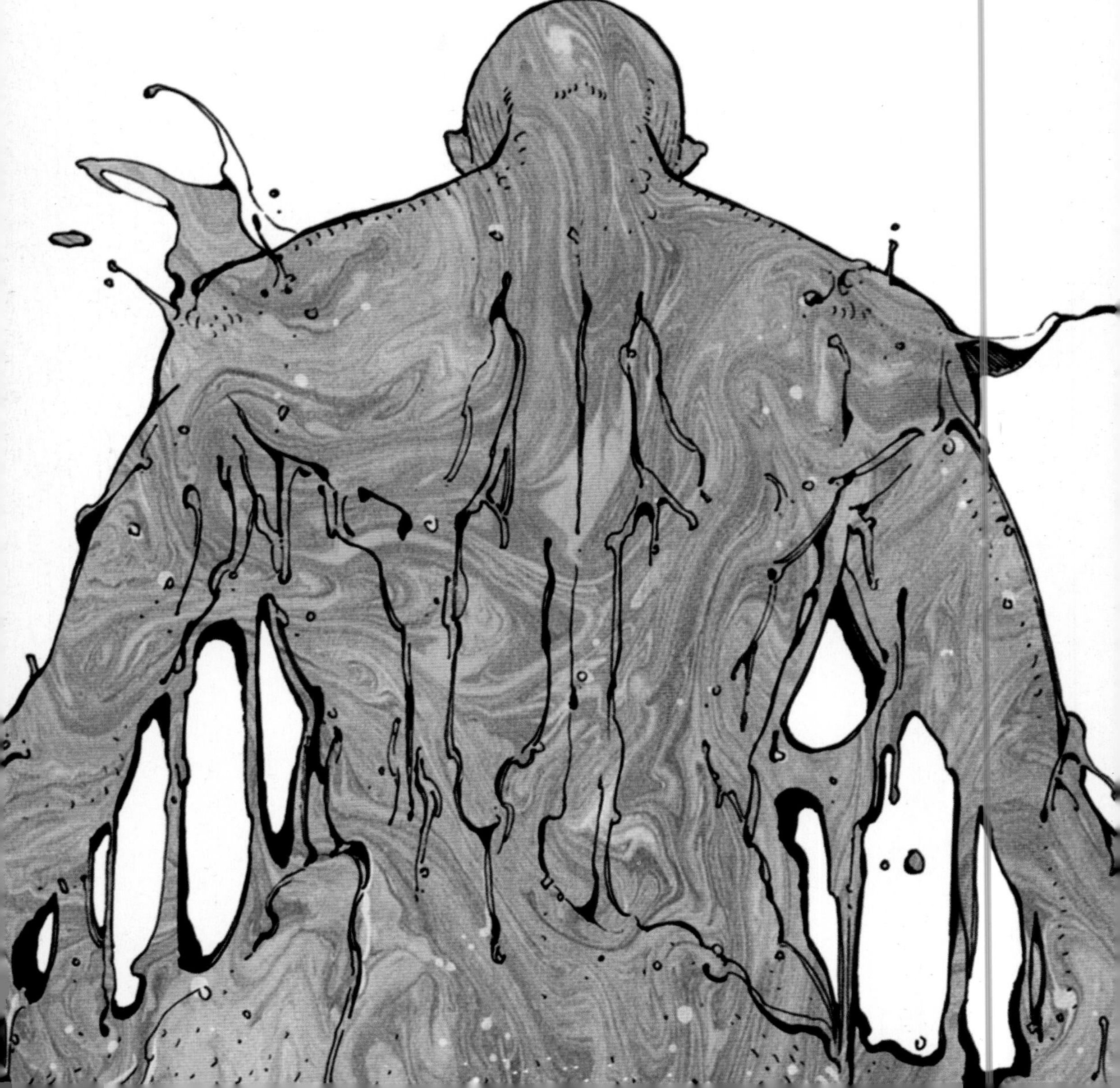

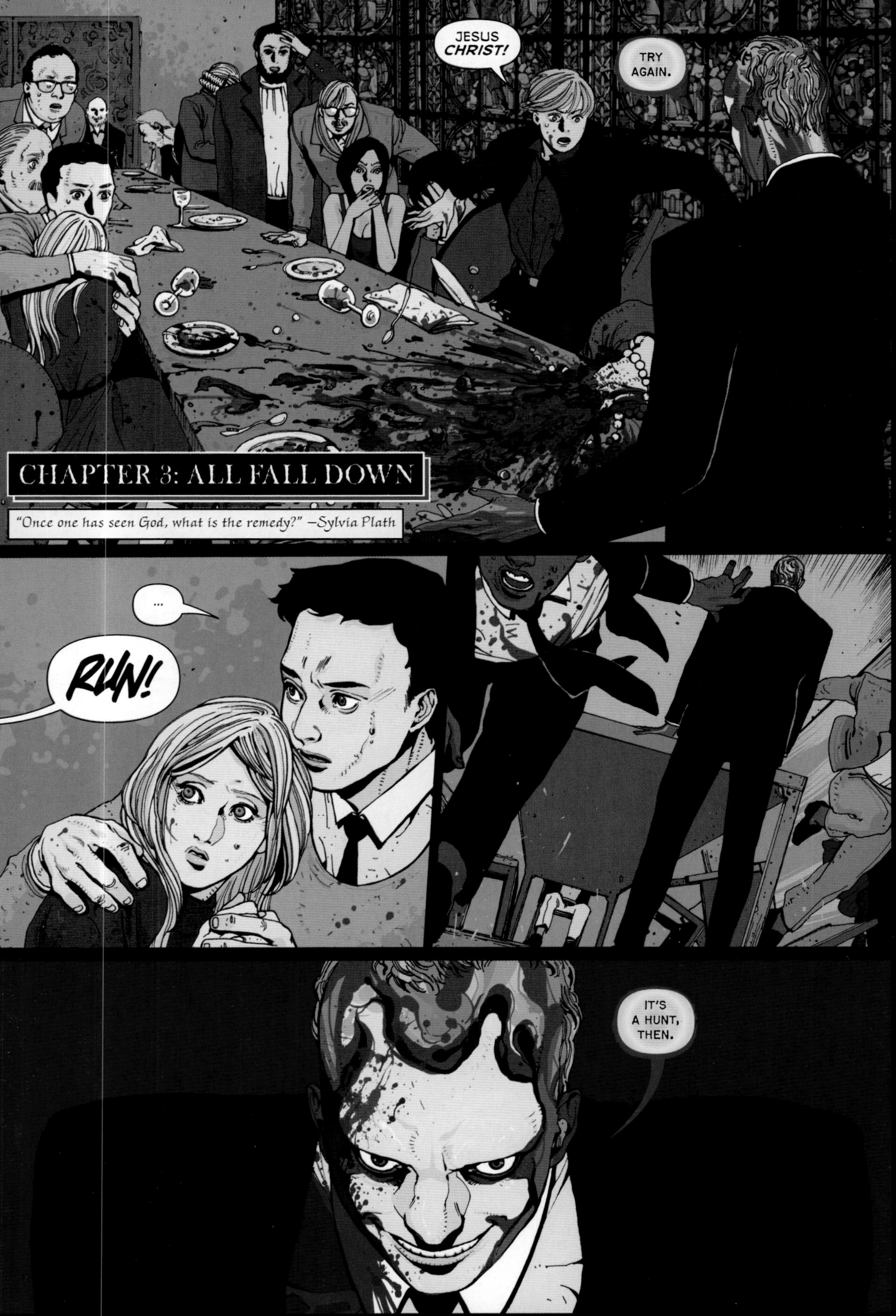
JESUS CHRIST!
TRY AGAIN.
CHAPTER 3: ALL FALL DOWN
"Once one has seen God, what is the remedy?" —Sylvia Plath
...
RUN!
IT'S A HUNT, THEN.

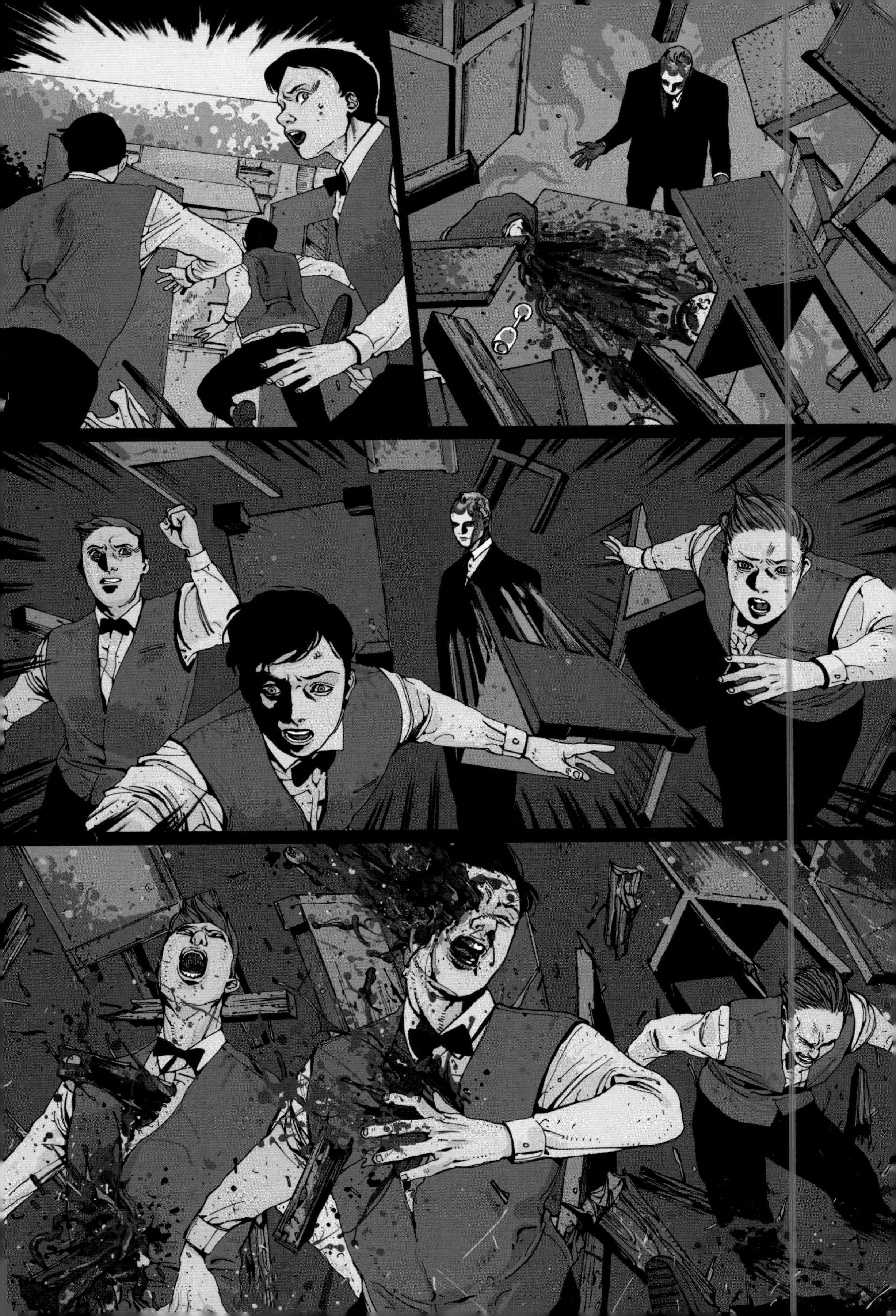

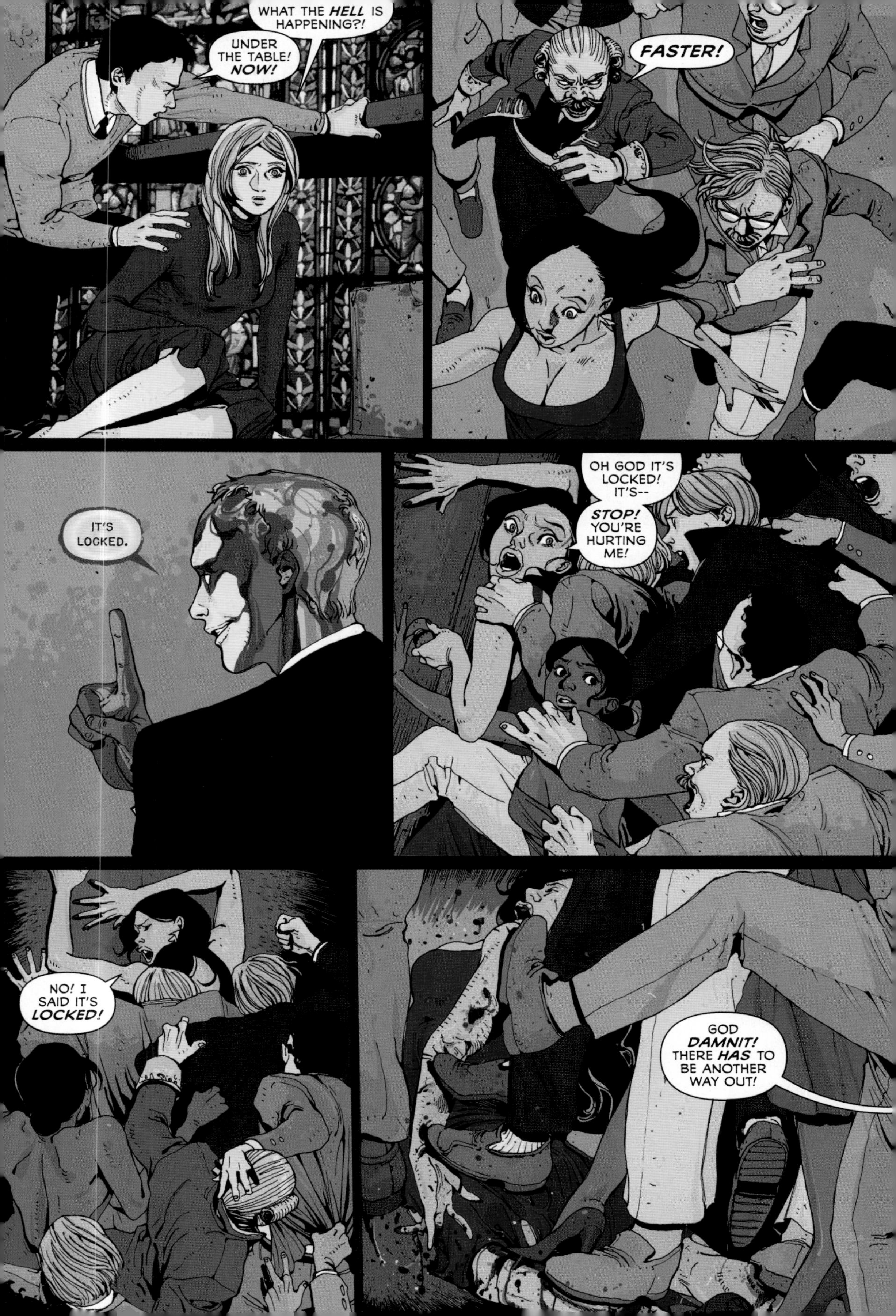

WHAT THE **HELL** IS HAPPENING?!
UNDER THE TABLE! **NOW!**
FASTER!
IT'S LOCKED.
OH GOD IT'S LOCKED! IT'S--
STOP! YOU'RE HURTING ME!
NO! I SAID IT'S **LOCKED!**
GOD **DAMNIT!** THERE **HAS** TO BE ANOTHER WAY OUT!

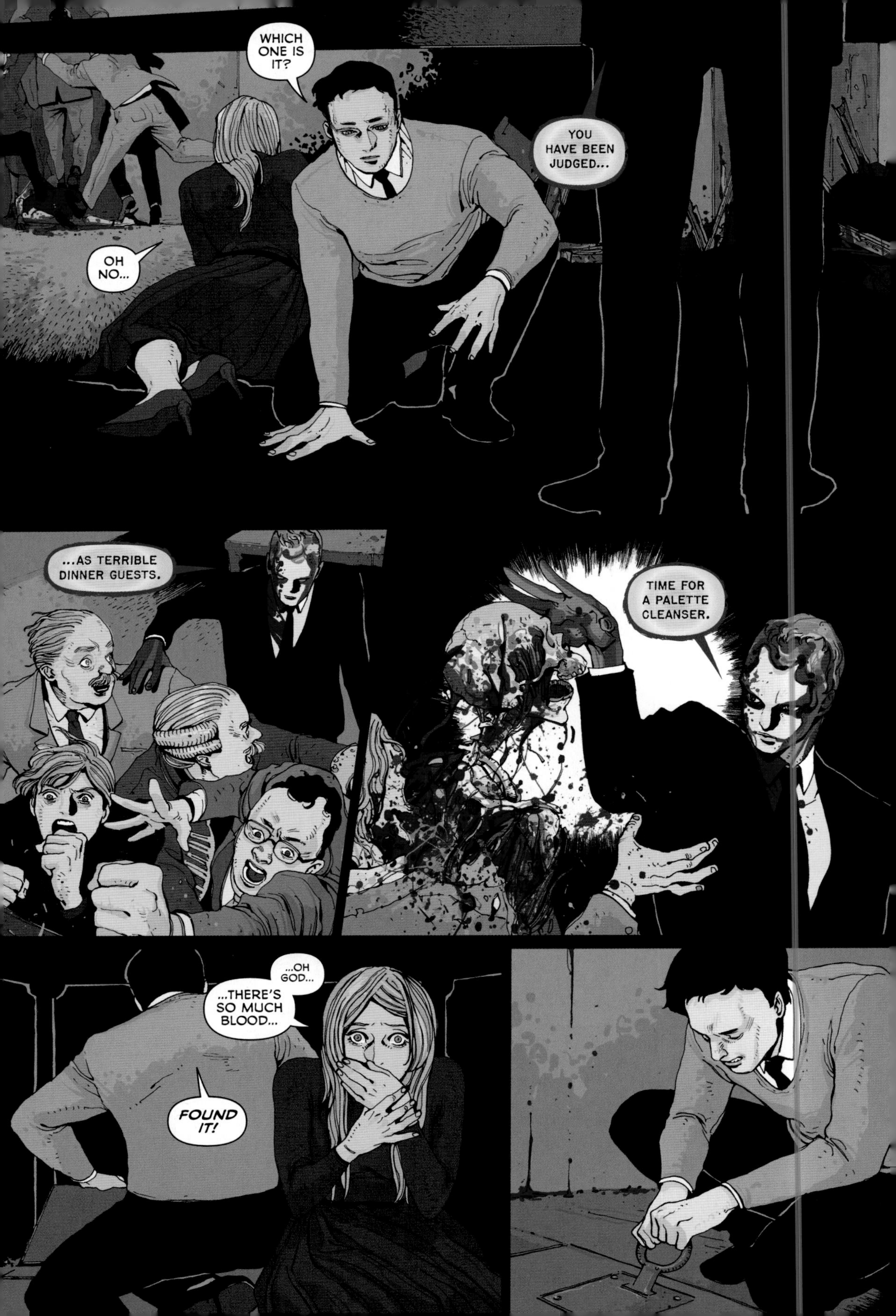
WHICH ONE IS IT?
YOU HAVE BEEN JUDGED...
OH NO...
...AS TERRIBLE DINNER GUESTS.
TIME FOR A PALETTE CLEANSER.
...OH GOD...
...THERE'S SO MUCH BLOOD...
FOUND IT!

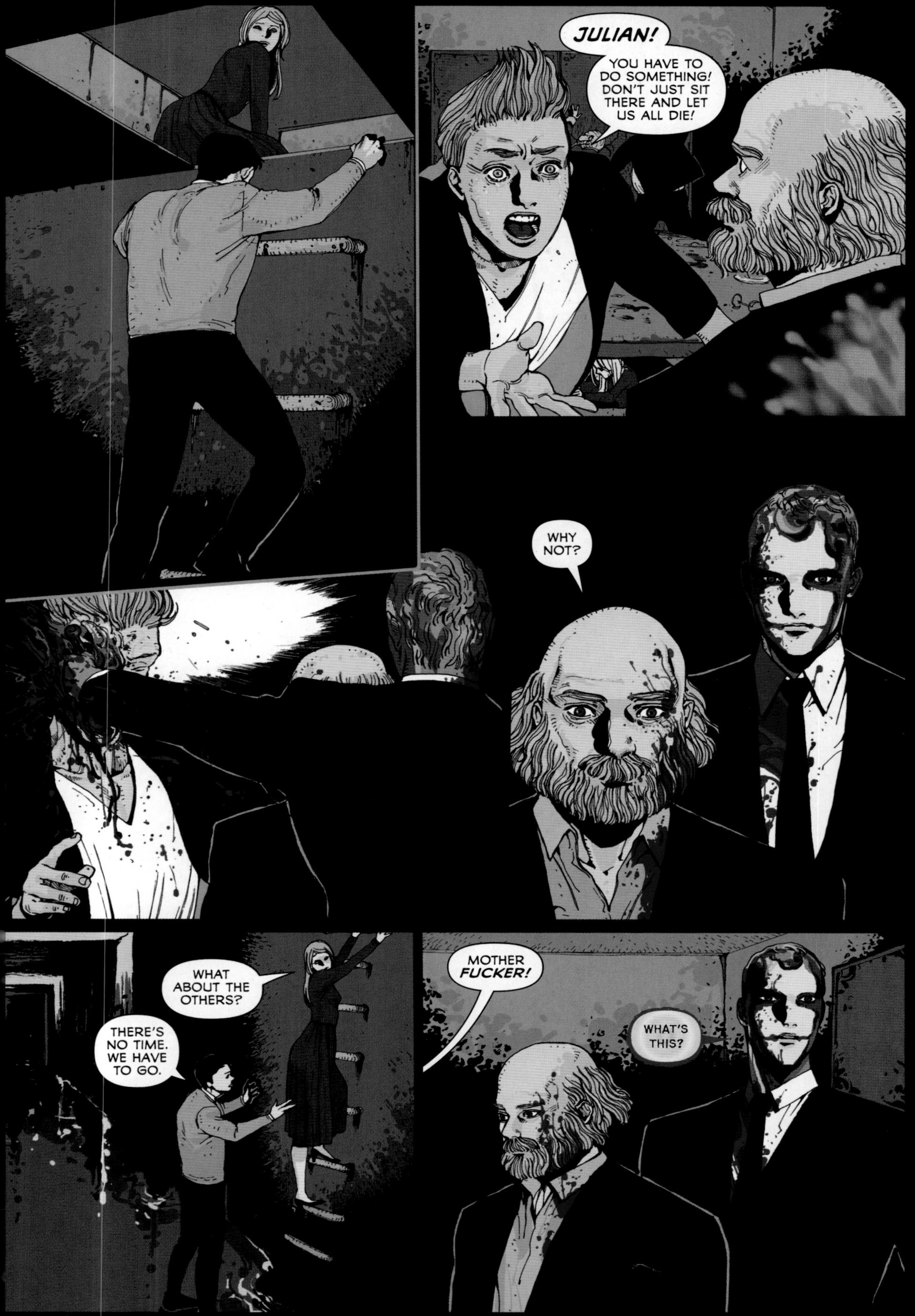
JULIAN!
YOU HAVE TO DO SOMETHING! DON'T JUST SIT THERE AND LET US ALL DIE!
WHY NOT?
WHAT ABOUT THE OTHERS?
THERE'S NO TIME. WE HAVE TO GO.
MOTHER *FUCKER!*
WHAT'S THIS?

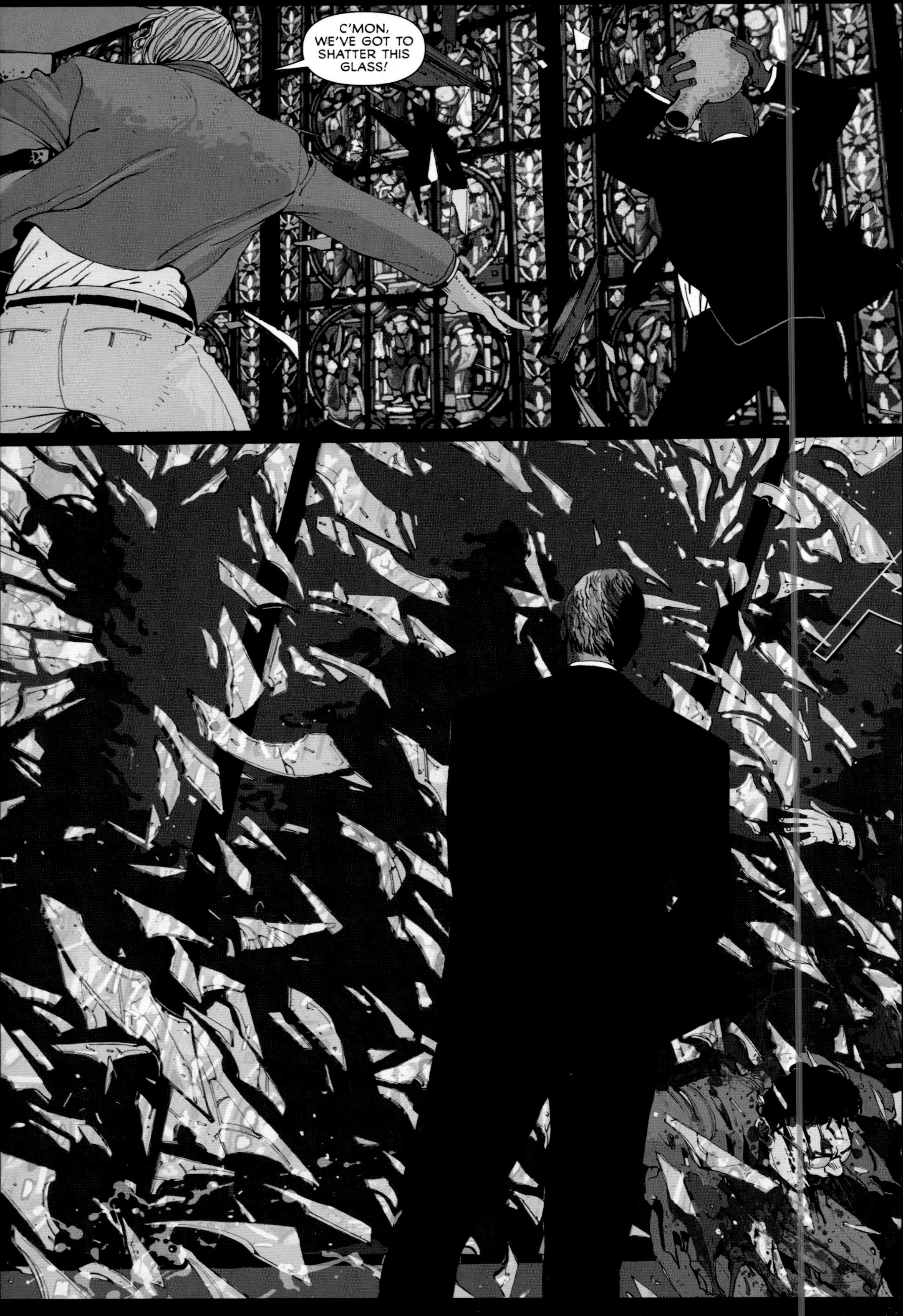
C'MON, WE'VE GOT TO SHATTER THIS GLASS!

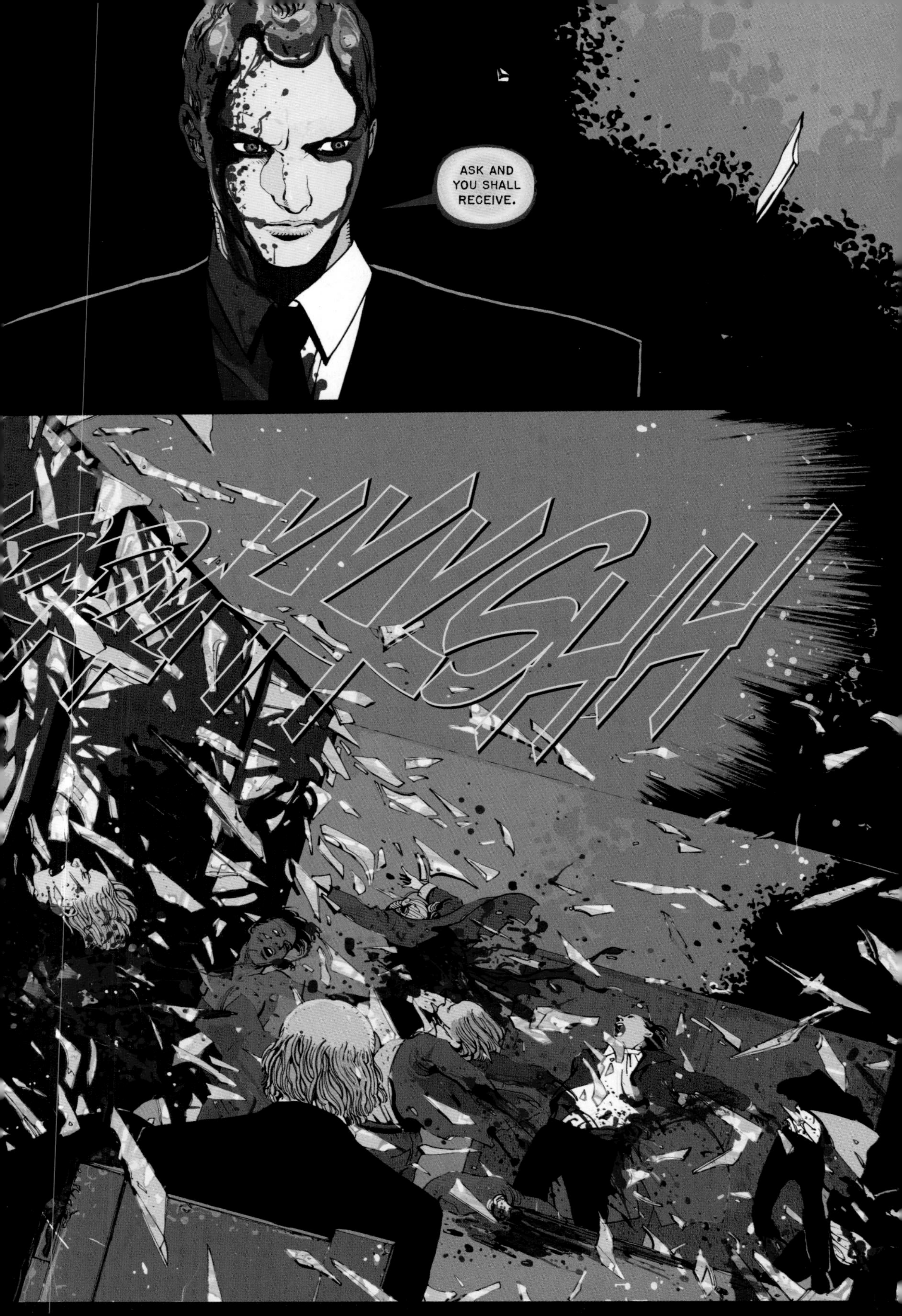
ASK AND YOU SHALL RECEIVE.

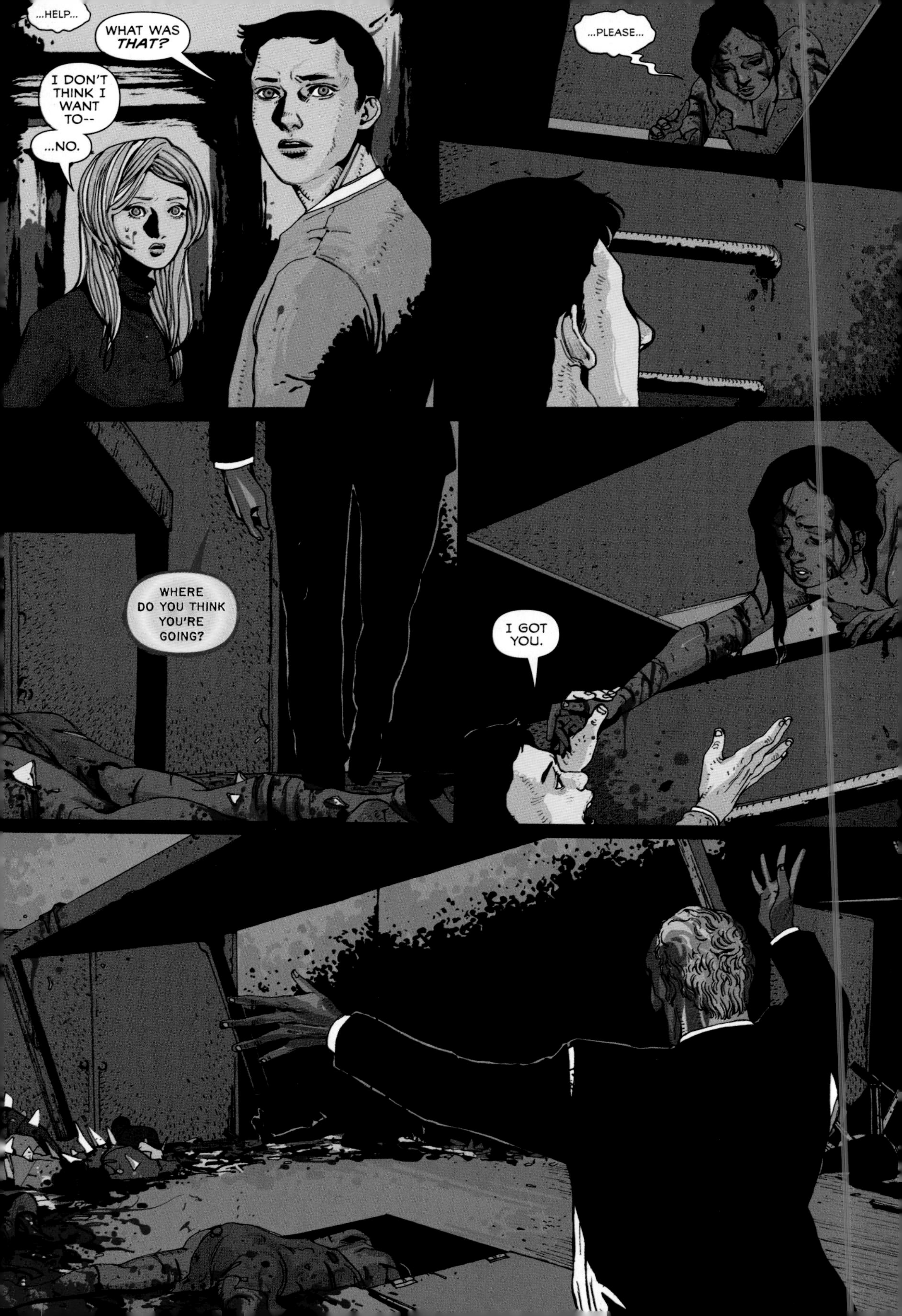

...HELP...
WHAT WAS *THAT?*
I DON'T THINK I WANT TO--
...NO.
...PLEASE...
WHERE DO YOU THINK YOU'RE GOING?
I GOT YOU.

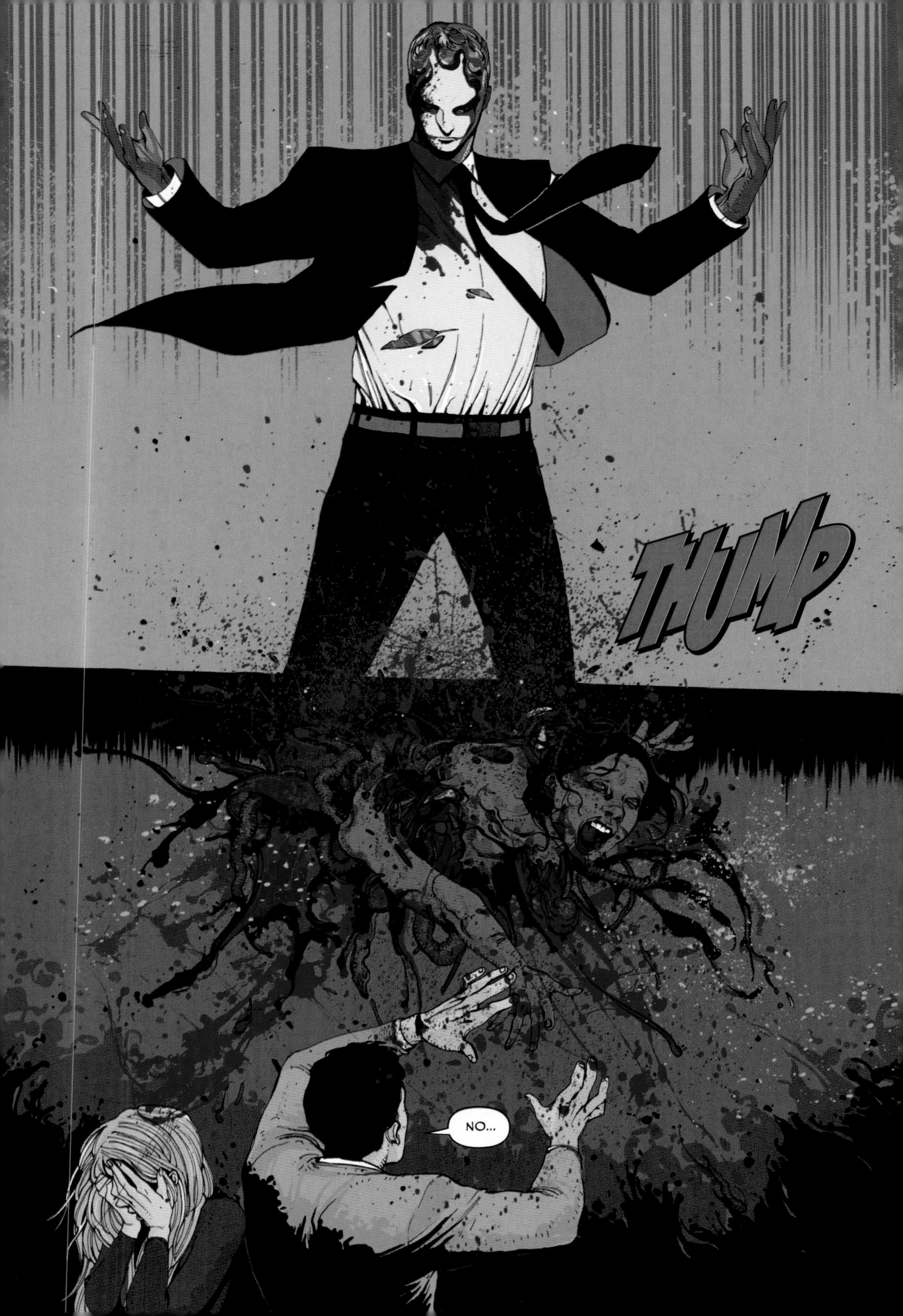
THUMP
NO...

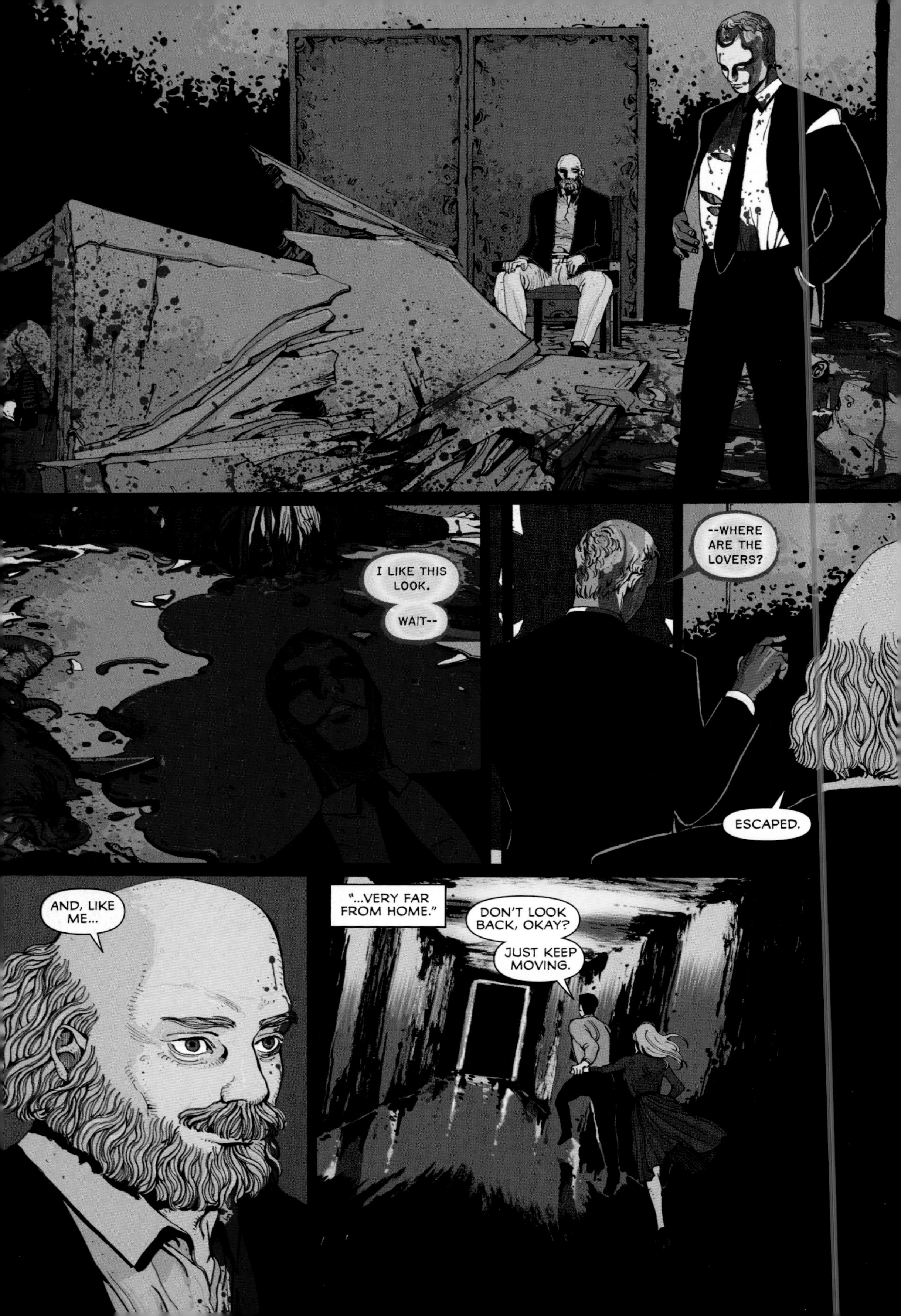

I LIKE THIS LOOK.
WAIT--
--WHERE ARE THE LOVERS?
ESCAPED.
AND, LIKE ME...
"...VERY FAR FROM HOME."
DON'T LOOK BACK, OKAY?
JUST KEEP MOVING.

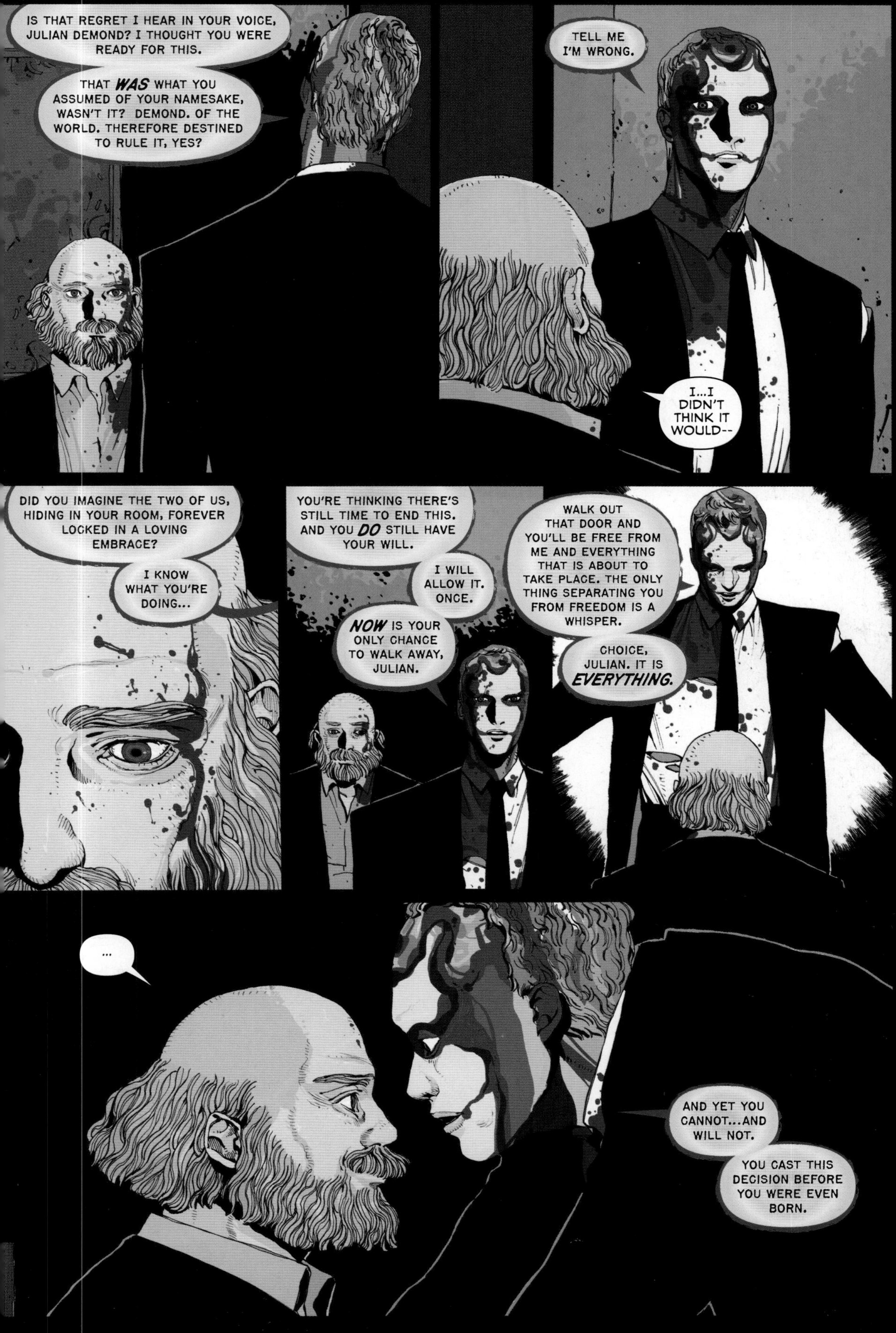
IS THAT REGRET I HEAR IN YOUR VOICE, JULIAN DEMOND? I THOUGHT YOU WERE READY FOR THIS.
THAT WAS WHAT YOU ASSUMED OF YOUR NAMESAKE, WASN'T IT? DEMOND. OF THE WORLD. THEREFORE DESTINED TO RULE IT, YES?
TELL ME I'M WRONG.
I...I DIDN'T THINK IT WOULD--
DID YOU IMAGINE THE TWO OF US, HIDING IN YOUR ROOM, FOREVER LOCKED IN A LOVING EMBRACE?
I KNOW WHAT YOU'RE DOING...
YOU'RE THINKING THERE'S STILL TIME TO END THIS. AND YOU DO STILL HAVE YOUR WILL.
I WILL ALLOW IT. ONCE.
NOW IS YOUR ONLY CHANCE TO WALK AWAY, JULIAN.
WALK OUT THAT DOOR AND YOU'LL BE FREE FROM ME AND EVERYTHING THAT IS ABOUT TO TAKE PLACE. THE ONLY THING SEPARATING YOU FROM FREEDOM IS A WHISPER.
CHOICE, JULIAN. IT IS EVERYTHING.
...
AND YET YOU CANNOT...AND WILL NOT.
YOU CAST THIS DECISION BEFORE YOU WERE EVEN BORN.

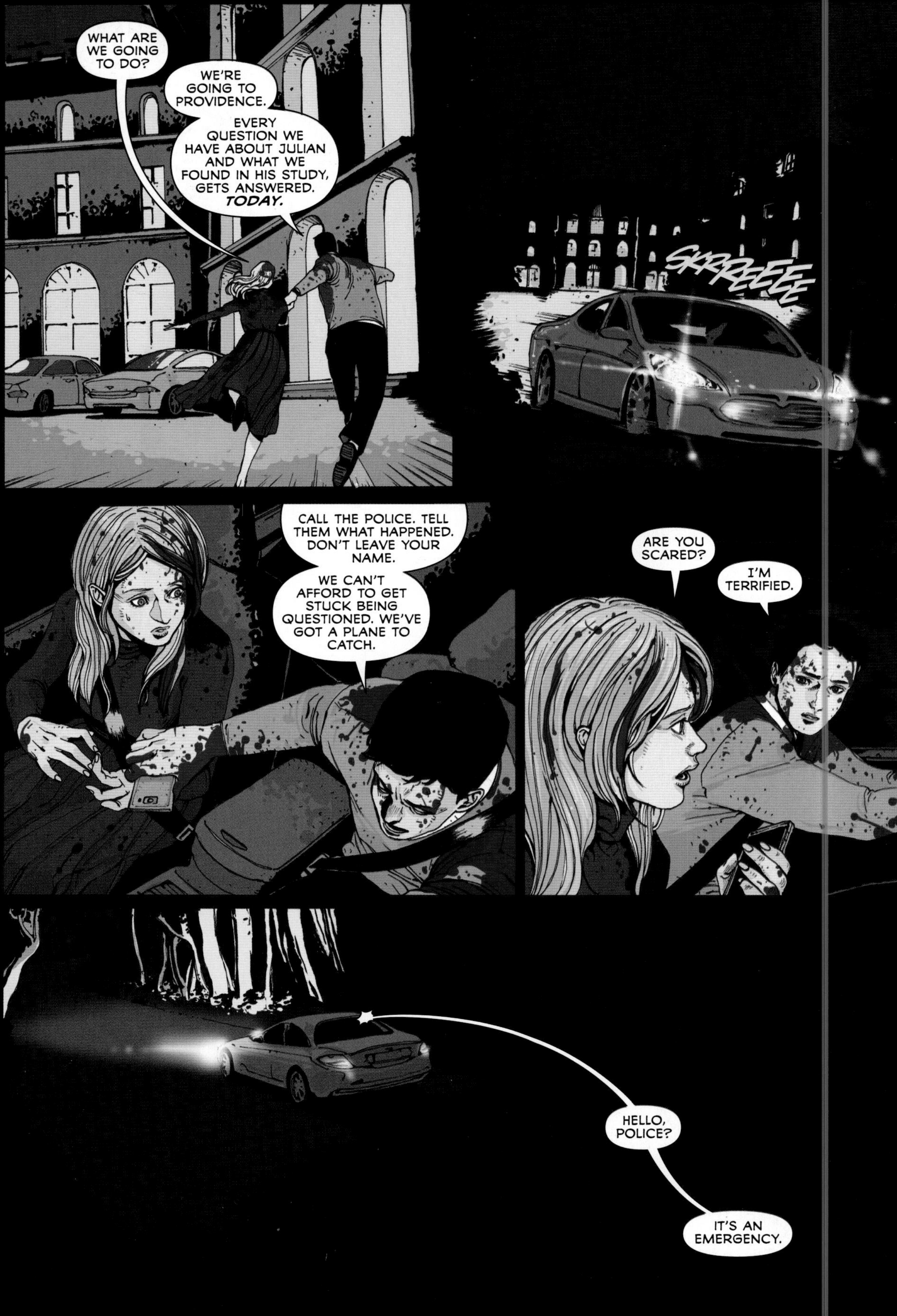
WHAT ARE WE GOING TO DO?
WE'RE GOING TO PROVIDENCE.
EVERY QUESTION WE HAVE ABOUT JULIAN AND WHAT WE FOUND IN HIS STUDY, GETS ANSWERED. *TODAY.*
SKRREEEE
CALL THE POLICE. TELL THEM WHAT HAPPENED. DON'T LEAVE YOUR NAME.
WE CAN'T AFFORD TO GET STUCK BEING QUESTIONED. WE'VE GOT A PLANE TO CATCH.
ARE YOU SCARED?
I'M TERRIFIED.
HELLO, POLICE?
IT'S AN EMERGENCY.

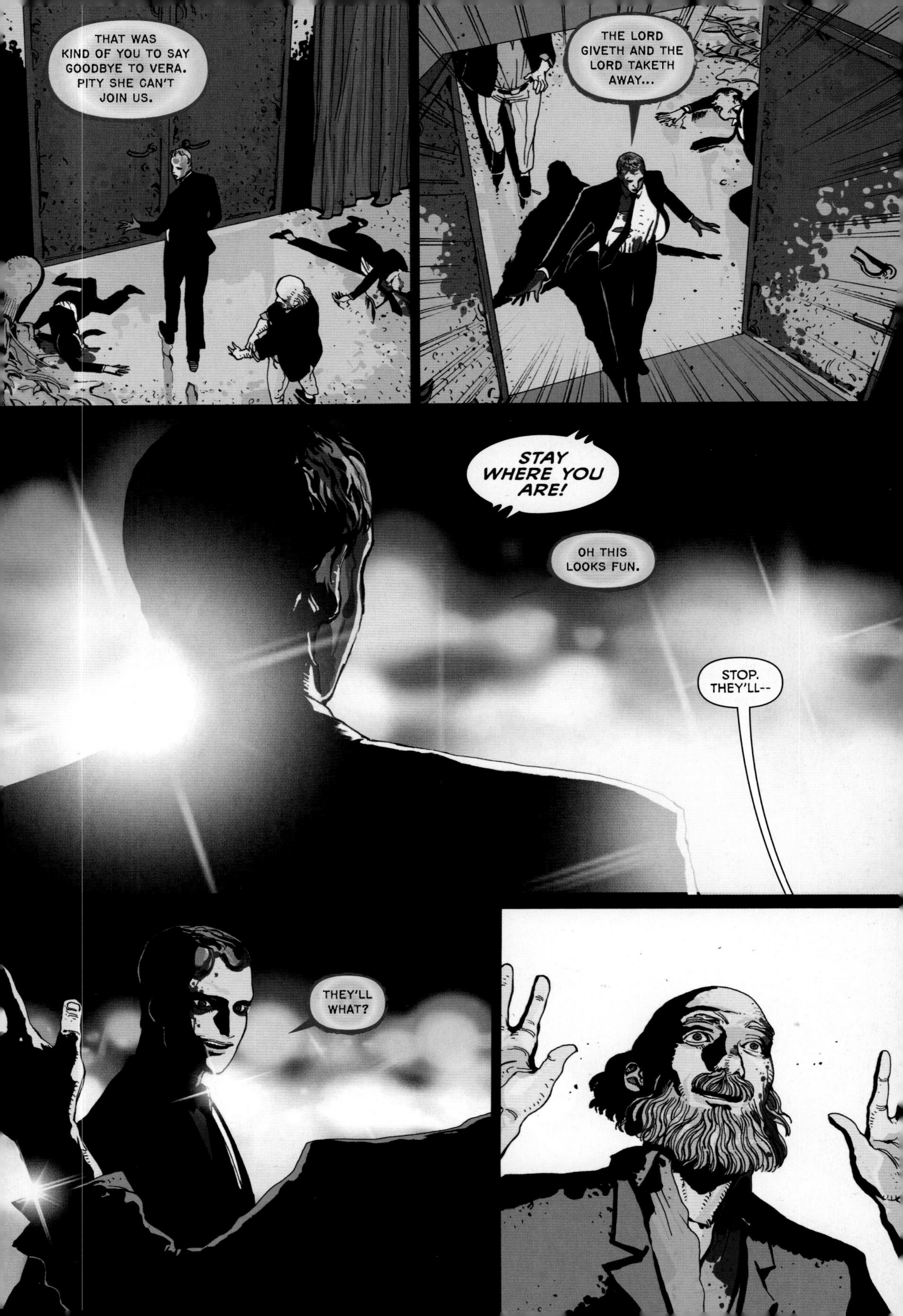
THAT WAS KIND OF YOU TO SAY GOODBYE TO VERA. PITY SHE CAN'T JOIN US.
THE LORD GIVETH AND THE LORD TAKETH AWAY...
STAY WHERE YOU ARE!
OH THIS LOOKS FUN.
STOP. THEY'LL--
THEY'LL WHAT?

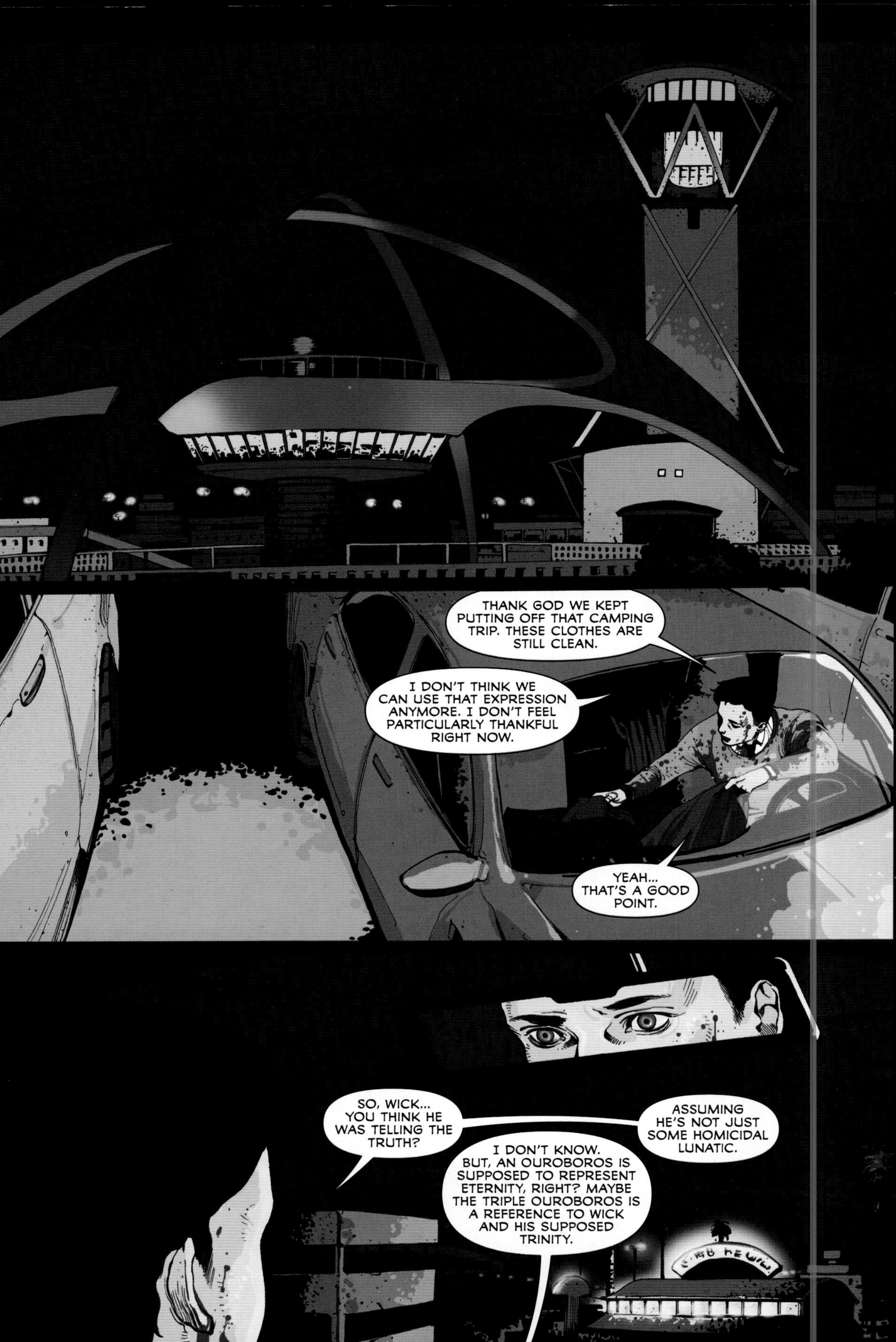
THANK GOD WE KEPT PUTTING OFF THAT CAMPING TRIP. THESE CLOTHES ARE STILL CLEAN.
I DON'T THINK WE CAN USE THAT EXPRESSION ANYMORE. I DON'T FEEL PARTICULARLY THANKFUL RIGHT NOW.
YEAH... THAT'S A GOOD POINT.
SO, WICK... YOU THINK HE WAS TELLING THE TRUTH?
ASSUMING HE'S NOT JUST SOME HOMICIDAL LUNATIC.
I DON'T KNOW. BUT, AN OUROBOROS IS SUPPOSED TO REPRESENT ETERNITY, RIGHT? MAYBE THE TRIPLE OUROBOROS IS A REFERENCE TO WICK AND HIS SUPPOSED TRINITY.

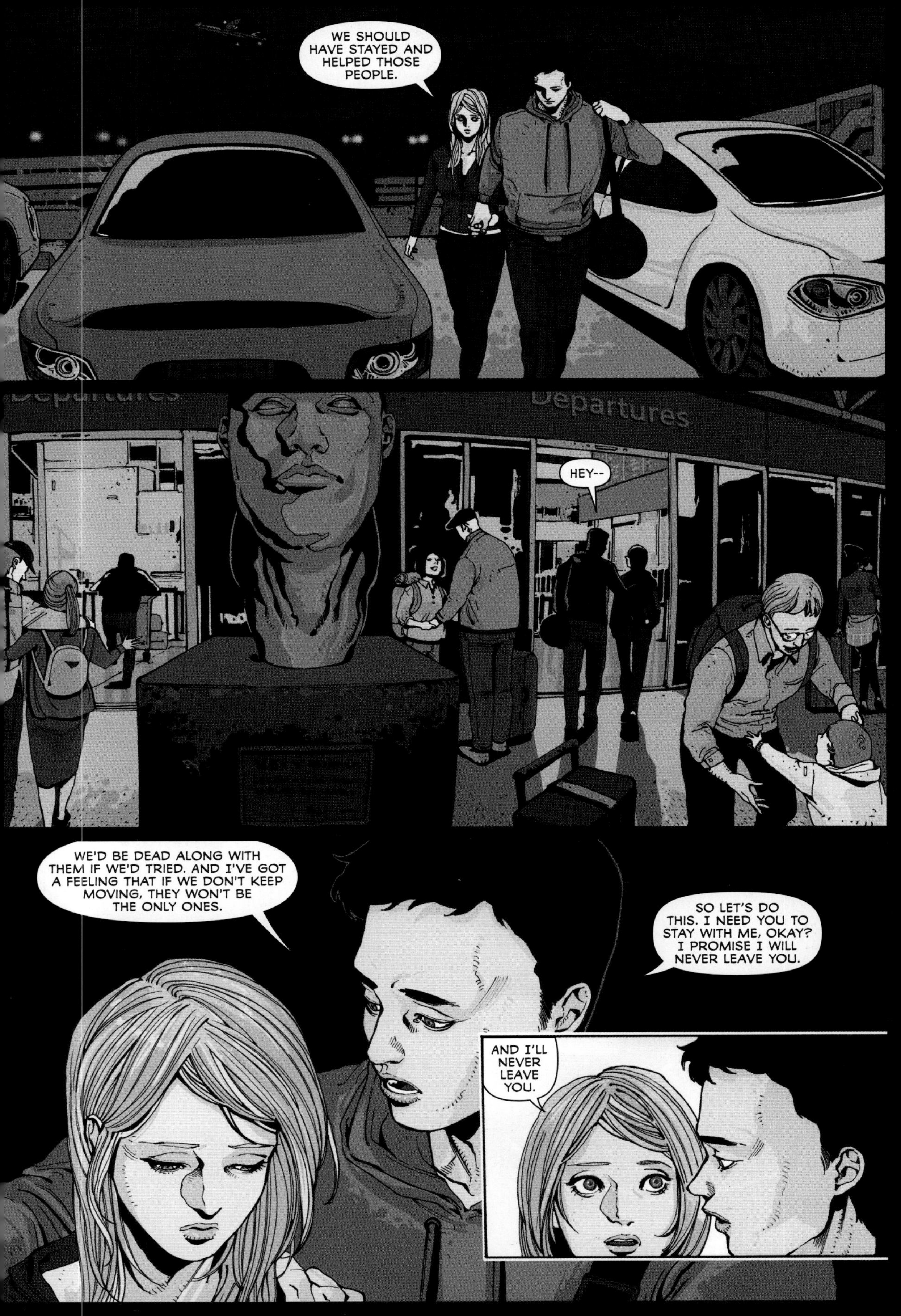
WE SHOULD HAVE STAYED AND HELPED THOSE PEOPLE.
Departures
Departures
HEY--
WE'D BE DEAD ALONG WITH THEM IF WE'D TRIED. AND I'VE GOT A FEELING THAT IF WE DON'T KEEP MOVING, THEY WON'T BE THE ONLY ONES.
SO LET'S DO THIS. I NEED YOU TO STAY WITH ME, OKAY? I PROMISE I WILL NEVER LEAVE YOU.
AND I'LL NEVER LEAVE YOU.

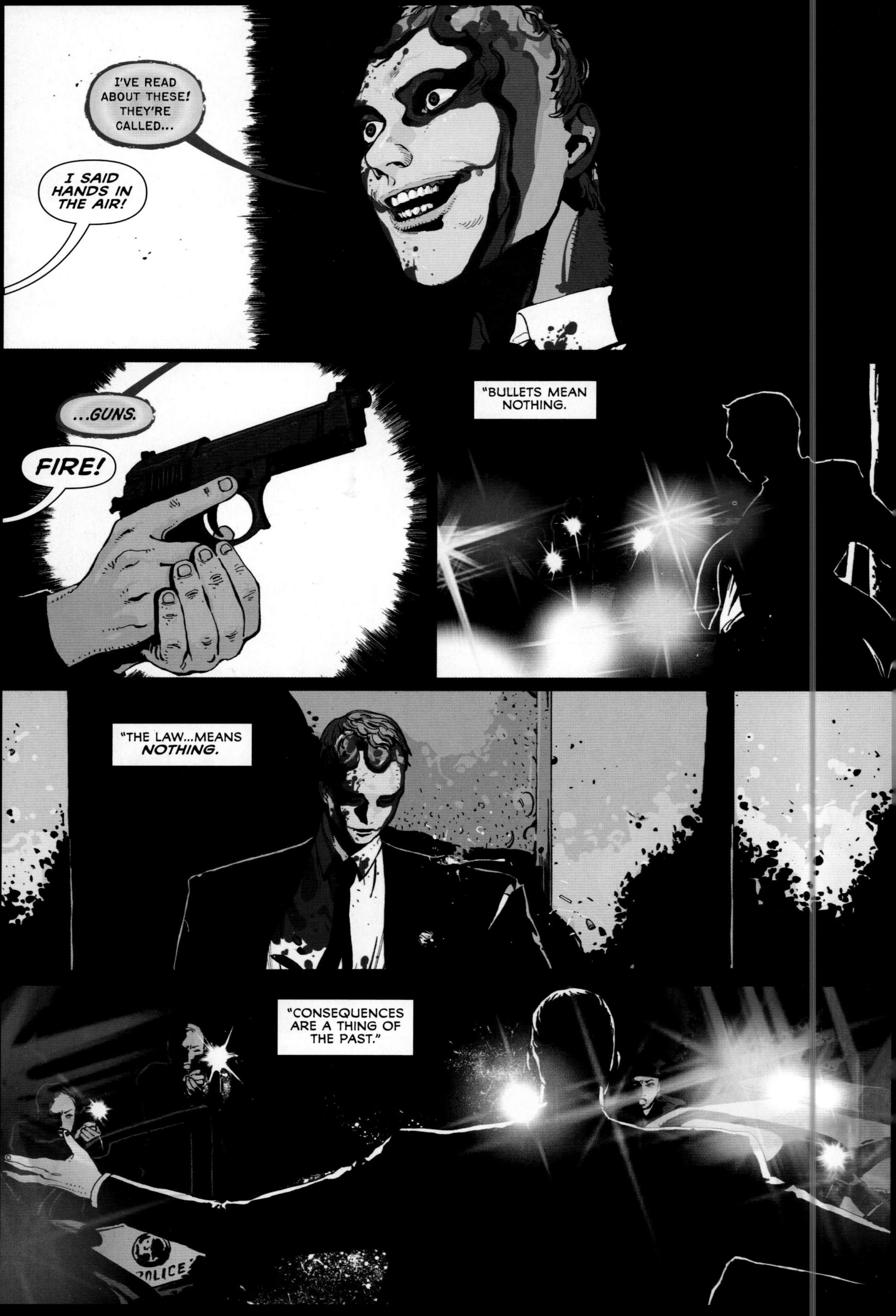
I'VE READ ABOUT THESE! THEY'RE CALLED...
I SAID HANDS IN THE AIR!
...GUNS.
FIRE!
"BULLETS MEAN NOTHING.
"THE LAW...MEANS *NOTHING.*
"CONSEQUENCES ARE A THING OF THE PAST."
POLICE

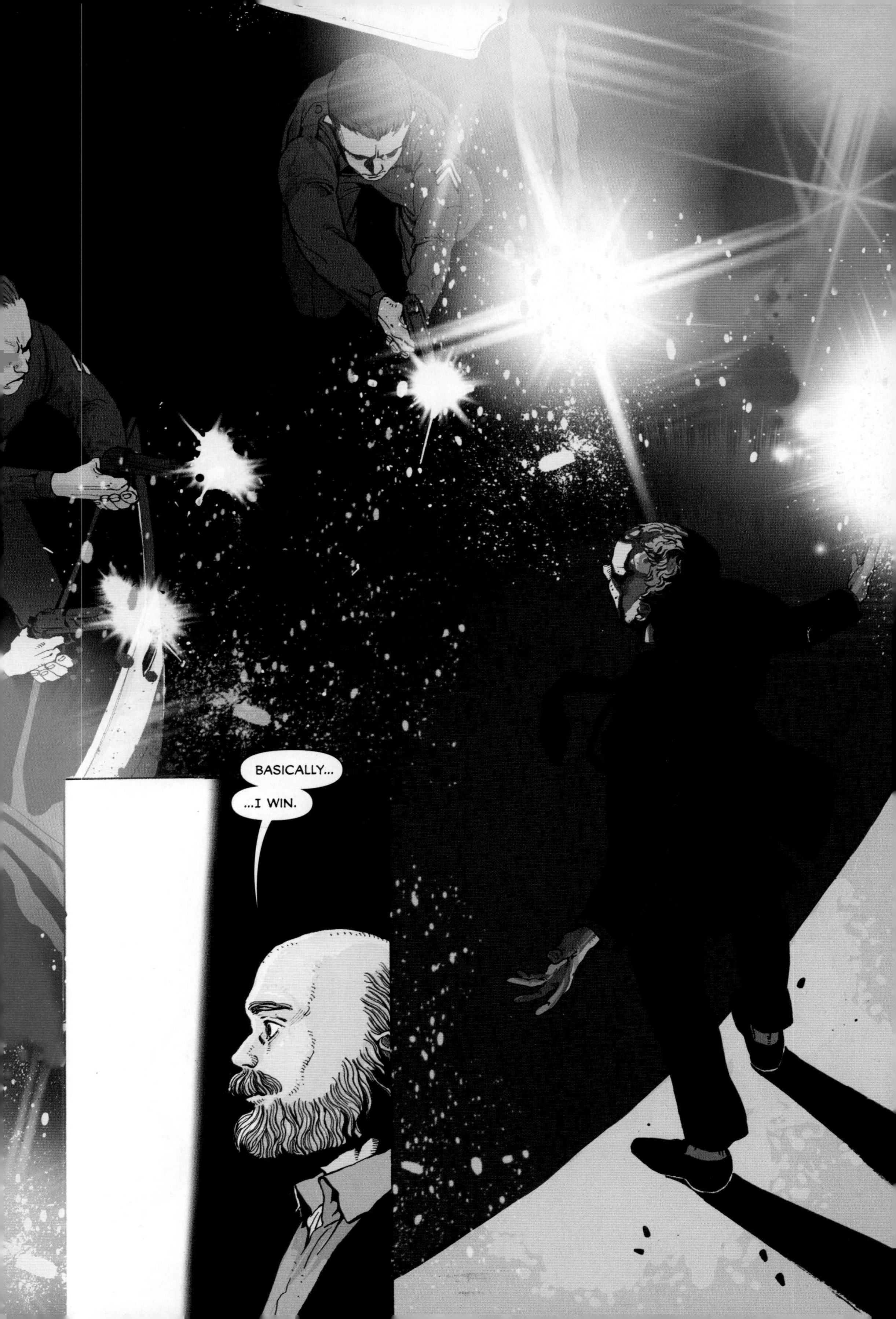
BASICALLY...
...I WIN.

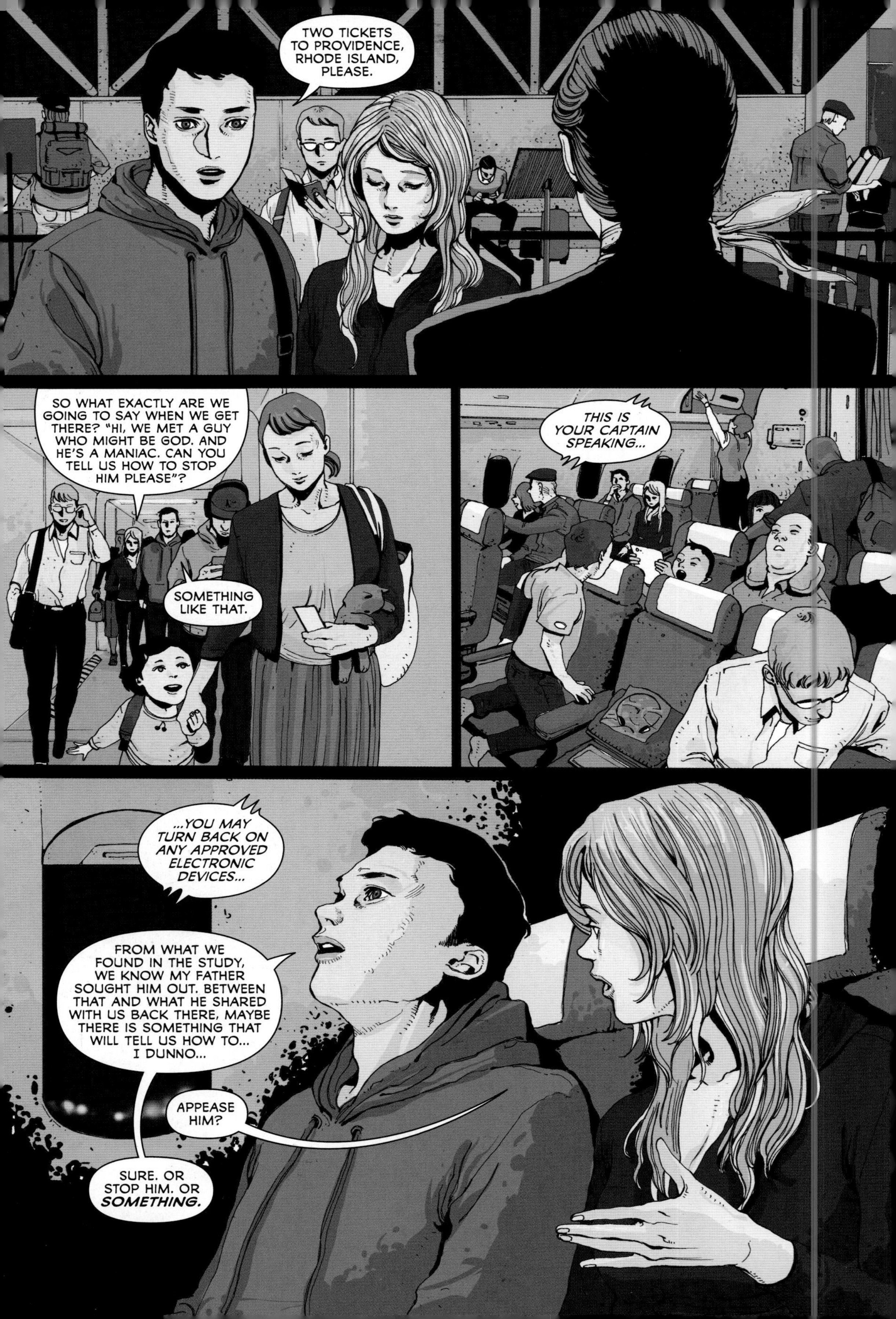
TWO TICKETS TO PROVIDENCE, RHODE ISLAND, PLEASE.
SO WHAT EXACTLY ARE WE GOING TO SAY WHEN WE GET THERE? "HI, WE MET A GUY WHO MIGHT BE GOD. AND HE'S A MANIAC. CAN YOU TELL US HOW TO STOP HIM PLEASE"?
SOMETHING LIKE THAT.
THIS IS YOUR CAPTAIN SPEAKING...
...YOU MAY TURN BACK ON ANY APPROVED ELECTRONIC DEVICES...
FROM WHAT WE FOUND IN THE STUDY, WE KNOW MY FATHER SOUGHT HIM OUT. BETWEEN THAT AND WHAT HE SHARED WITH US BACK THERE, MAYBE THERE IS SOMETHING THAT WILL TELL US HOW TO... I DUNNO...
APPEASE HIM?
SURE. OR STOP HIM. OR ***SOMETHING.***

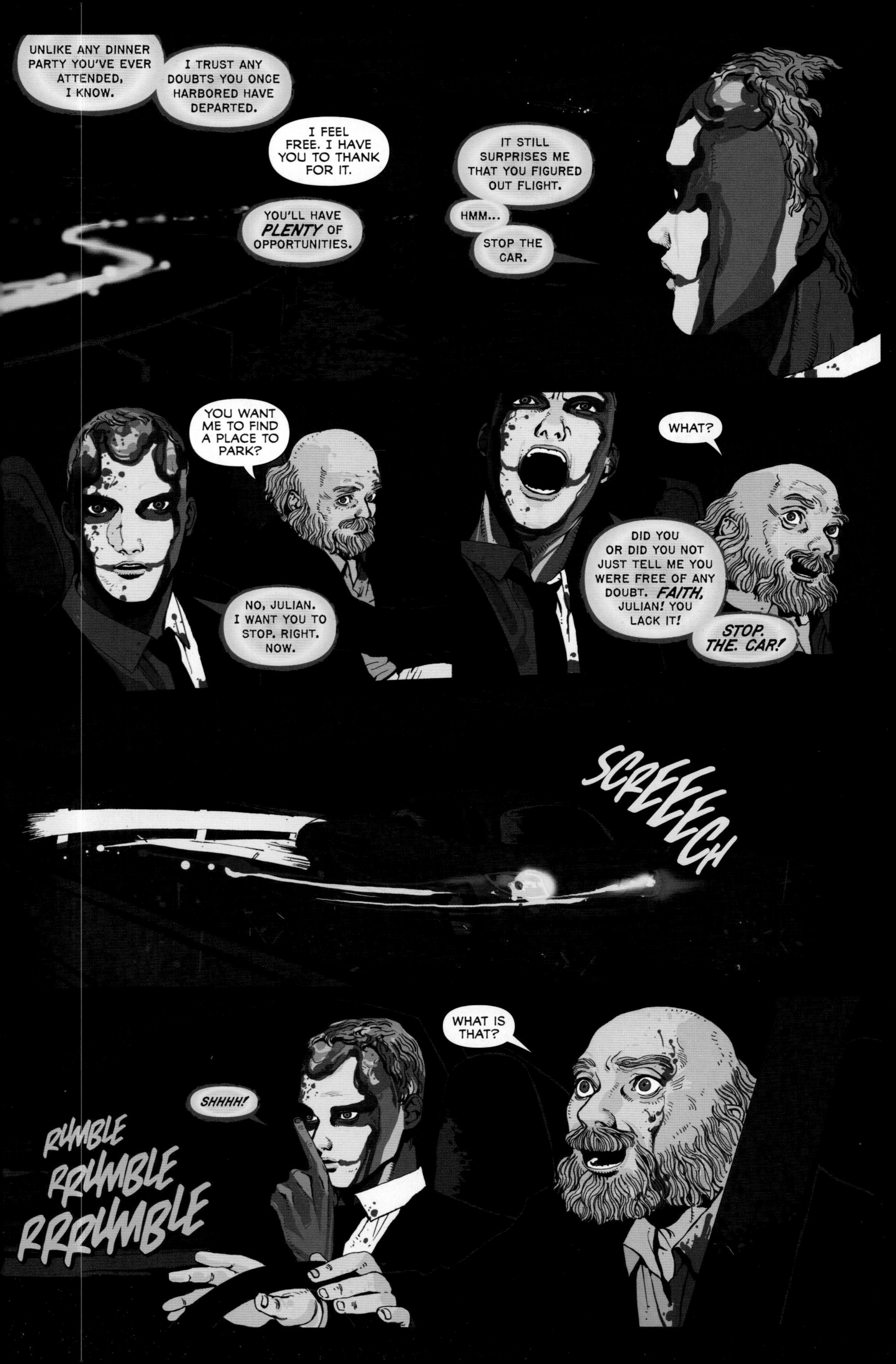
UNLIKE ANY DINNER PARTY YOU'VE EVER ATTENDED, I KNOW.
I TRUST ANY DOUBTS YOU ONCE HARBORED HAVE DEPARTED.
I FEEL FREE. I HAVE YOU TO THANK FOR IT.
YOU'LL HAVE PLENTY OF OPPORTUNITIES.
IT STILL SURPRISES ME THAT YOU FIGURED OUT FLIGHT.
HMM...
STOP THE CAR.
YOU WANT ME TO FIND A PLACE TO PARK?
NO, JULIAN. I WANT YOU TO STOP. RIGHT. NOW.
WHAT?
DID YOU OR DID YOU NOT JUST TELL ME YOU WERE FREE OF ANY DOUBT. FAITH, JULIAN! YOU LACK IT!
STOP. THE. CAR!
SCREEEECH
WHAT IS THAT?
SHHHH!
RUMBLE
RRUMBLE
RRRUMBLE

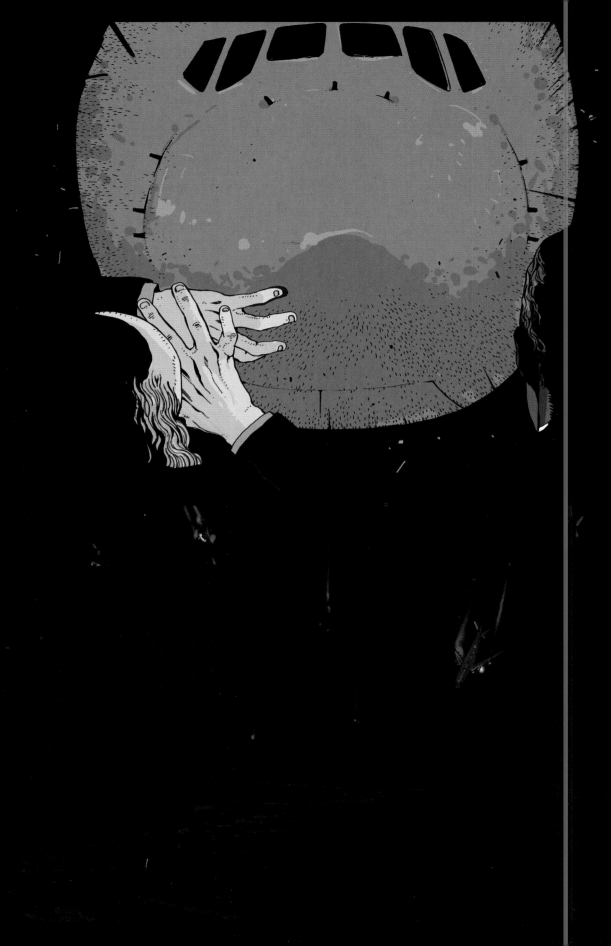

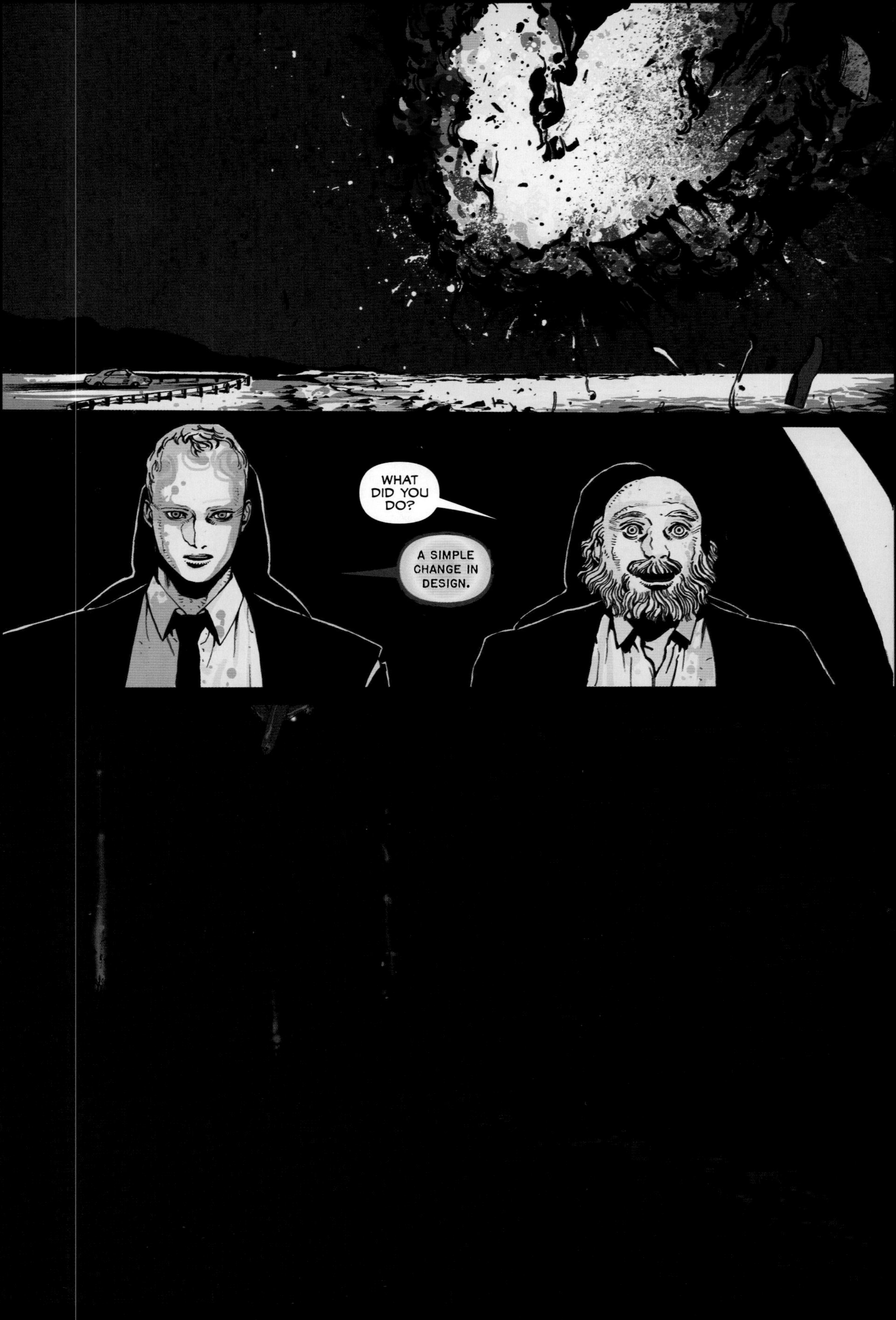
WHAT DID YOU DO?
A SIMPLE CHANGE IN DESIGN.

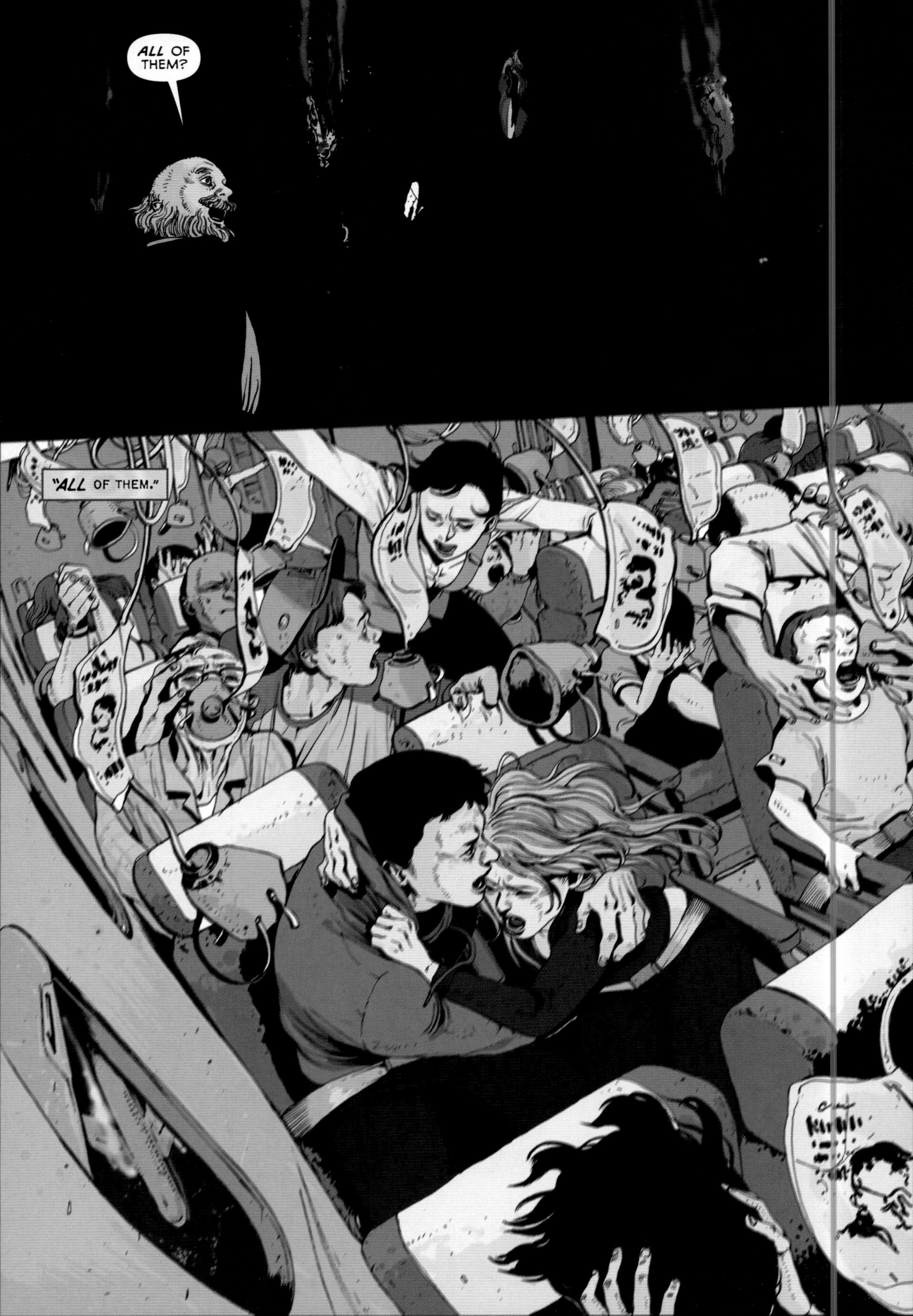
ALL OF THEM?
"ALL OF THEM."

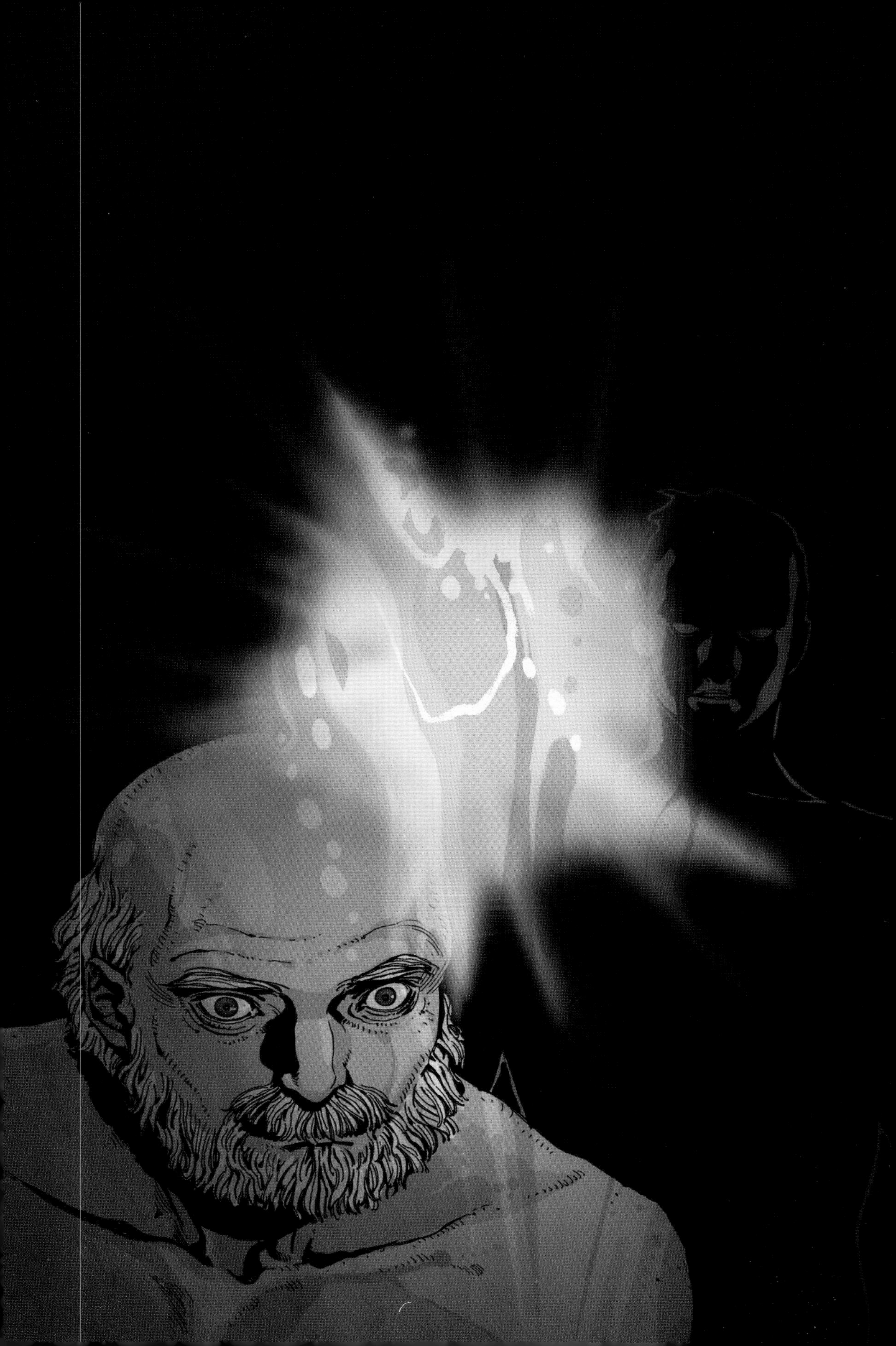

CHAPTER FOUR

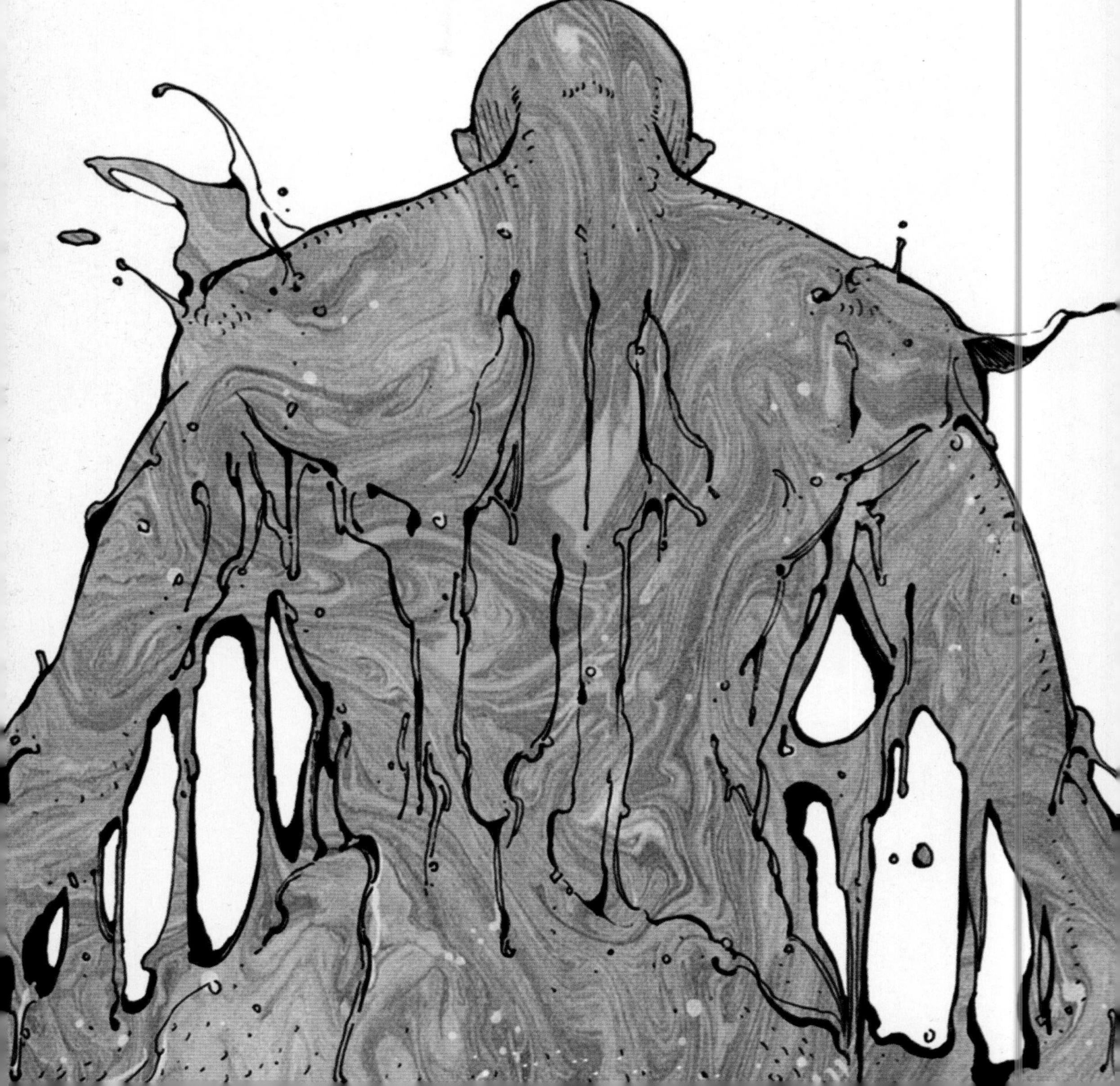

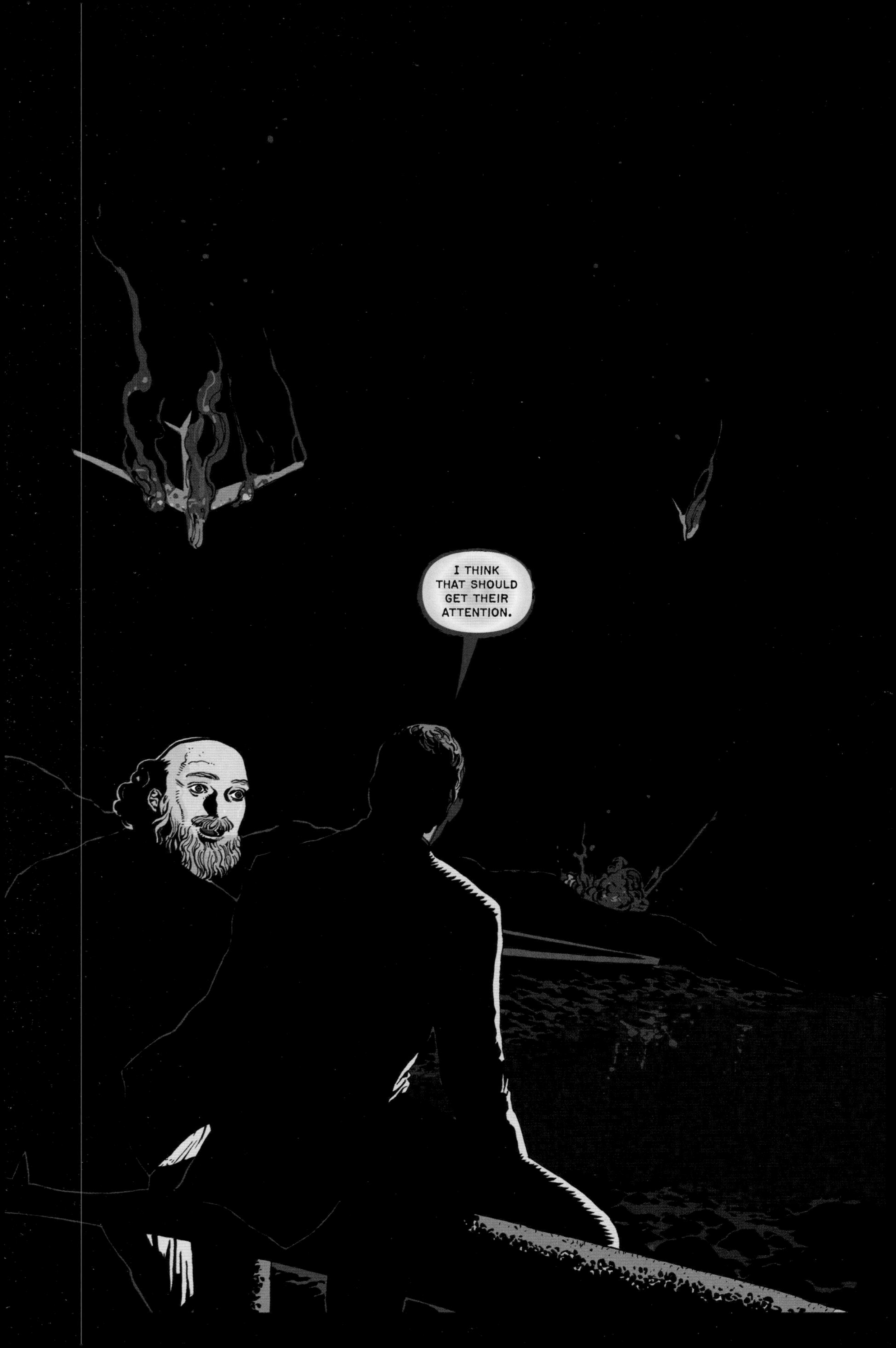
I THINK THAT SHOULD GET THEIR ATTENTION.

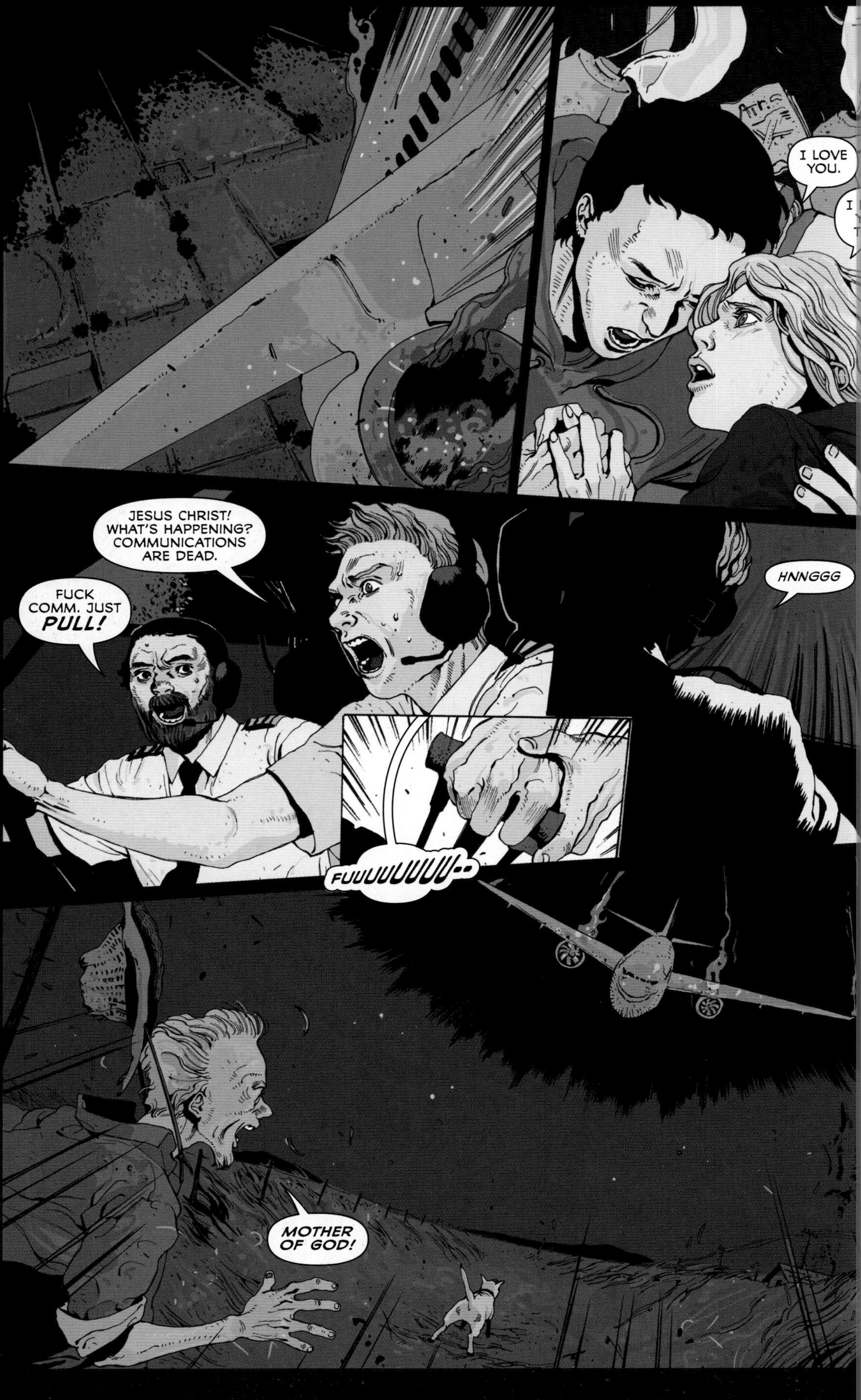
I LOVE YOU.
I LOVE YOU TOO.
JESUS CHRIST! WHAT'S HAPPENING? COMMUNICATIONS ARE DEAD.
FUCK COMM. JUST PULL!
HNNGGG
FUUUUUUUU--
MOTHER OF GOD!

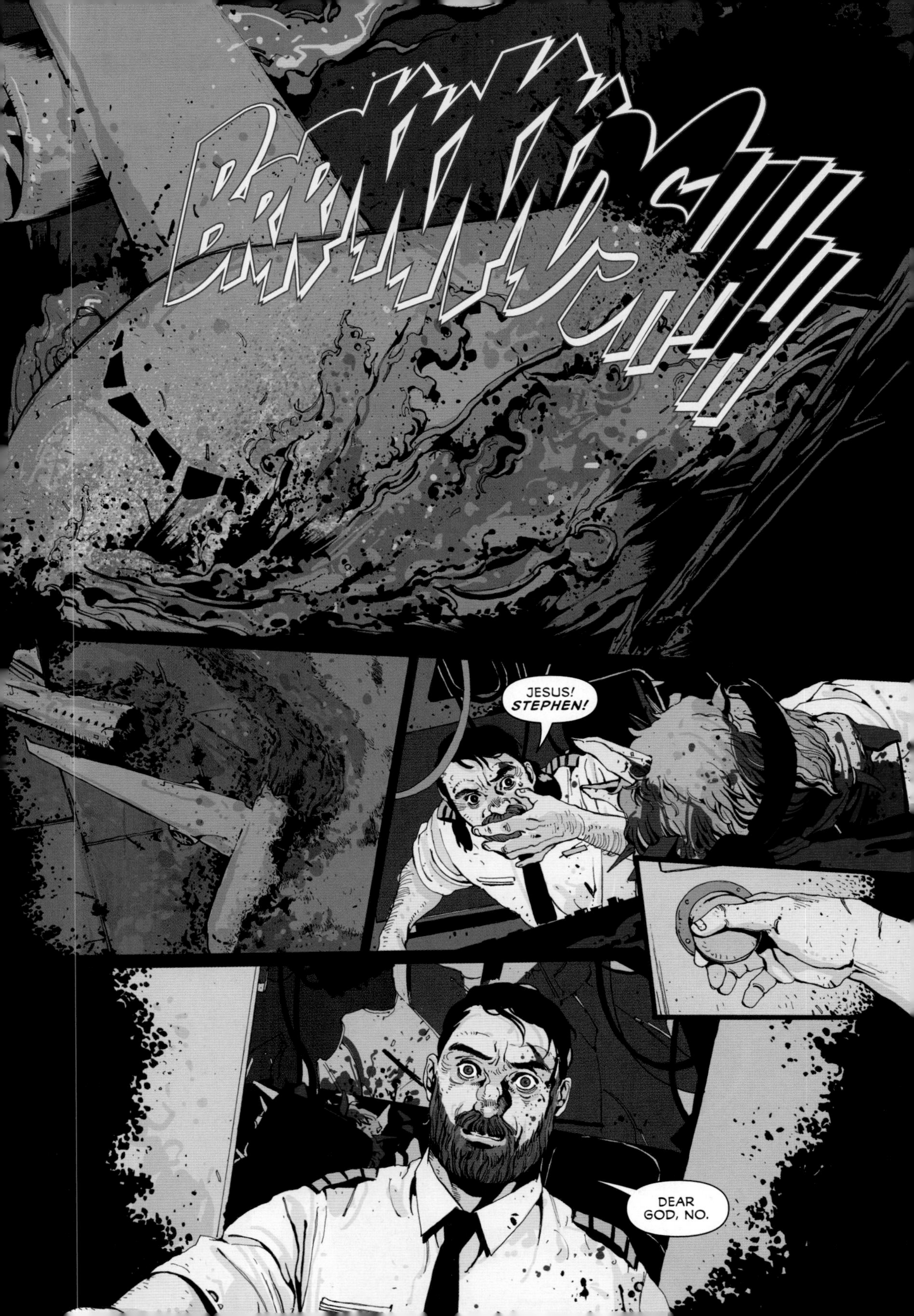
BRRUMMSCHH
JESUS! STEPHEN!
DEAR GOD, NO.

CHAPTER 4: THE NEW ROME

"What would be left of our tragedies if an insect were to present us his?" —Emil Cioran

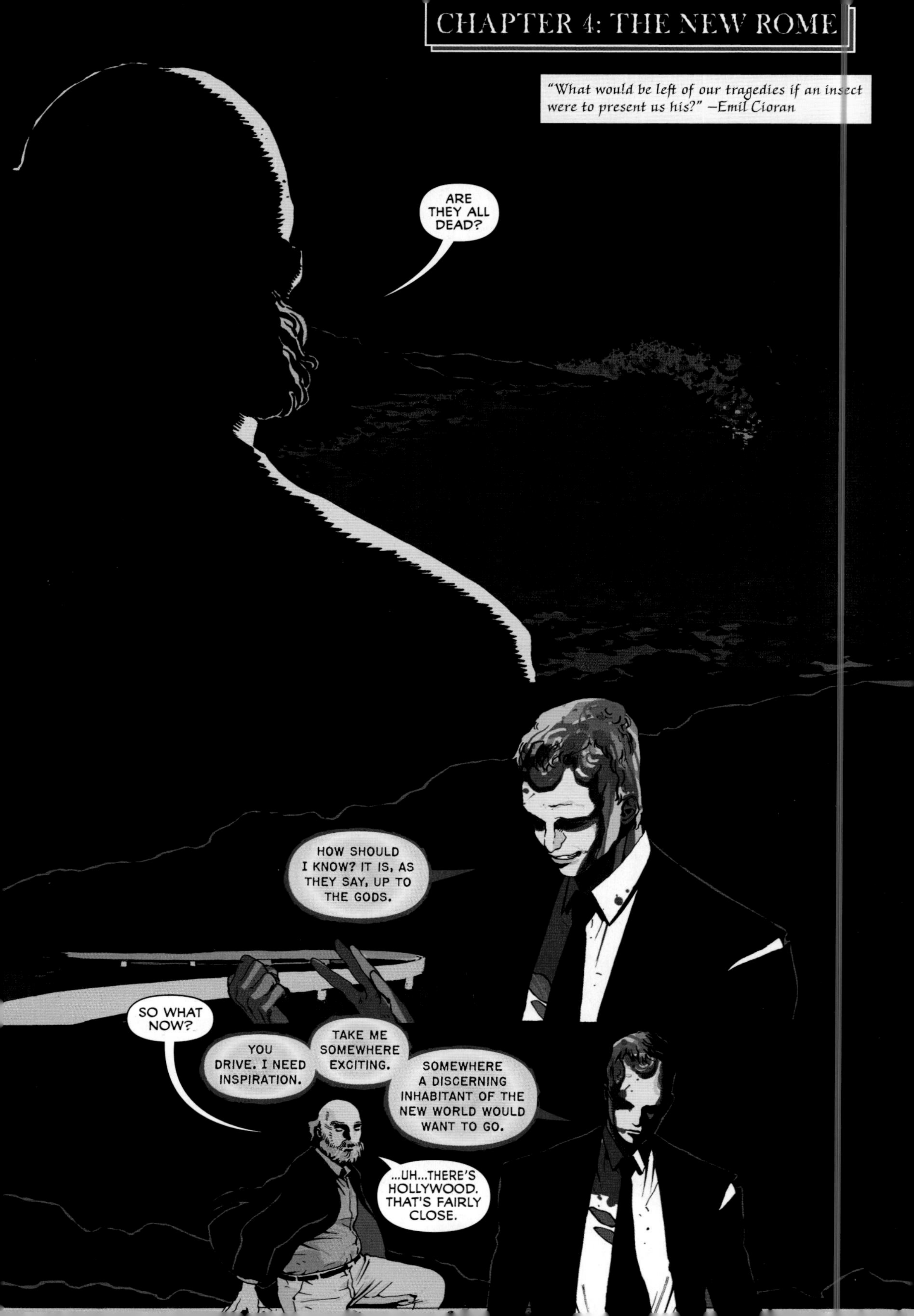
ARE THEY ALL DEAD?
HOW SHOULD I KNOW? IT IS, AS THEY SAY, UP TO THE GODS.
SO WHAT NOW?
YOU DRIVE. I NEED INSPIRATION.
TAKE ME SOMEWHERE EXCITING.
SOMEWHERE A DISCERNING INHABITANT OF THE NEW WORLD WOULD WANT TO GO.
...UH...THERE'S HOLLYWOOD. THAT'S FAIRLY CLOSE.

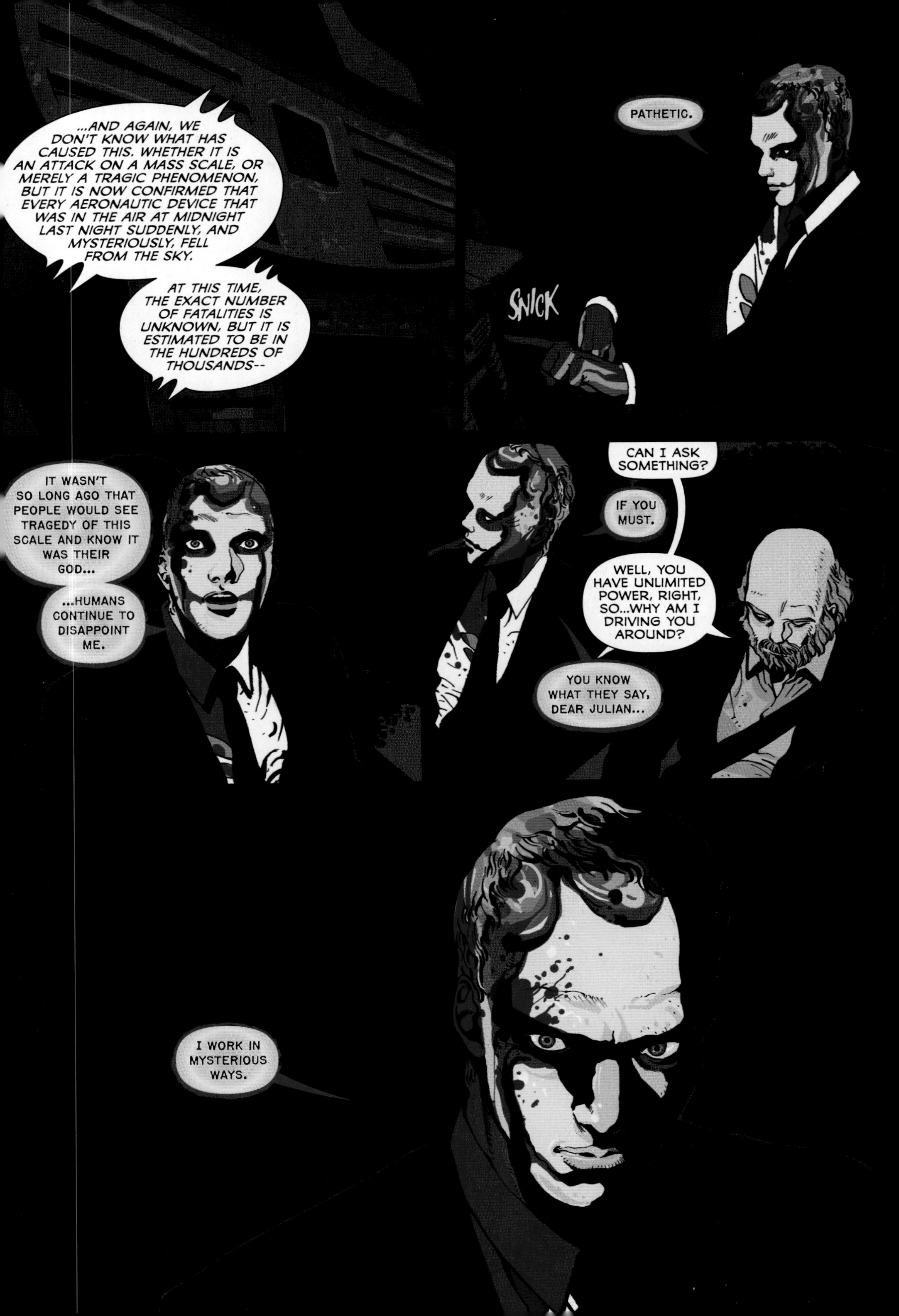
...AND AGAIN, WE DON'T KNOW WHAT HAS CAUSED THIS. WHETHER IT IS AN ATTACK ON A MASS SCALE, OR MERELY A TRAGIC PHENOMENON, BUT IT IS NOW CONFIRMED THAT EVERY AERONAUTIC DEVICE THAT WAS IN THE AIR AT MIDNIGHT LAST NIGHT SUDDENLY, AND MYSTERIOUSLY, FELL FROM THE SKY.
AT THIS TIME, THE EXACT NUMBER OF FATALITIES IS UNKNOWN, BUT IT IS ESTIMATED TO BE IN THE HUNDREDS OF THOUSANDS--
PATHETIC.
SNICK
IT WASN'T SO LONG AGO THAT PEOPLE WOULD SEE TRAGEDY OF THIS SCALE AND KNOW IT WAS THEIR GOD...
...HUMANS CONTINUE TO DISAPPOINT ME.
CAN I ASK SOMETHING?
IF YOU MUST.
WELL, YOU HAVE UNLIMITED POWER, RIGHT, SO...WHY AM I DRIVING YOU AROUND?
YOU KNOW WHAT THEY SAY, DEAR JULIAN...
I WORK IN MYSTERIOUS WAYS.

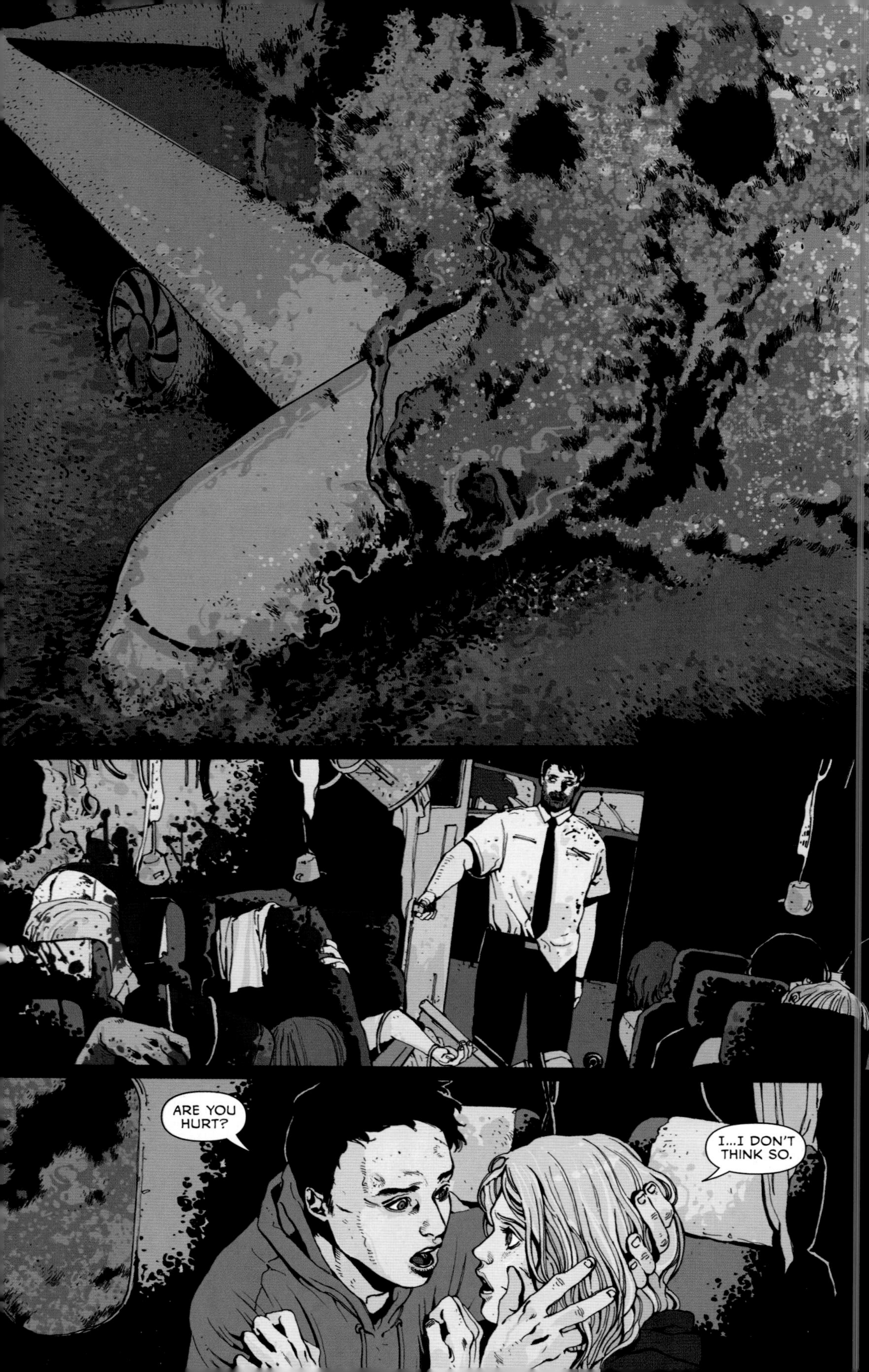
ARE YOU HURT?
I...I DON'T THINK SO.

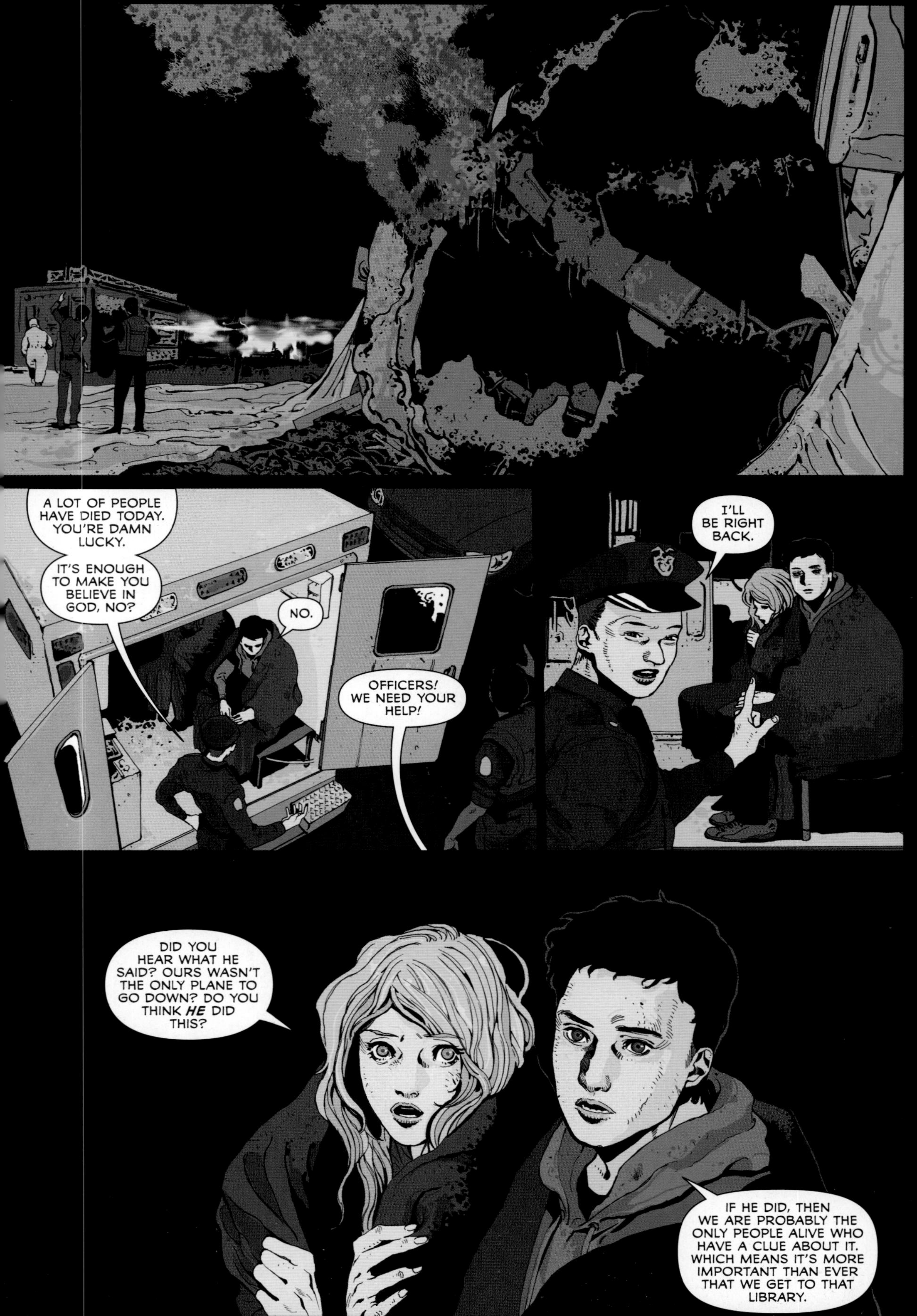
A LOT OF PEOPLE HAVE DIED TODAY. YOU'RE DAMN LUCKY.
IT'S ENOUGH TO MAKE YOU BELIEVE IN GOD, NO?
NO.
OFFICERS! WE NEED YOUR HELP!
I'LL BE RIGHT BACK.
DID YOU HEAR WHAT HE SAID? OURS WASN'T THE ONLY PLANE TO GO DOWN? DO YOU THINK *HE* DID THIS?
IF HE DID, THEN WE ARE PROBABLY THE ONLY PEOPLE ALIVE WHO HAVE A CLUE ABOUT IT. WHICH MEANS IT'S MORE IMPORTANT THAN EVER THAT WE GET TO THAT LIBRARY.

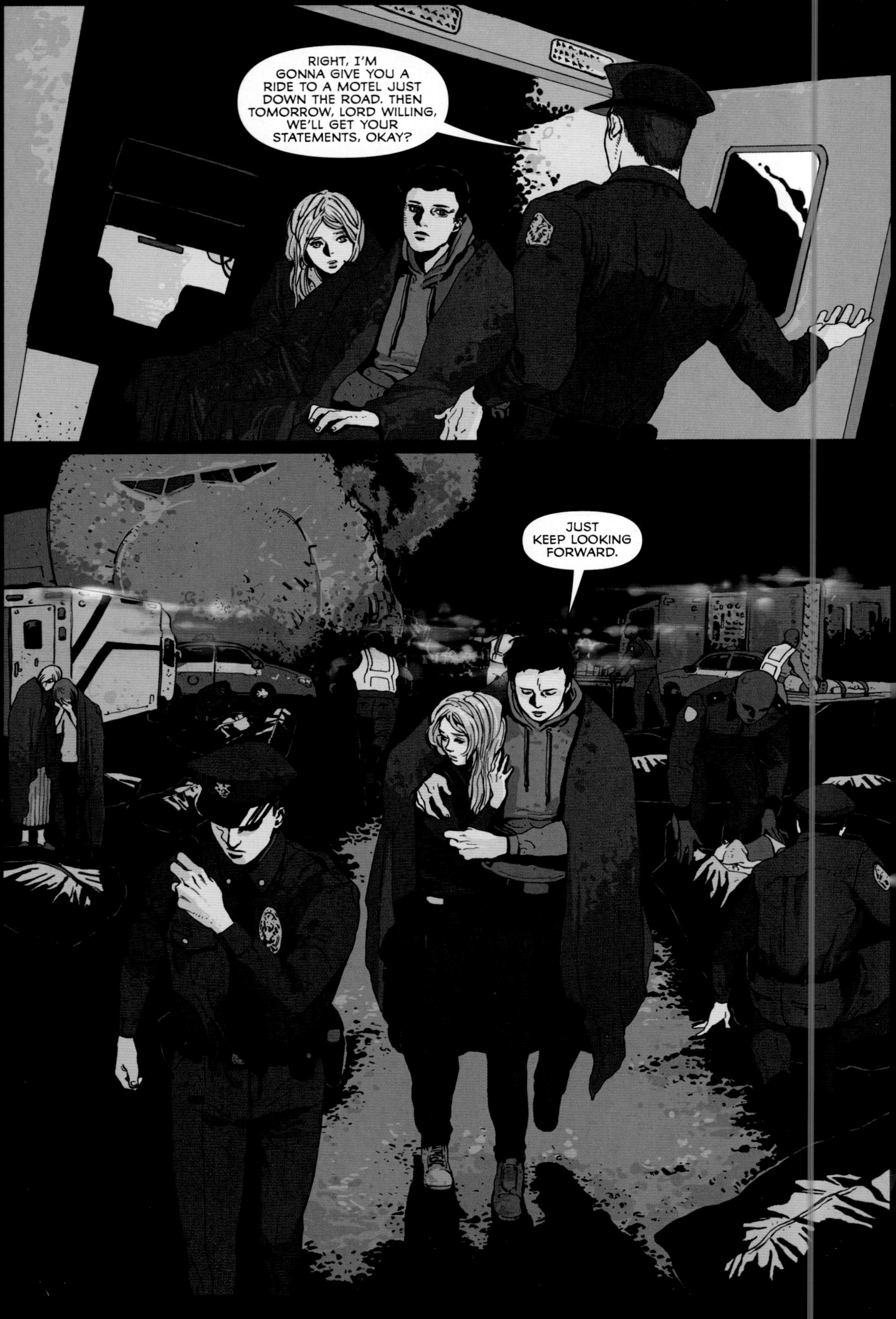
RIGHT, I'M GONNA GIVE YOU A RIDE TO A MOTEL JUST DOWN THE ROAD. THEN TOMORROW, LORD WILLING, WE'LL GET YOUR STATEMENTS, OKAY?
JUST KEEP LOOKING FORWARD.

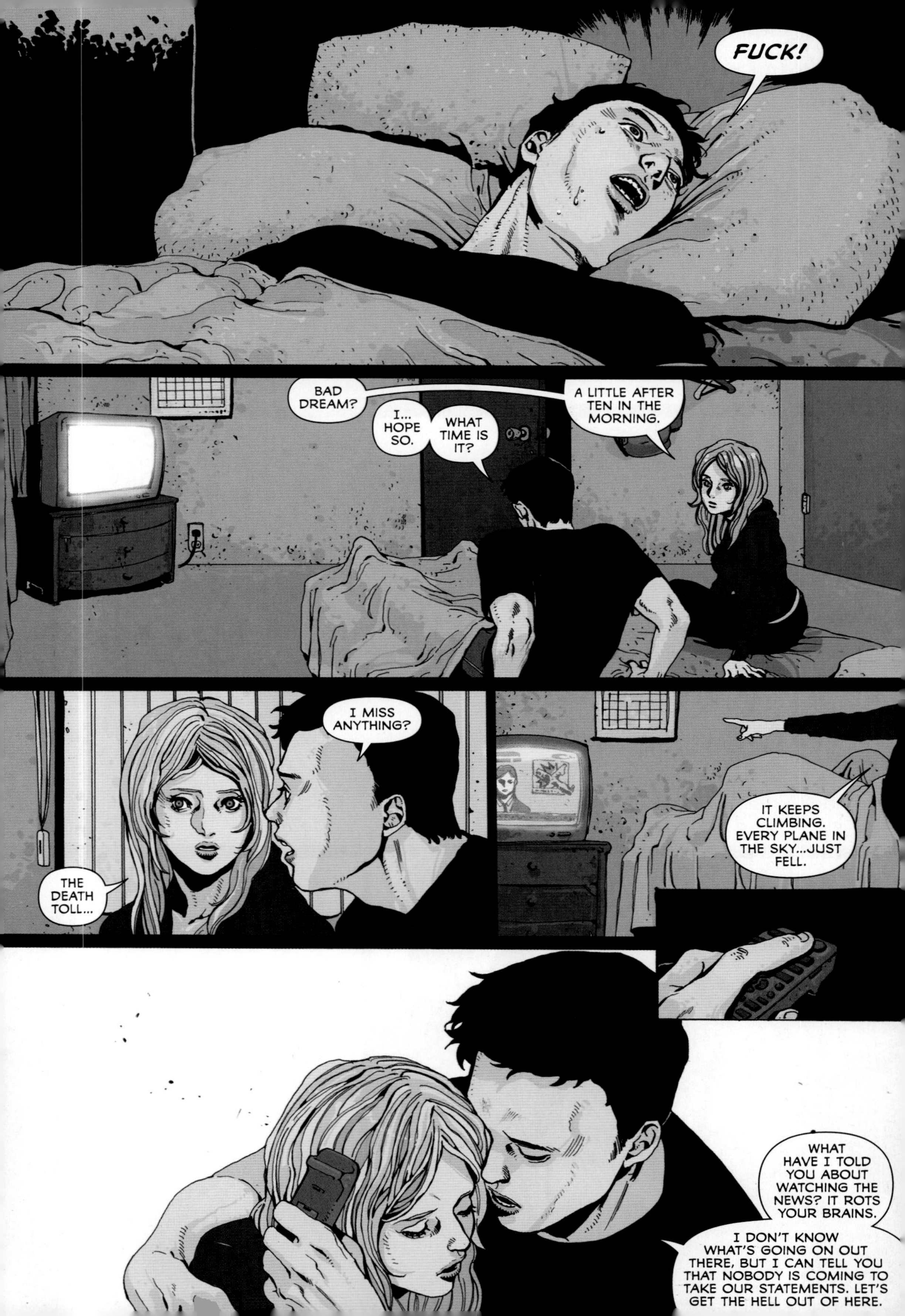

FUCK!
BAD DREAM?
I... HOPE SO.
WHAT TIME IS IT?
A LITTLE AFTER TEN IN THE MORNING.
I MISS ANYTHING?
THE DEATH TOLL...
IT KEEPS CLIMBING. EVERY PLANE IN THE SKY...JUST FELL.
WHAT HAVE I TOLD YOU ABOUT WATCHING THE NEWS? IT ROTS YOUR BRAINS.
I DON'T KNOW WHAT'S GOING ON OUT THERE, BUT I CAN TELL YOU THAT NOBODY IS COMING TO TAKE OUR STATEMENTS. LET'S GET THE HELL OUT OF HERE.

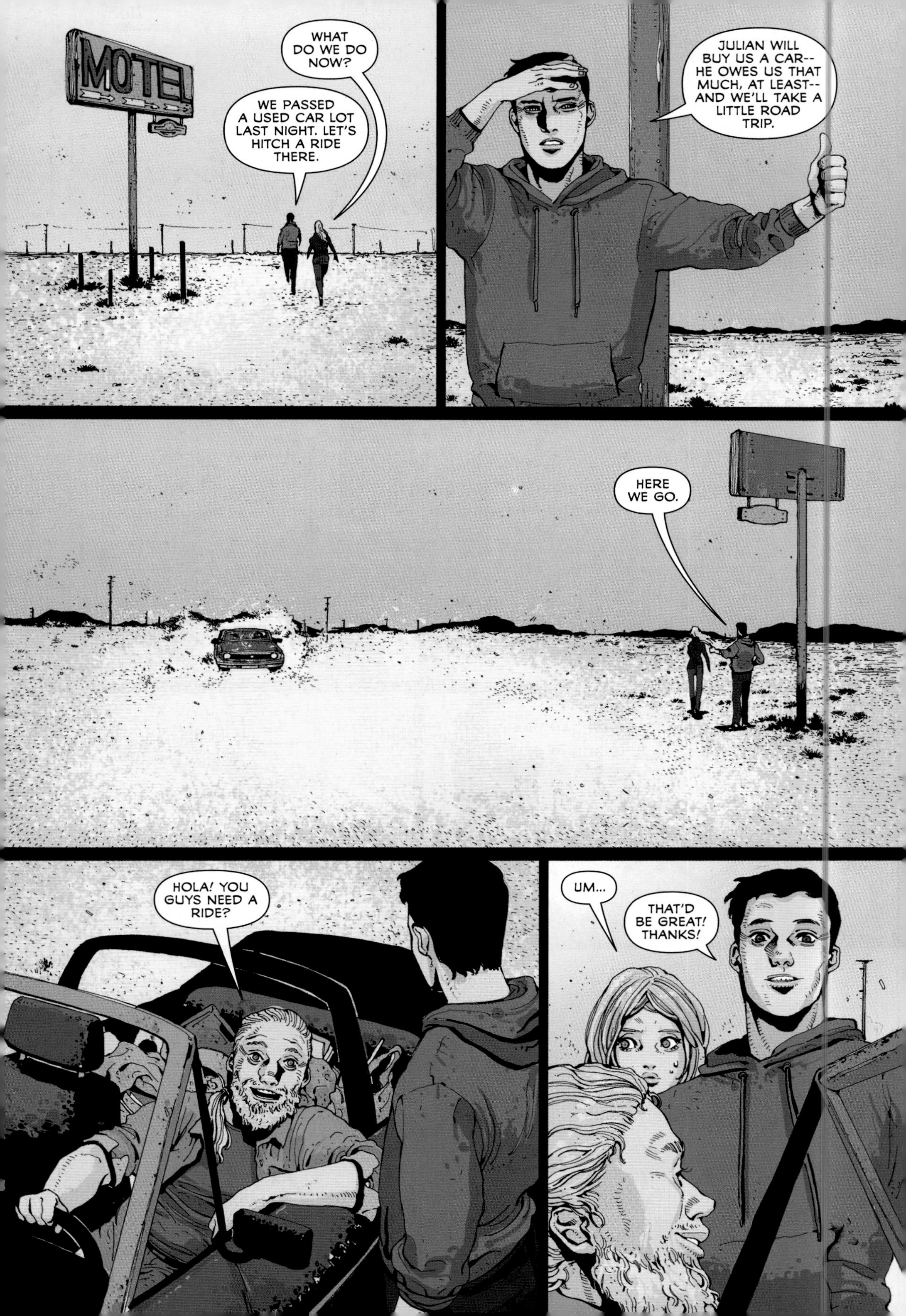
MOTEL
WHAT DO WE DO NOW?
WE PASSED A USED CAR LOT LAST NIGHT. LET'S HITCH A RIDE THERE.
JULIAN WILL BUY US A CAR-- HE OWES US THAT MUCH, AT LEAST-- AND WE'LL TAKE A LITTLE ROAD TRIP.
HERE WE GO.
HOLA! YOU GUYS NEED A RIDE?
UM...
THAT'D BE GREAT! THANKS!

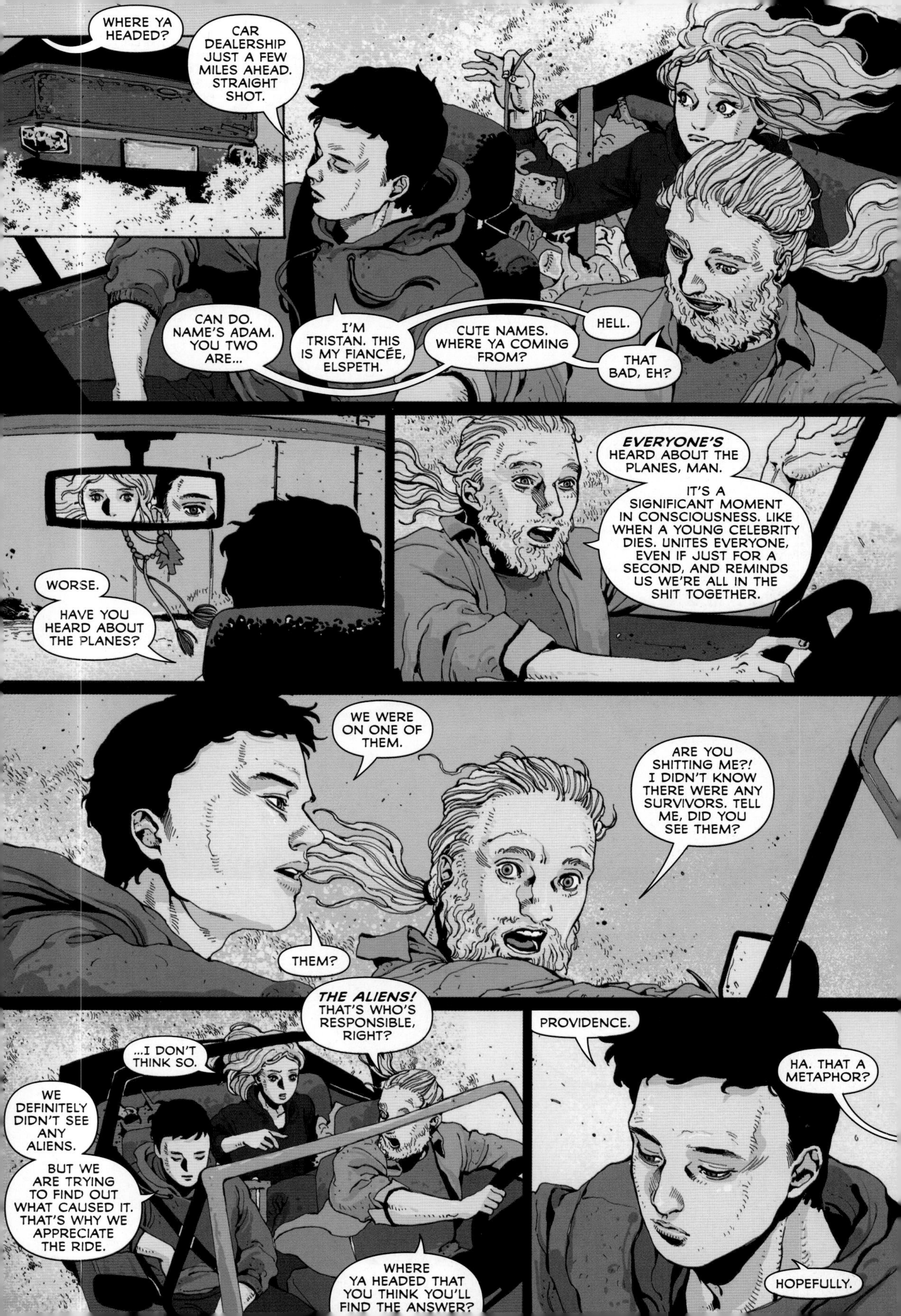
WHERE YA HEADED?
CAR DEALERSHIP JUST A FEW MILES AHEAD. STRAIGHT SHOT.
CAN DO. NAME'S ADAM. YOU TWO ARE...
I'M TRISTAN. THIS IS MY FIANCÉE, ELSPETH.
CUTE NAMES. WHERE YA COMING FROM?
HELL.
THAT BAD, EH?
WORSE.
HAVE YOU HEARD ABOUT THE PLANES?
EVERYONE'S HEARD ABOUT THE PLANES, MAN.
IT'S A SIGNIFICANT MOMENT IN CONSCIOUSNESS. LIKE WHEN A YOUNG CELEBRITY DIES. UNITES EVERYONE, EVEN IF JUST FOR A SECOND, AND REMINDS US WE'RE ALL IN THE SHIT TOGETHER.
WE WERE ON ONE OF THEM.
ARE YOU SHITTING ME?! I DIDN'T KNOW THERE WERE ANY SURVIVORS. TELL ME, DID YOU SEE THEM?
THEM?
THE ALIENS! THAT'S WHO'S RESPONSIBLE, RIGHT?
...I DON'T THINK SO.
WE DEFINITELY DIDN'T SEE ANY ALIENS.
BUT WE ARE TRYING TO FIND OUT WHAT CAUSED IT. THAT'S WHY WE APPRECIATE THE RIDE.
WHERE YA HEADED THAT YOU THINK YOU'LL FIND THE ANSWER?
PROVIDENCE.
HA. THAT A METAPHOR?
HOPEFULLY.

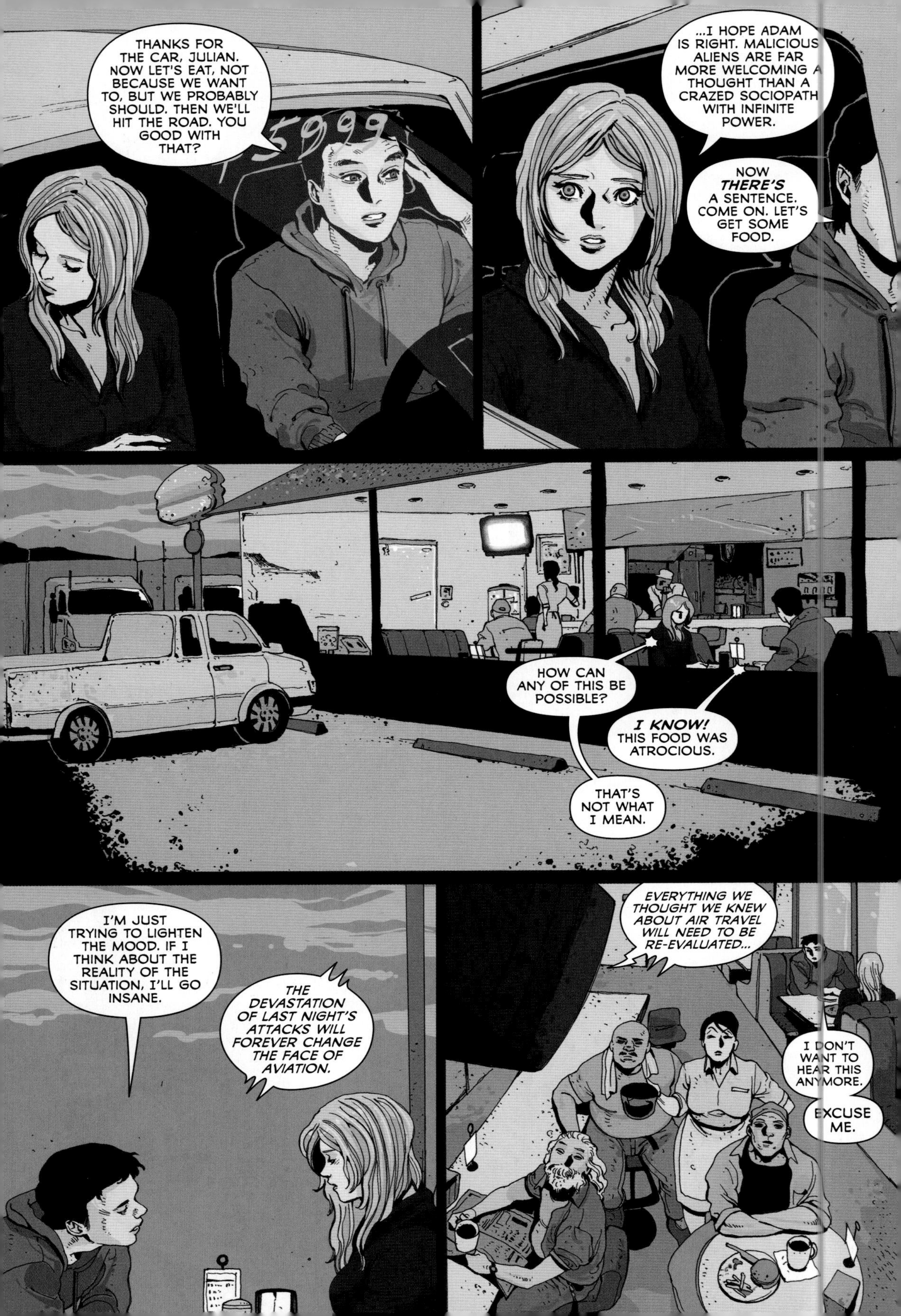
THANKS FOR THE CAR, JULIAN. NOW LET'S EAT, NOT BECAUSE WE WANT TO, BUT WE PROBABLY SHOULD. THEN WE'LL HIT THE ROAD. YOU GOOD WITH THAT?
...I HOPE ADAM IS RIGHT. MALICIOUS ALIENS ARE FAR MORE WELCOMING A THOUGHT THAN A CRAZED SOCIOPATH WITH INFINITE POWER.
NOW *THERE'S* A SENTENCE. COME ON. LET'S GET SOME FOOD.
HOW CAN ANY OF THIS BE POSSIBLE?
I KNOW! THIS FOOD WAS ATROCIOUS.
THAT'S NOT WHAT I MEAN.
I'M JUST TRYING TO LIGHTEN THE MOOD. IF I THINK ABOUT THE REALITY OF THE SITUATION, I'LL GO INSANE.
THE DEVASTATION OF LAST NIGHT'S ATTACKS WILL FOREVER CHANGE THE FACE OF AVIATION.
EVERYTHING WE THOUGHT WE KNEW ABOUT AIR TRAVEL WILL NEED TO BE RE-EVALUATED...
I DON'T WANT TO HEAR THIS ANYMORE.
EXCUSE ME.

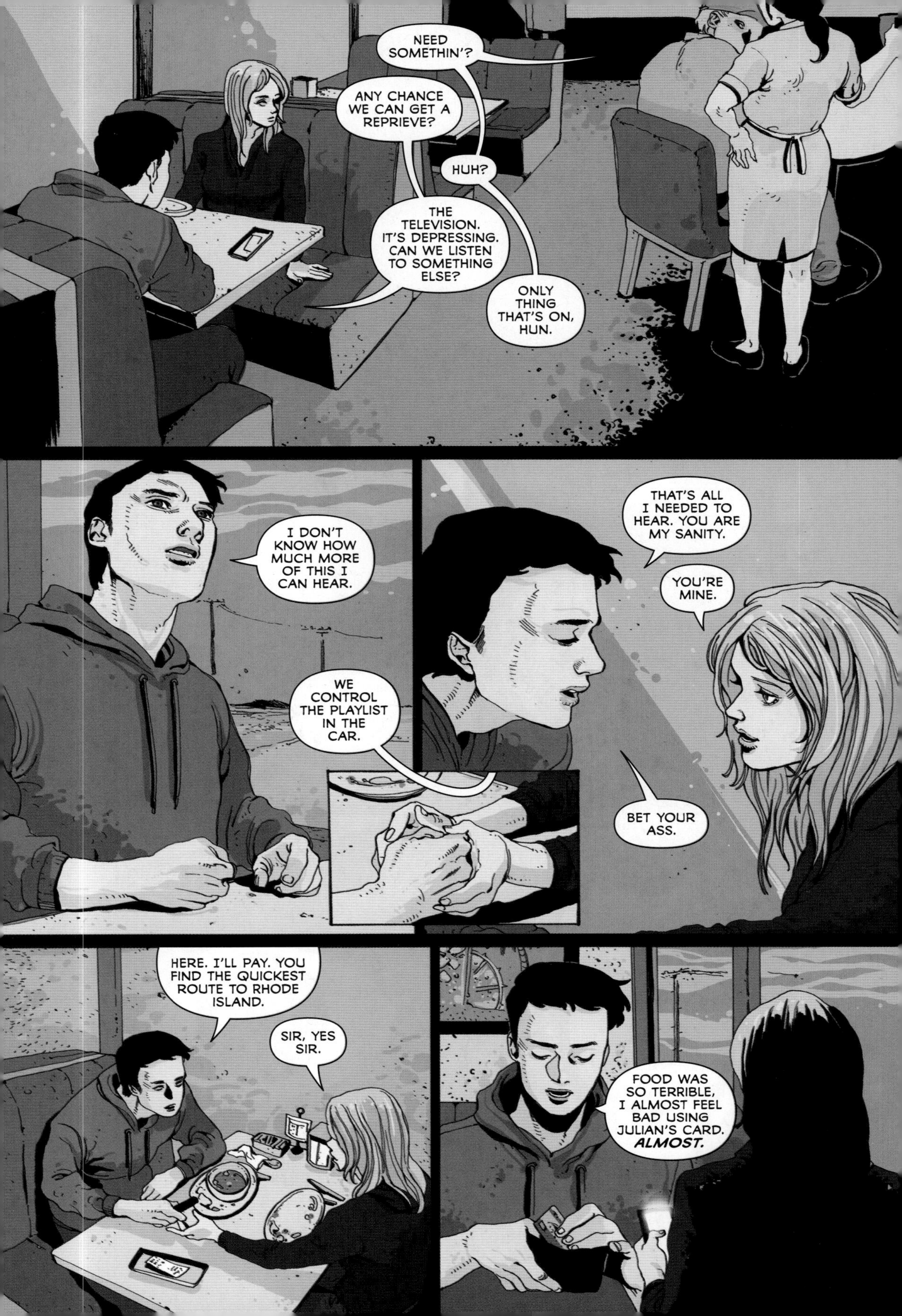
NEED SOMETHIN'?
ANY CHANCE WE CAN GET A REPRIEVE?
HUH?
THE TELEVISION. IT'S DEPRESSING. CAN WE LISTEN TO SOMETHING ELSE?
ONLY THING THAT'S ON, HUN.
I DON'T KNOW HOW MUCH MORE OF THIS I CAN HEAR.
WE CONTROL THE PLAYLIST IN THE CAR.
THAT'S ALL I NEEDED TO HEAR. YOU ARE MY SANITY.
YOU'RE MINE.
BET YOUR ASS.
HERE. I'LL PAY. YOU FIND THE QUICKEST ROUTE TO RHODE ISLAND.
SIR, YES SIR.
FOOD WAS SO TERRIBLE, I ALMOST FEEL BAD USING JULIAN'S CARD. ***ALMOST.***

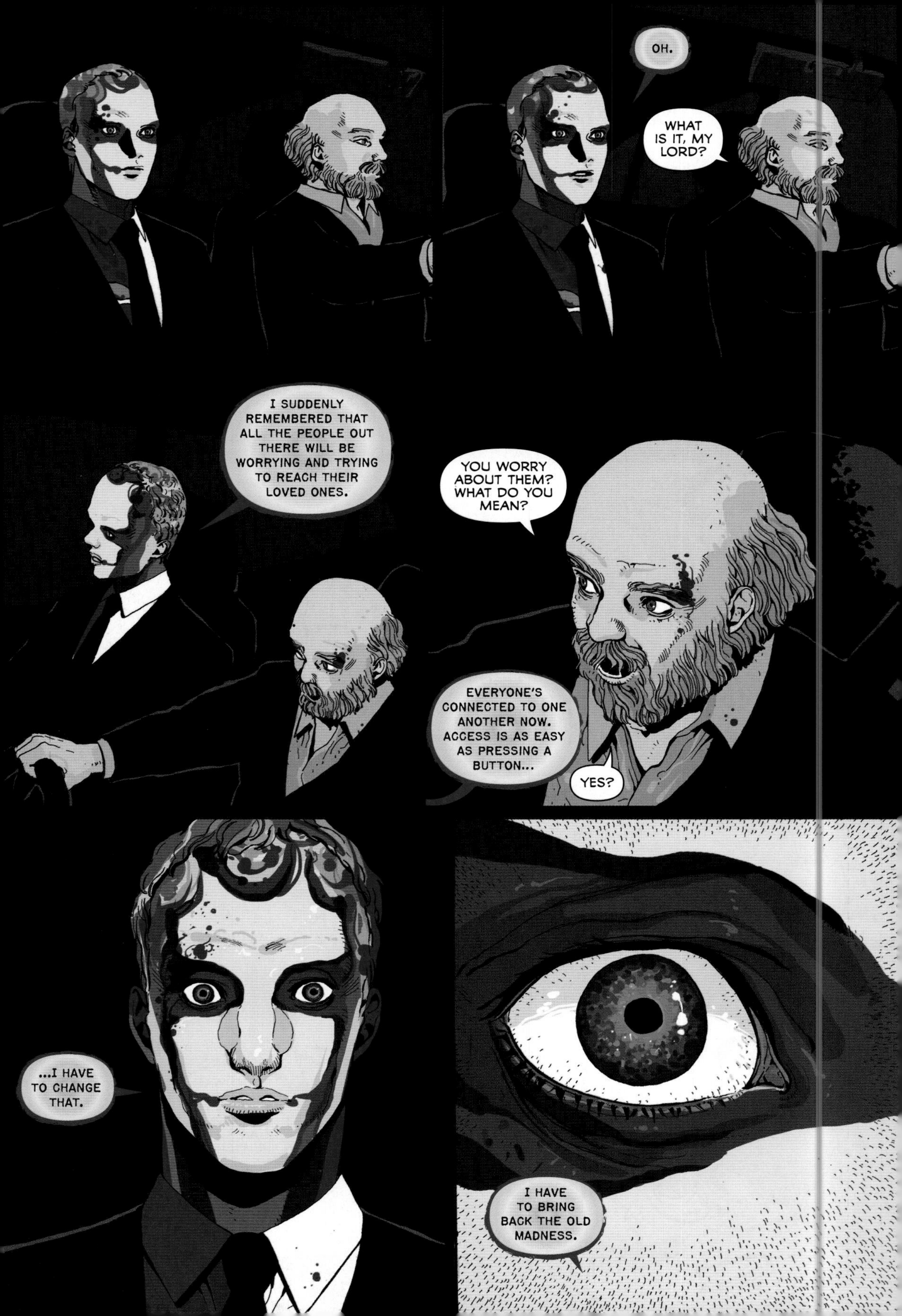
OH.
WHAT IS IT, MY LORD?
I SUDDENLY REMEMBERED THAT ALL THE PEOPLE OUT THERE WILL BE WORRYING AND TRYING TO REACH THEIR LOVED ONES.
YOU WORRY ABOUT THEM? WHAT DO YOU MEAN?
EVERYONE'S CONNECTED TO ONE ANOTHER NOW. ACCESS IS AS EASY AS PRESSING A BUTTON...
YES?
...I HAVE TO CHANGE THAT.
I HAVE TO BRING BACK THE OLD MADNESS.

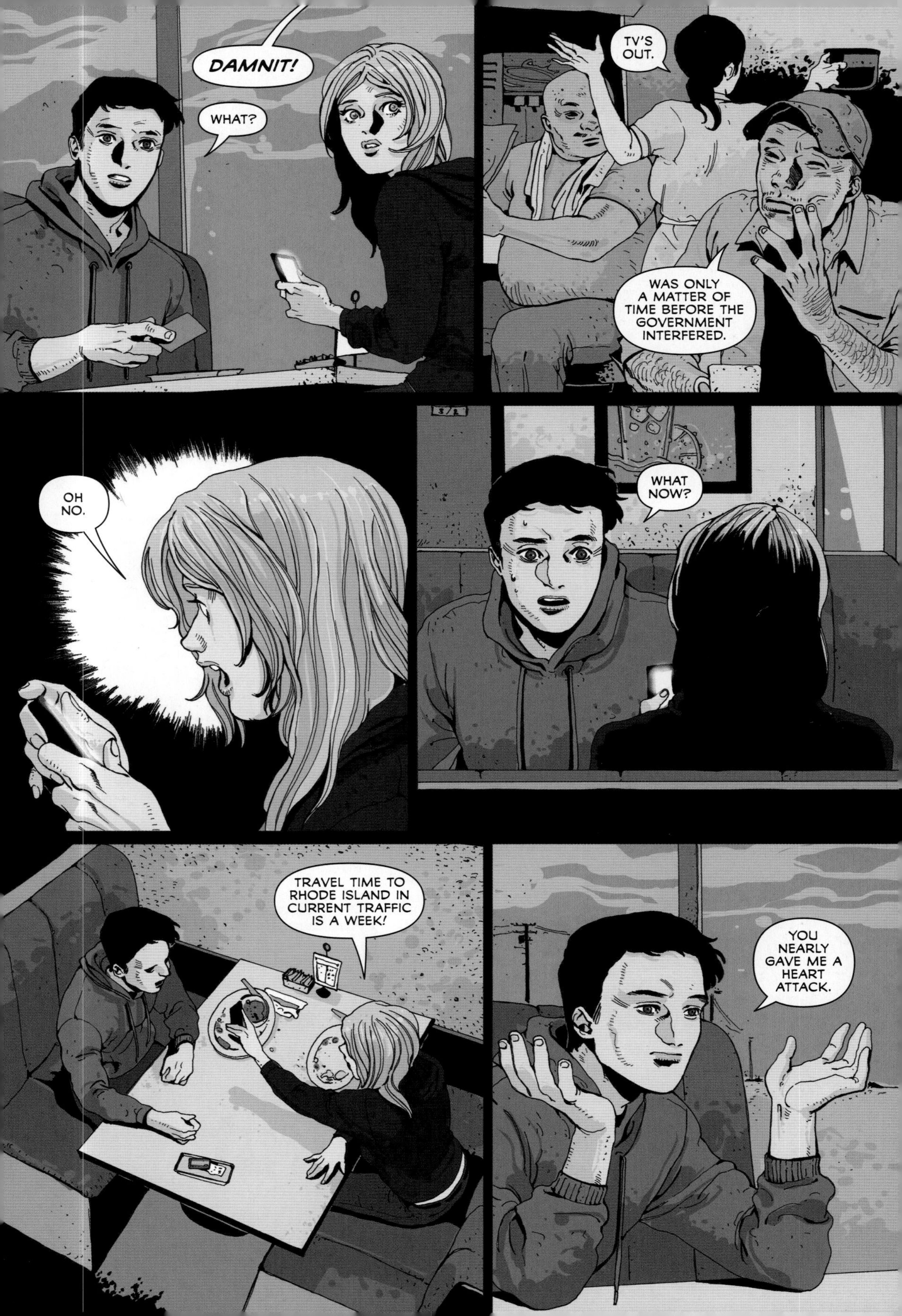
DAMNIT!
WHAT?
TV'S OUT.
WAS ONLY A MATTER OF TIME BEFORE THE GOVERNMENT INTERFERED.
OH NO.
WHAT NOW?
TRAVEL TIME TO RHODE ISLAND IN CURRENT TRAFFIC IS A WEEK!
YOU NEARLY GAVE ME A HEART ATTACK.

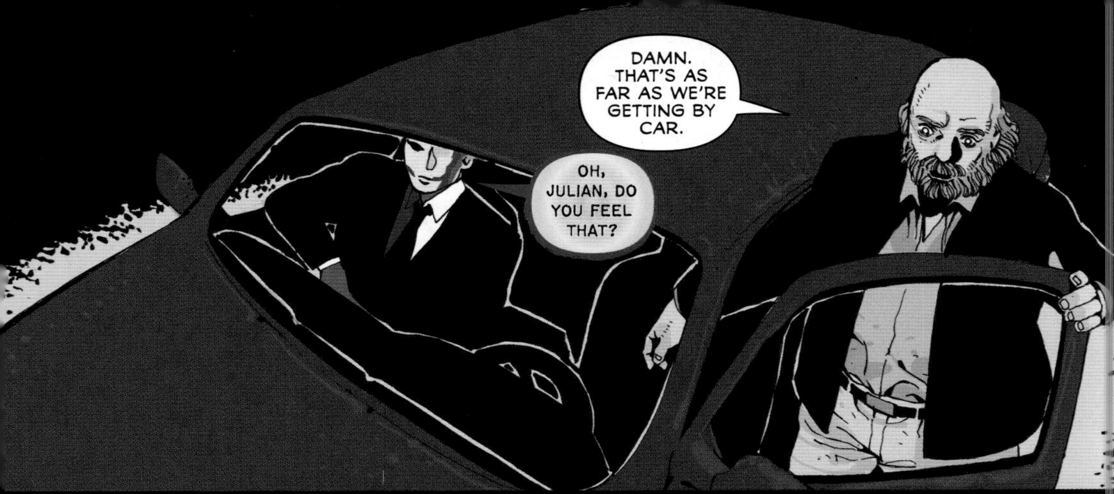
DAMN. THAT'S AS FAR AS WE'RE GETTING BY CAR.
OH, JULIAN, DO YOU FEEL THAT?

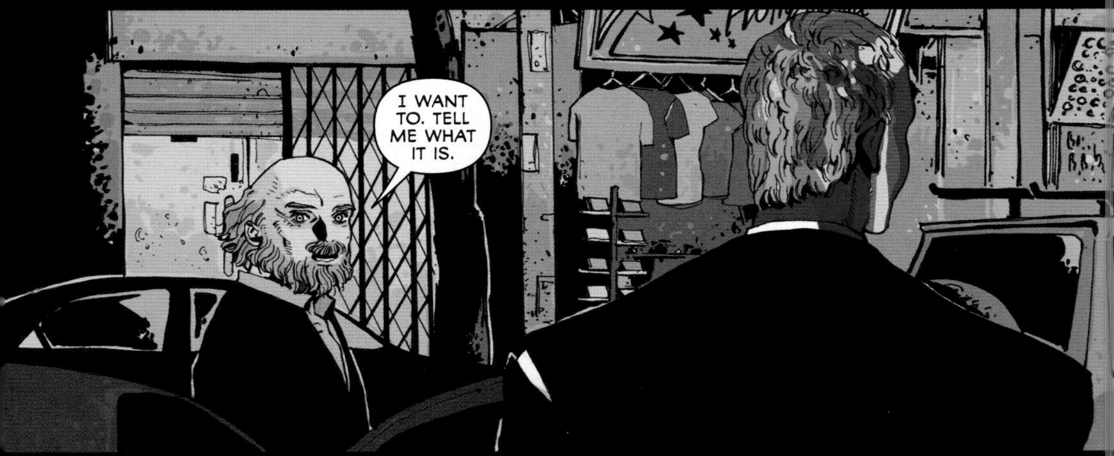
I WANT TO. TELL ME WHAT IT IS.

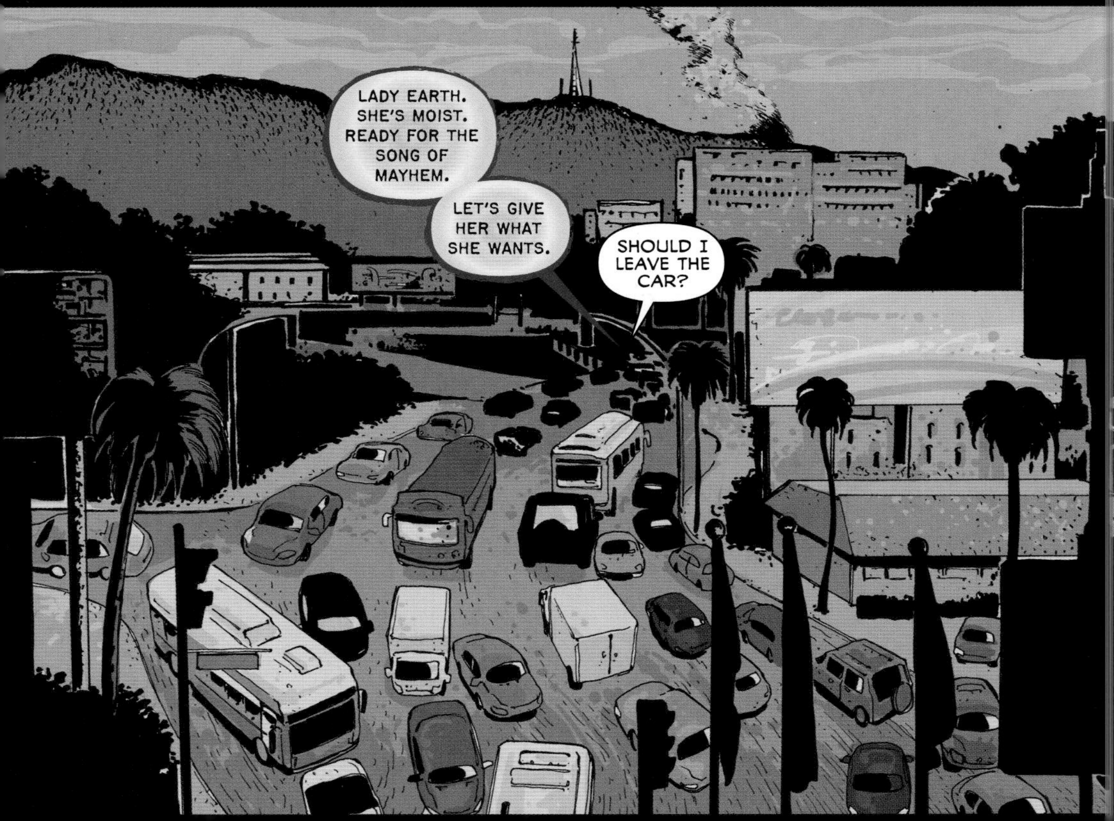
LADY EARTH. SHE'S MOIST. READY FOR THE SONG OF MAYHEM.
LET'S GIVE HER WHAT SHE WANTS.
SHOULD I LEAVE THE CAR?

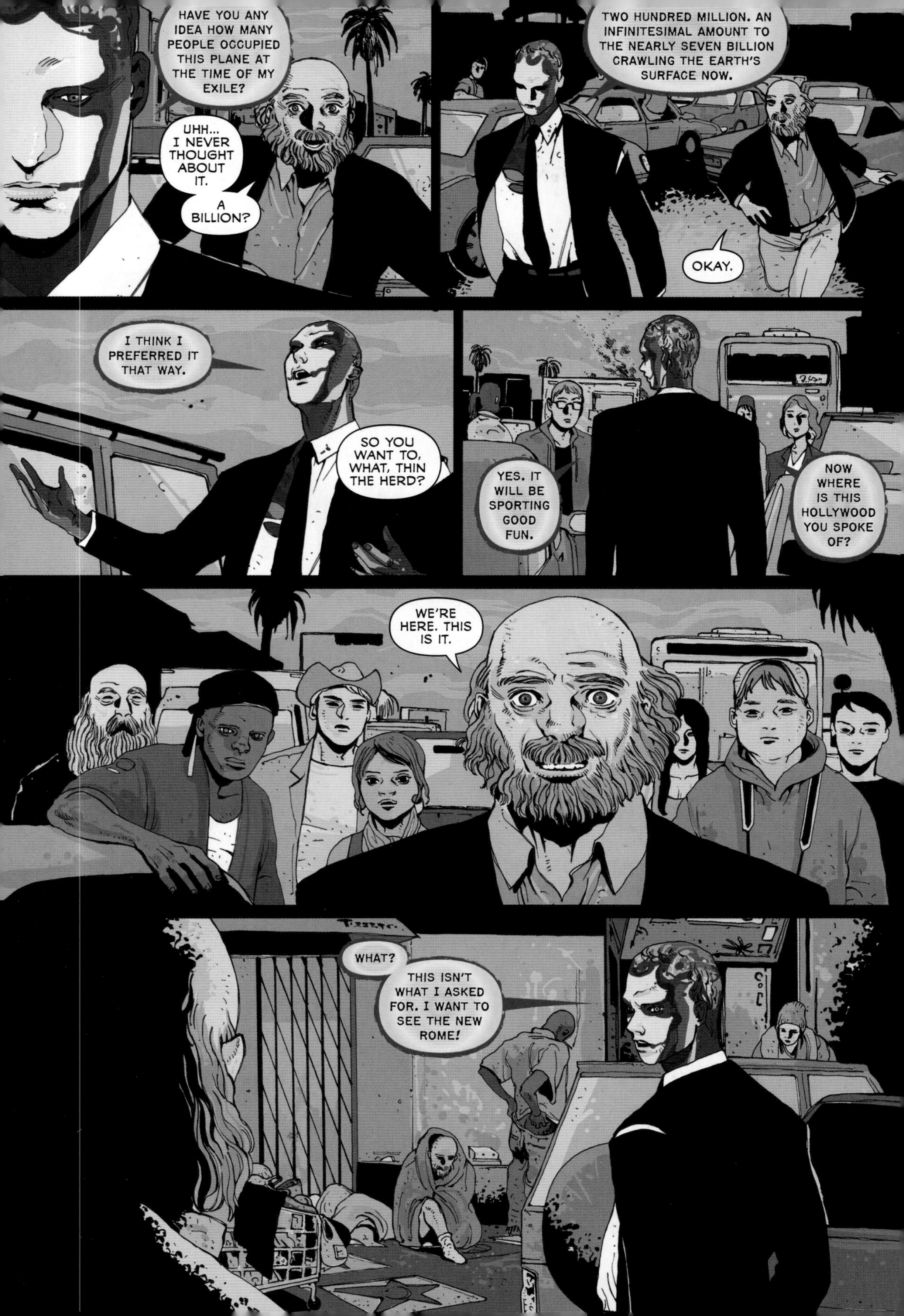
HAVE YOU ANY IDEA HOW MANY PEOPLE OCCUPIED THIS PLANE AT THE TIME OF MY EXILE?
UHH... I NEVER THOUGHT ABOUT IT.
A BILLION?
TWO HUNDRED MILLION. AN INFINITESIMAL AMOUNT TO THE NEARLY SEVEN BILLION CRAWLING THE EARTH'S SURFACE NOW.
OKAY.
I THINK I PREFERRED IT THAT WAY.
SO YOU WANT TO, WHAT, THIN THE HERD?
YES. IT WILL BE SPORTING GOOD FUN.
NOW WHERE IS THIS HOLLYWOOD YOU SPOKE OF?
WE'RE HERE. THIS IS IT.
WHAT?
THIS ISN'T WHAT I ASKED FOR. I WANT TO SEE THE NEW ROME!

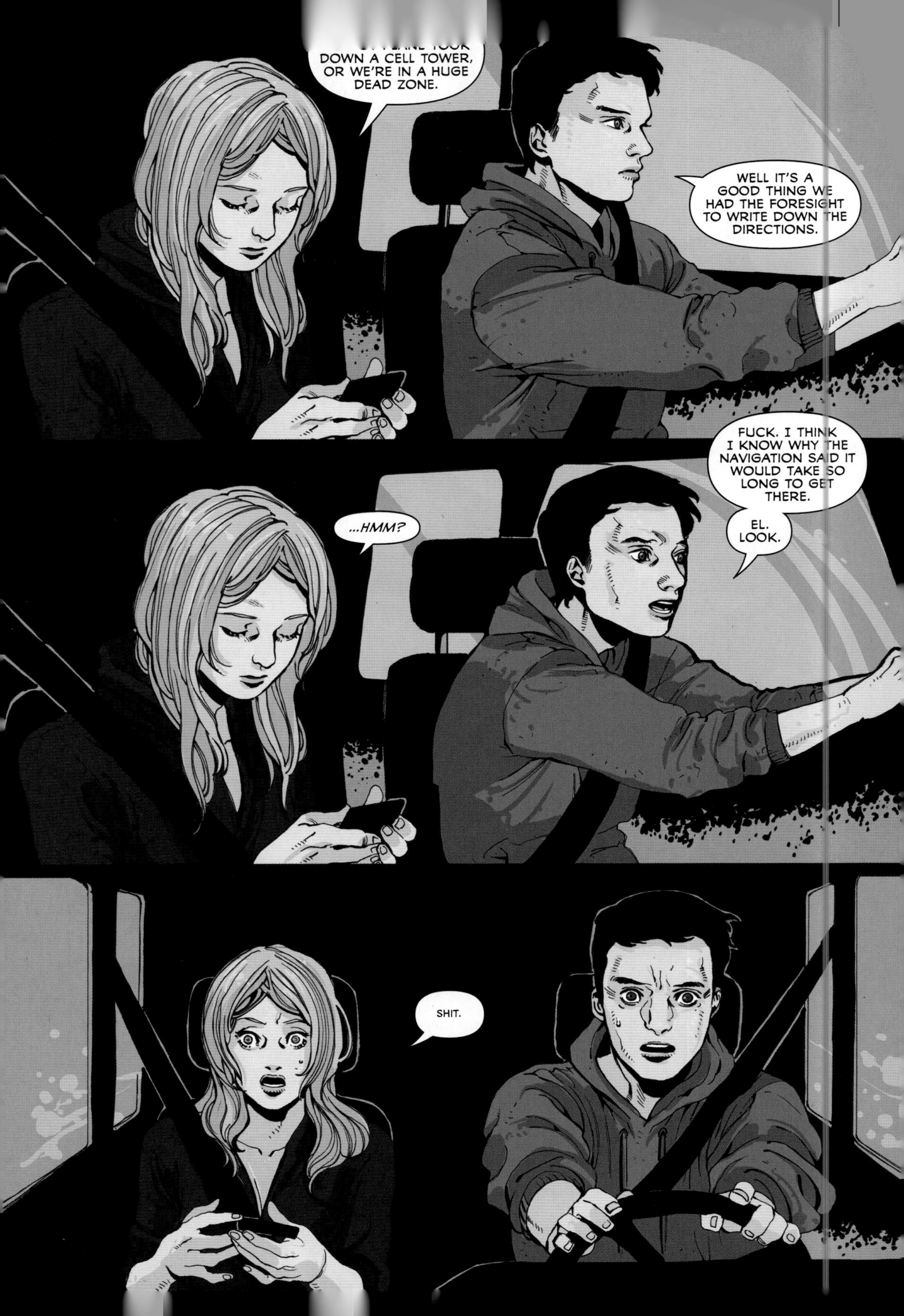
DOWN A CELL TOWER, OR WE'RE IN A HUGE DEAD ZONE.
WELL IT'S A GOOD THING WE HAD THE FORESIGHT TO WRITE DOWN THE DIRECTIONS.
FUCK. I THINK I KNOW WHY THE NAVIGATION SAID IT WOULD TAKE SO LONG TO GET THERE.
...HMM?
EL. LOOK.
SHIT.

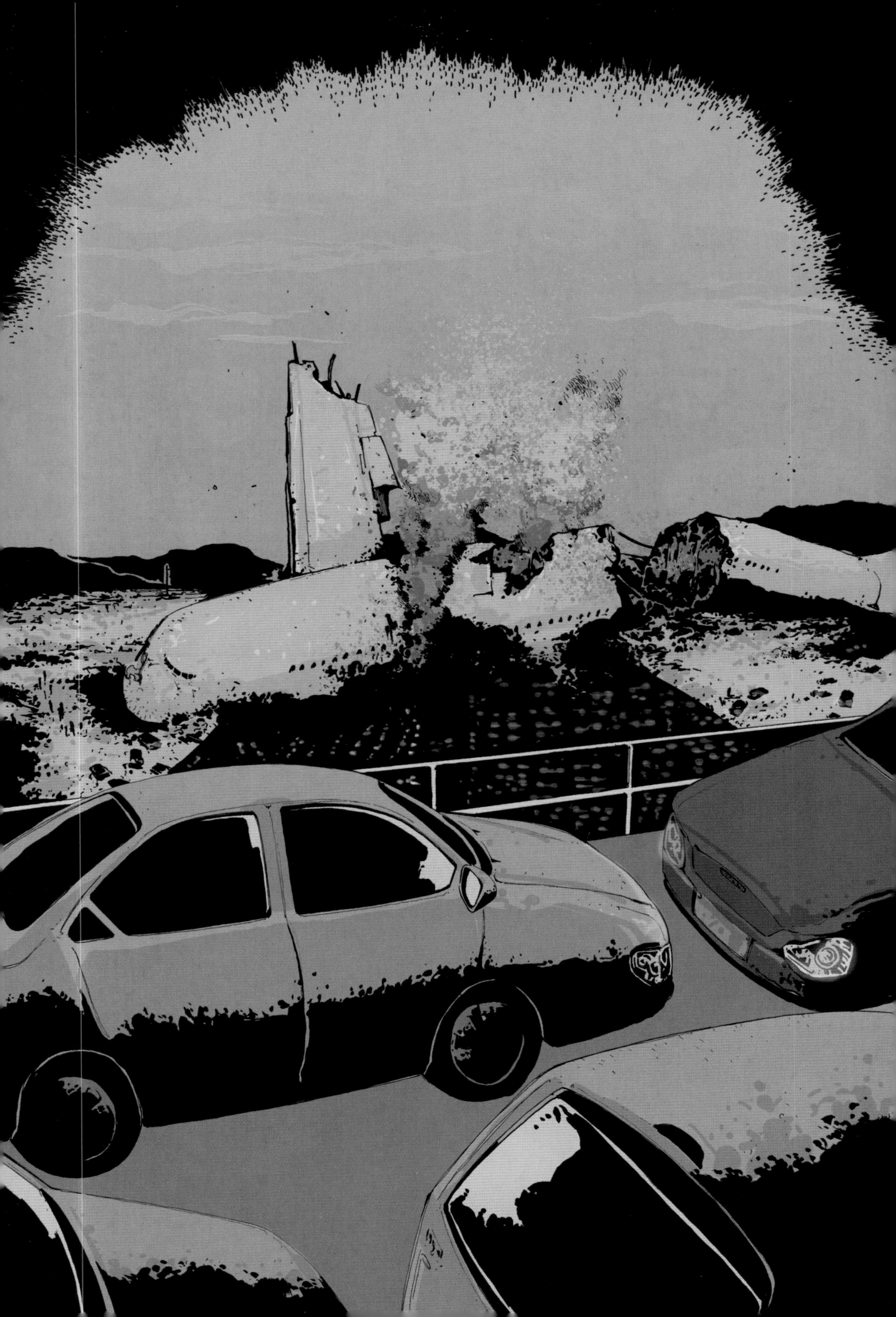

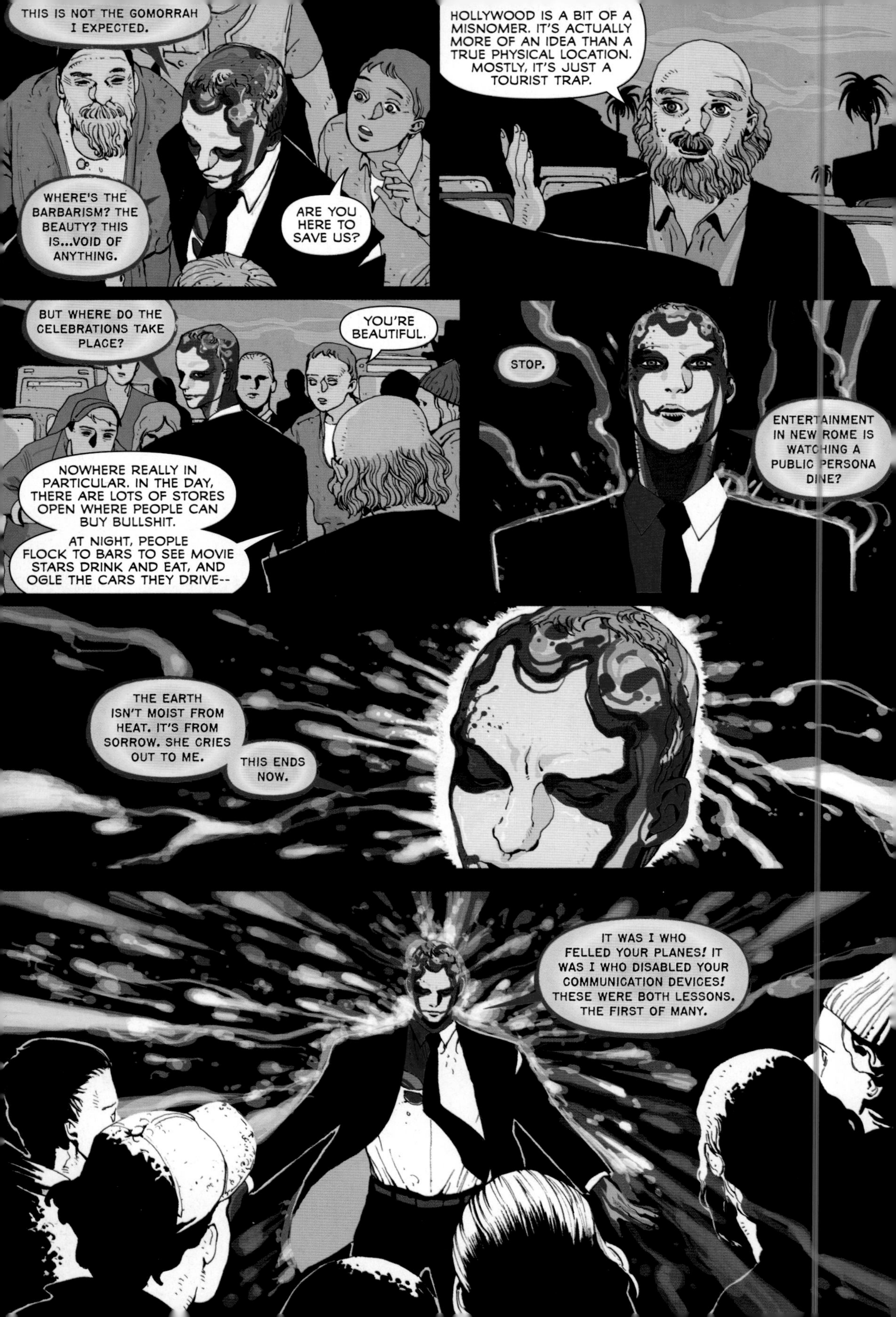
THIS IS NOT THE GOMORRAH I EXPECTED.
WHERE'S THE BARBARISM? THE BEAUTY? THIS IS...VOID OF ANYTHING.
ARE YOU HERE TO SAVE US?
HOLLYWOOD IS A BIT OF A MISNOMER. IT'S ACTUALLY MORE OF AN IDEA THAN A TRUE PHYSICAL LOCATION. MOSTLY, IT'S JUST A TOURIST TRAP.
BUT WHERE DO THE CELEBRATIONS TAKE PLACE?
YOU'RE BEAUTIFUL.
NOWHERE REALLY IN PARTICULAR. IN THE DAY, THERE ARE LOTS OF STORES OPEN WHERE PEOPLE CAN BUY BULLSHIT.
AT NIGHT, PEOPLE FLOCK TO BARS TO SEE MOVIE STARS DRINK AND EAT, AND OGLE THE CARS THEY DRIVE--
STOP.
ENTERTAINMENT IN NEW ROME IS WATCHING A PUBLIC PERSONA DINE?
THE EARTH ISN'T MOIST FROM HEAT. IT'S FROM SORROW. SHE CRIES OUT TO ME.
THIS ENDS NOW.
IT WAS I WHO FELLED YOUR PLANES! IT WAS I WHO DISABLED YOUR COMMUNICATION DEVICES! THESE WERE BOTH LESSONS. THE FIRST OF MANY.

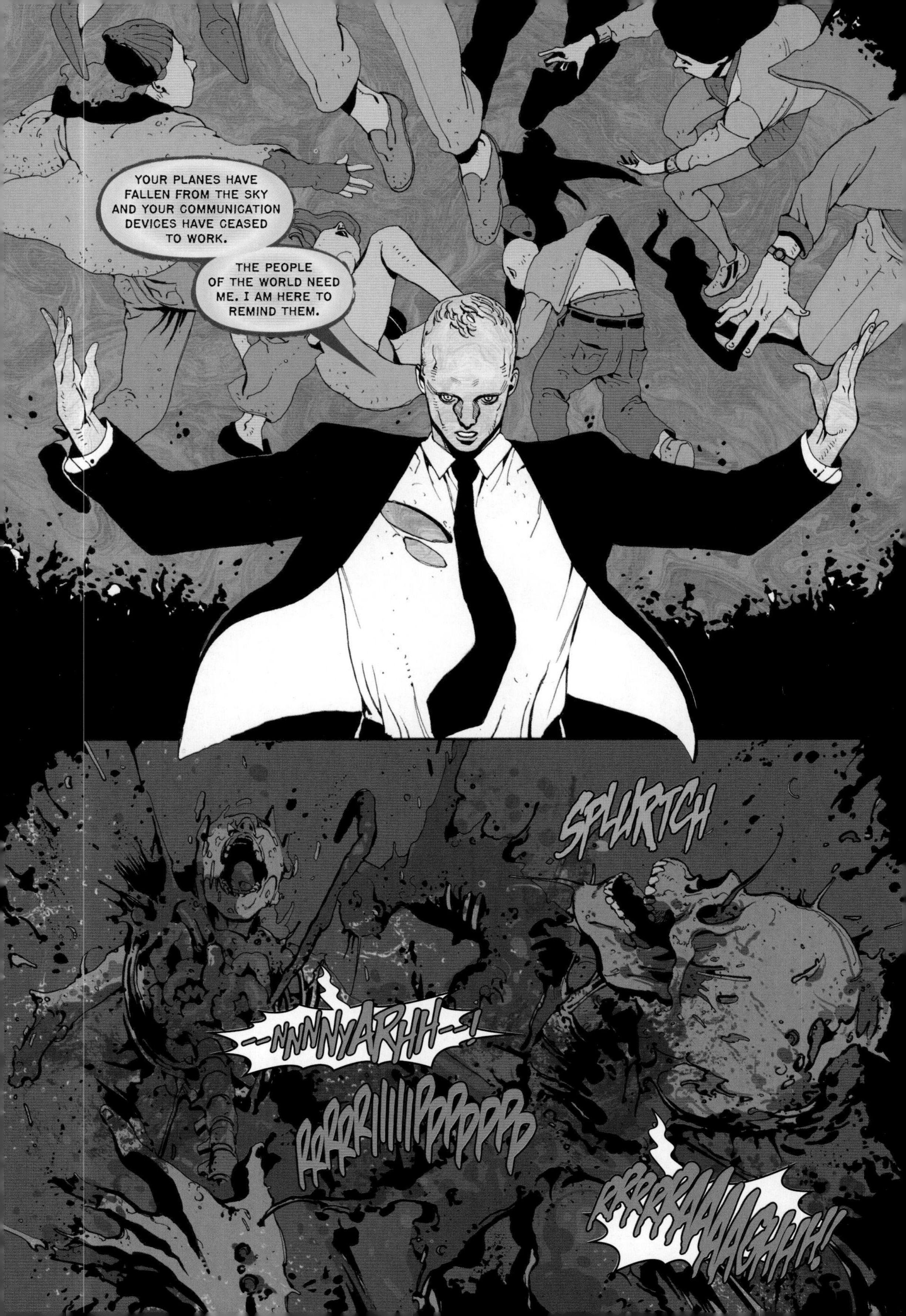

YOUR PLANES HAVE FALLEN FROM THE SKY AND YOUR COMMUNICATION DEVICES HAVE CEASED TO WORK.
THE PEOPLE OF THE WORLD NEED ME. I AM HERE TO REMIND THEM.
SPLURTCH
--NNNNYARHH--!
RRRRIIIIIPPPPPPP
RRRRAAAAAGHHH!

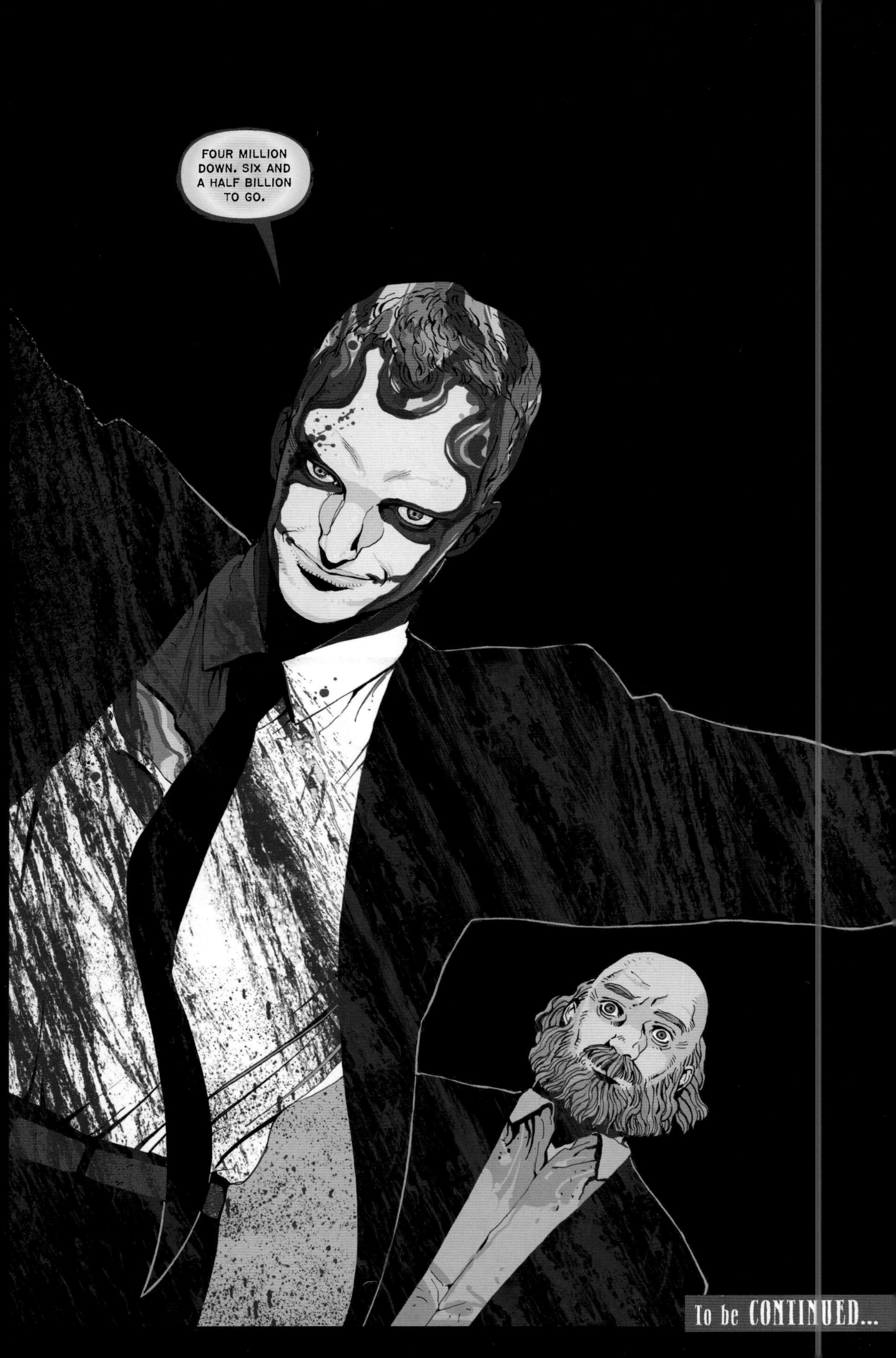
FOUR MILLION DOWN. SIX AND A HALF BILLION TO GO.
To be CONTINUED...

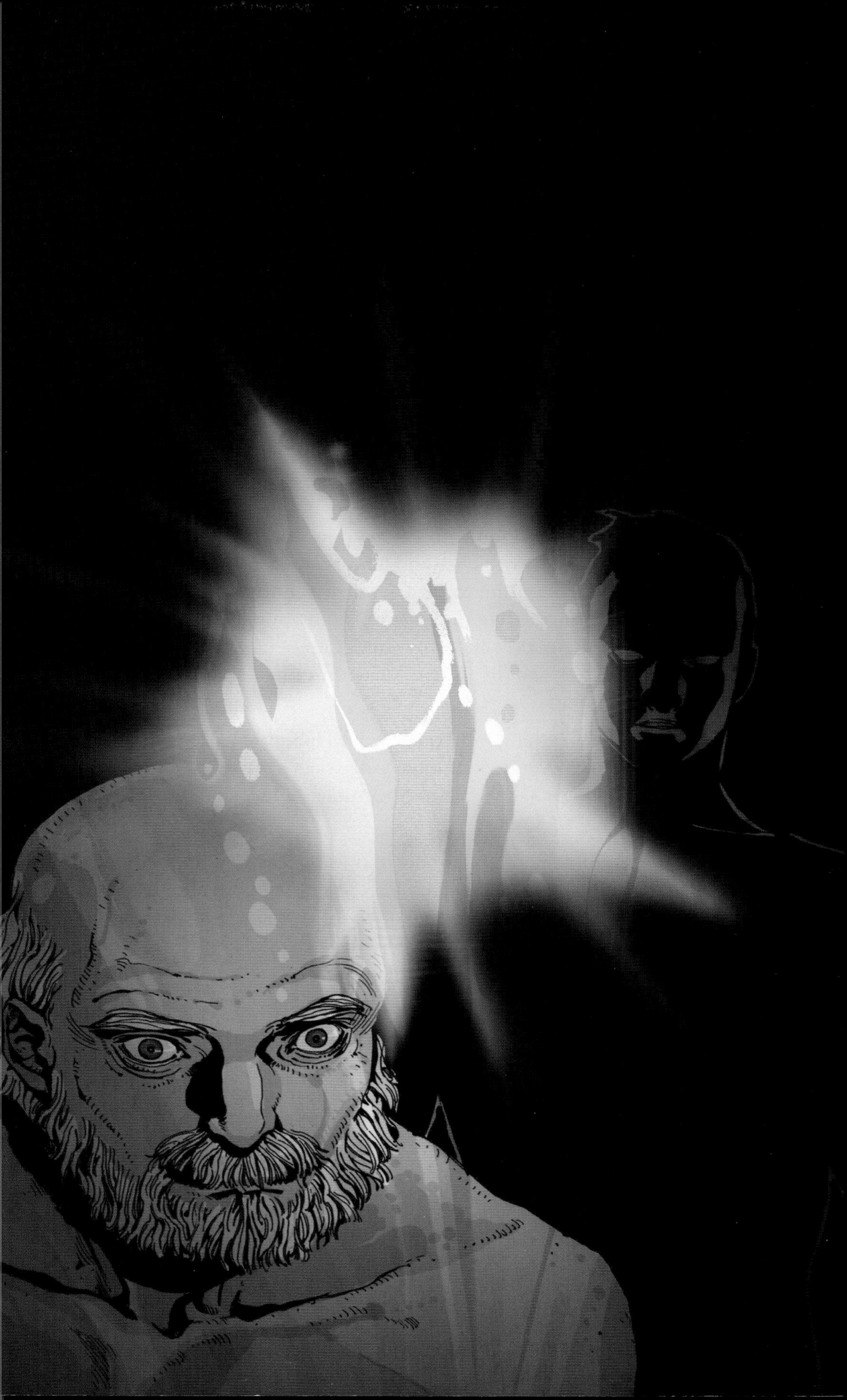

Afterword by Rodrigo Gudiño *(Rue Morgue)*

I cannot think of a more difficult subject to write about than god. God the Creator, God the Supreme Being, God the... Father. The eternal nemesis, Satan, seems like such an easier and welcoming bet; an earthbound angel fully devoted to the carnal appetites of the instinctual animal self. Seems like a guy we can all relate to. But god... the title is less a word and more of a sign – a myth symbol in the shape of a question mark, a signpost mirage in a fog of open guesses. God is an ideal and, more importantly, god is the universal ideal, which makes him/her/it a particularly daunting personality to capture in the modest mechanics of ink and paper.

And yet a good deal has been written about god. Ancient history has bequeathed us tome after comprehensive tome detailing the deity's loves and likes, wants and desires, schemes and regulations, presumably to get to know him better. And as anyone who has ever poured over these books with a candid heart knows, god isn't exactly the Benevolent Father that the faithful believe him to be. God is driven to anger as to love, has jealousies and spites, isn't above drawing blood to prove a point, and looks on approvingly as entire multitudes of men, women and children disintegrate in his name. God is a prick. And yet he is god – that being to which the human being presumably aspires to at his or her spiritual zenith. An intriguing paradox.

Throughout history, kings and queens, and labourers and laymen alike have sought out prophets and mystics, ever seeking the living voice of their creator, ever attentive to those few words that could make existence bearable: "I love you. I am here for you. Death is not the end."

Words of comfort that seem as elusive now as they have been through the long millennia. Following our technological adolescence in the 20th century, we seem to have matured into an intellectual materialism that does not want to admit that the desire to hear god – to feel his presence – is more acute than it ever was. A dull ache stiffens our spirit as we stand upright for the very first time, gaze at the stars as equals, and sense the possibility of direct communion with the cosmic Self.

Clive Barker and Mark Miller's Next Testament is strong ointment for that ache. It dares proclaim that now is the time to raise god from the books, to see him as he is, to step into the riddle, to explode the symbol. The birthing will be painful, no doubt, and as with matters of the flesh, blood flow will follow the hemorrhaging of the soul. And yet enlightenment seldom happens any other way.

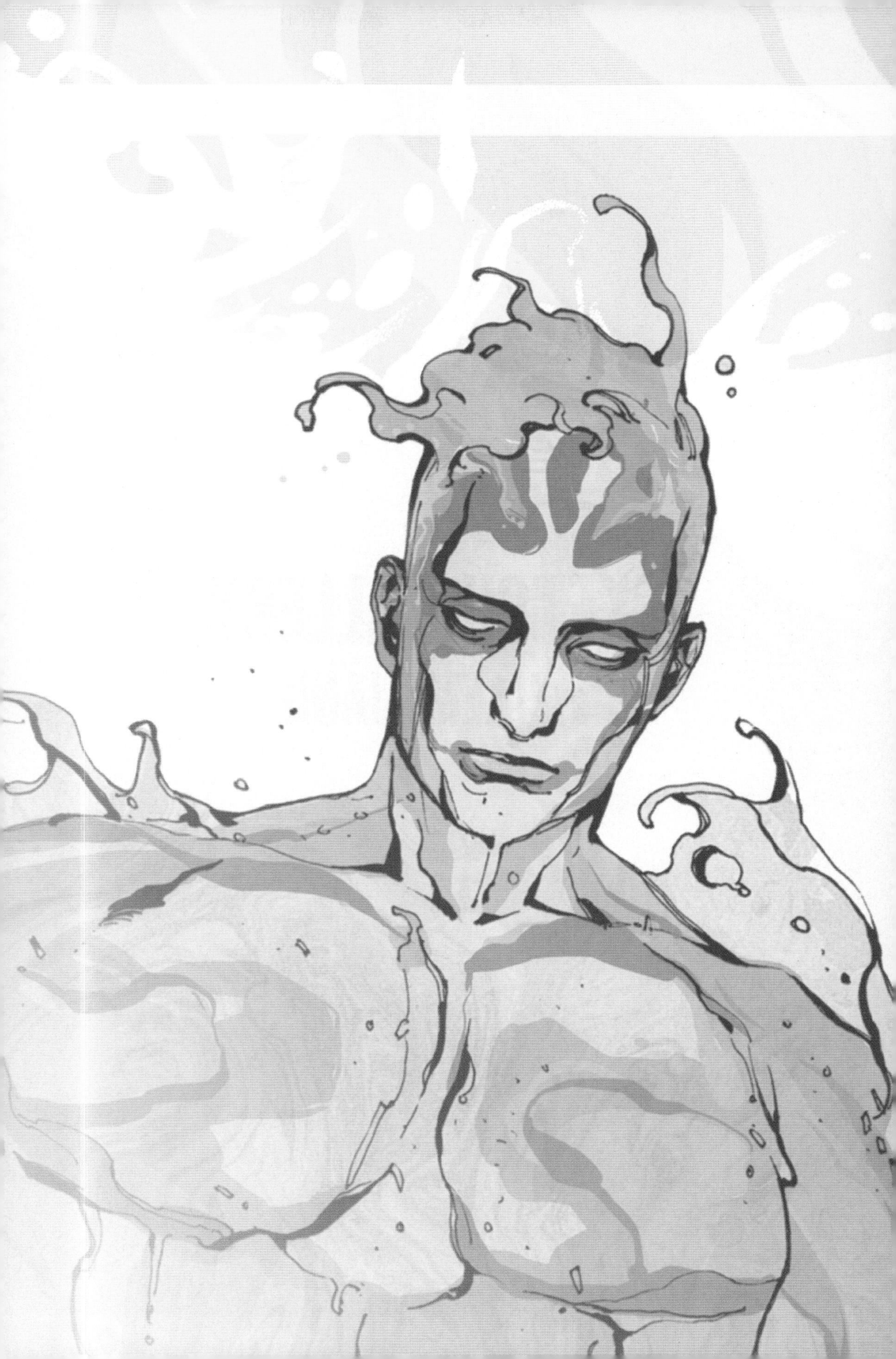

SKETCH GALLERY
BY HAEMI JANG

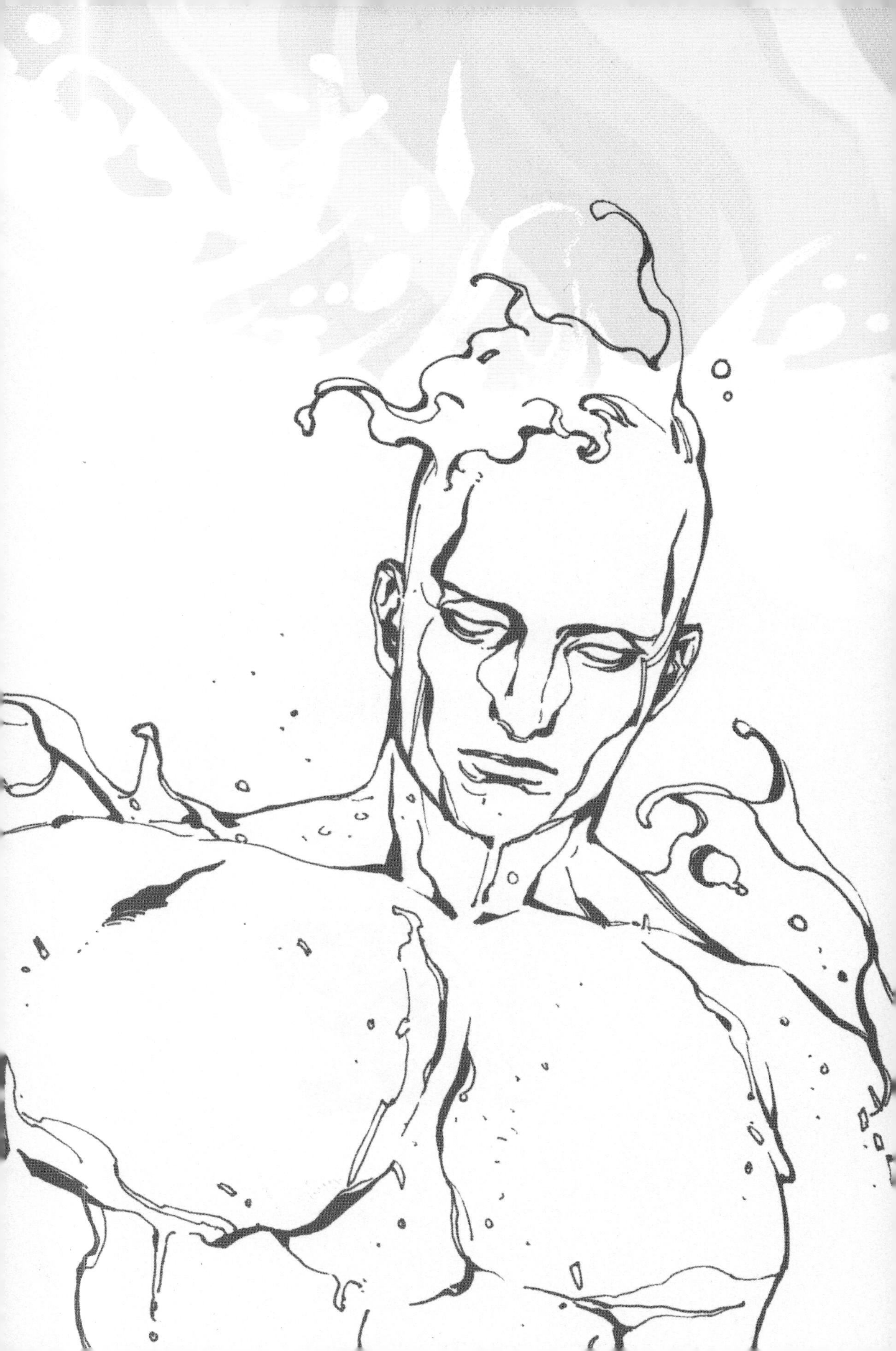

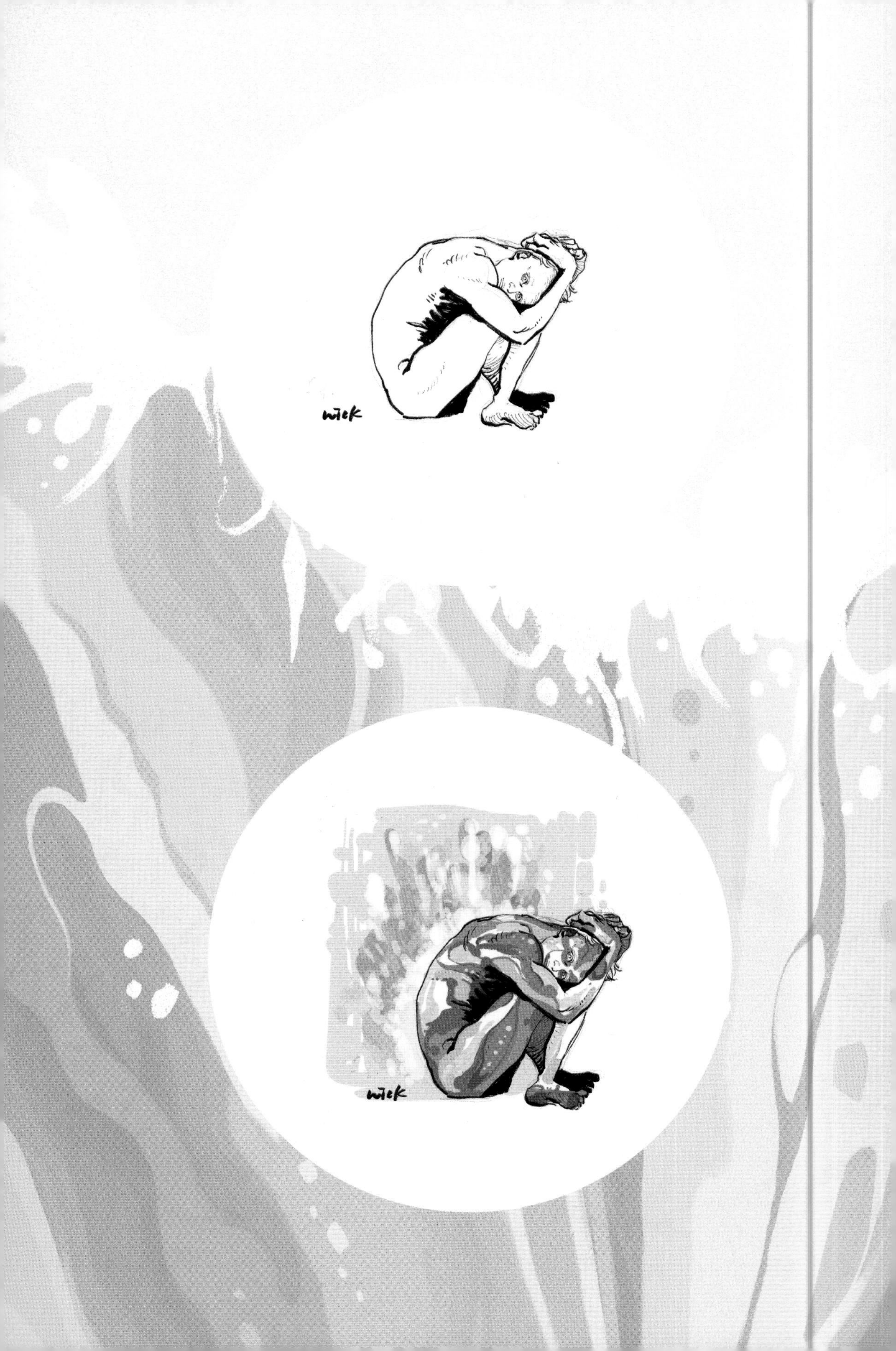
wick
wick

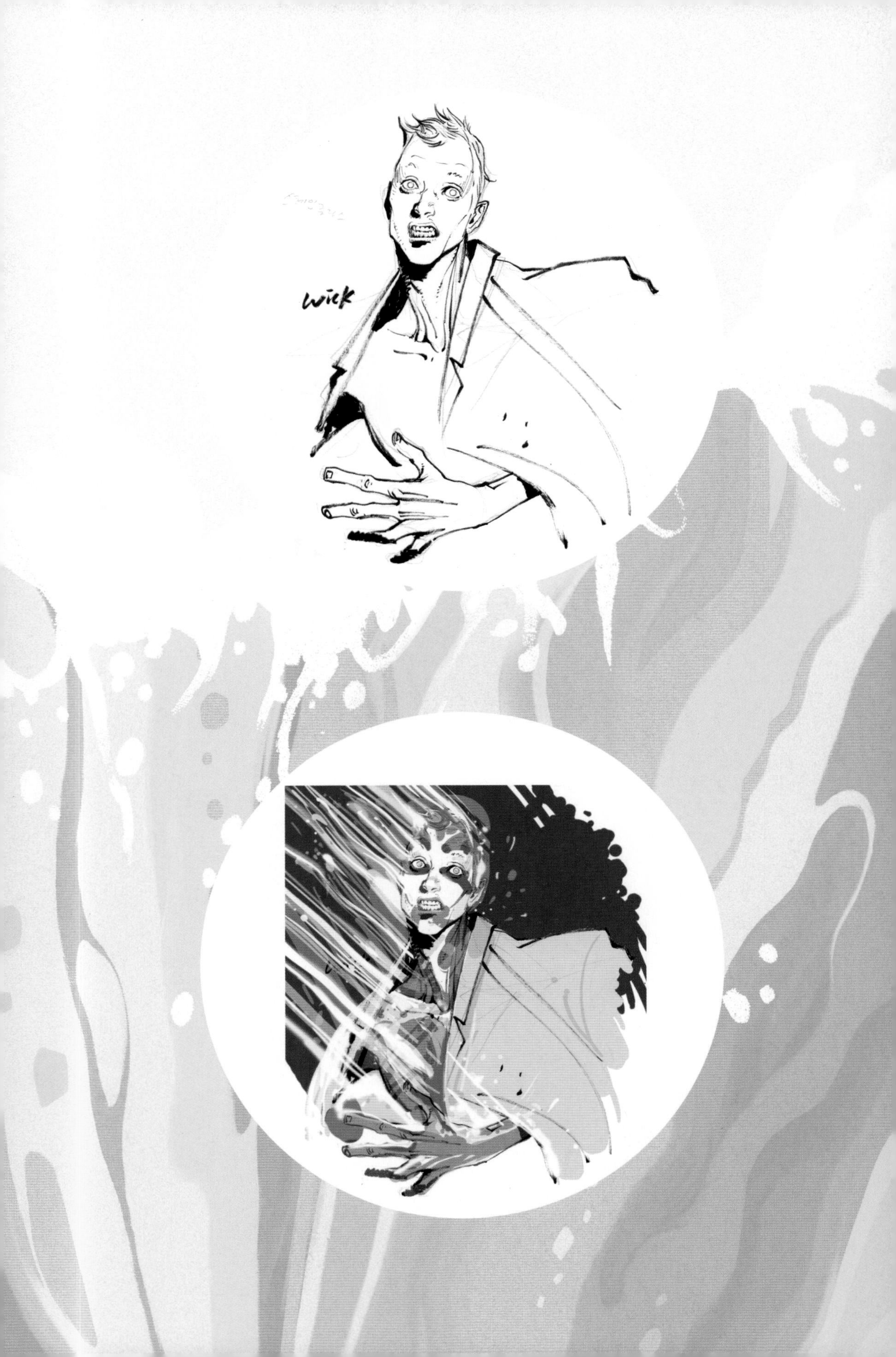
wick

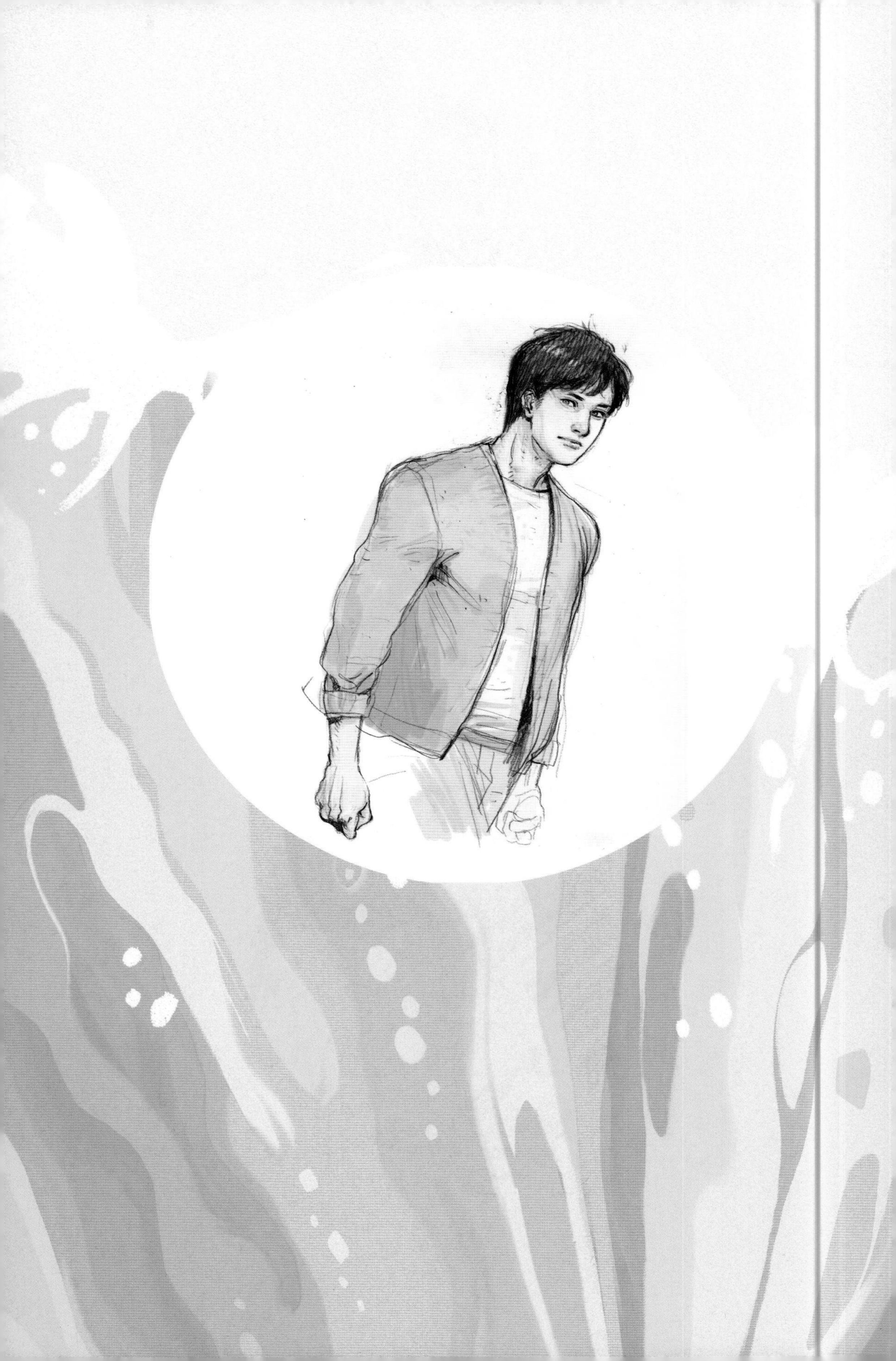

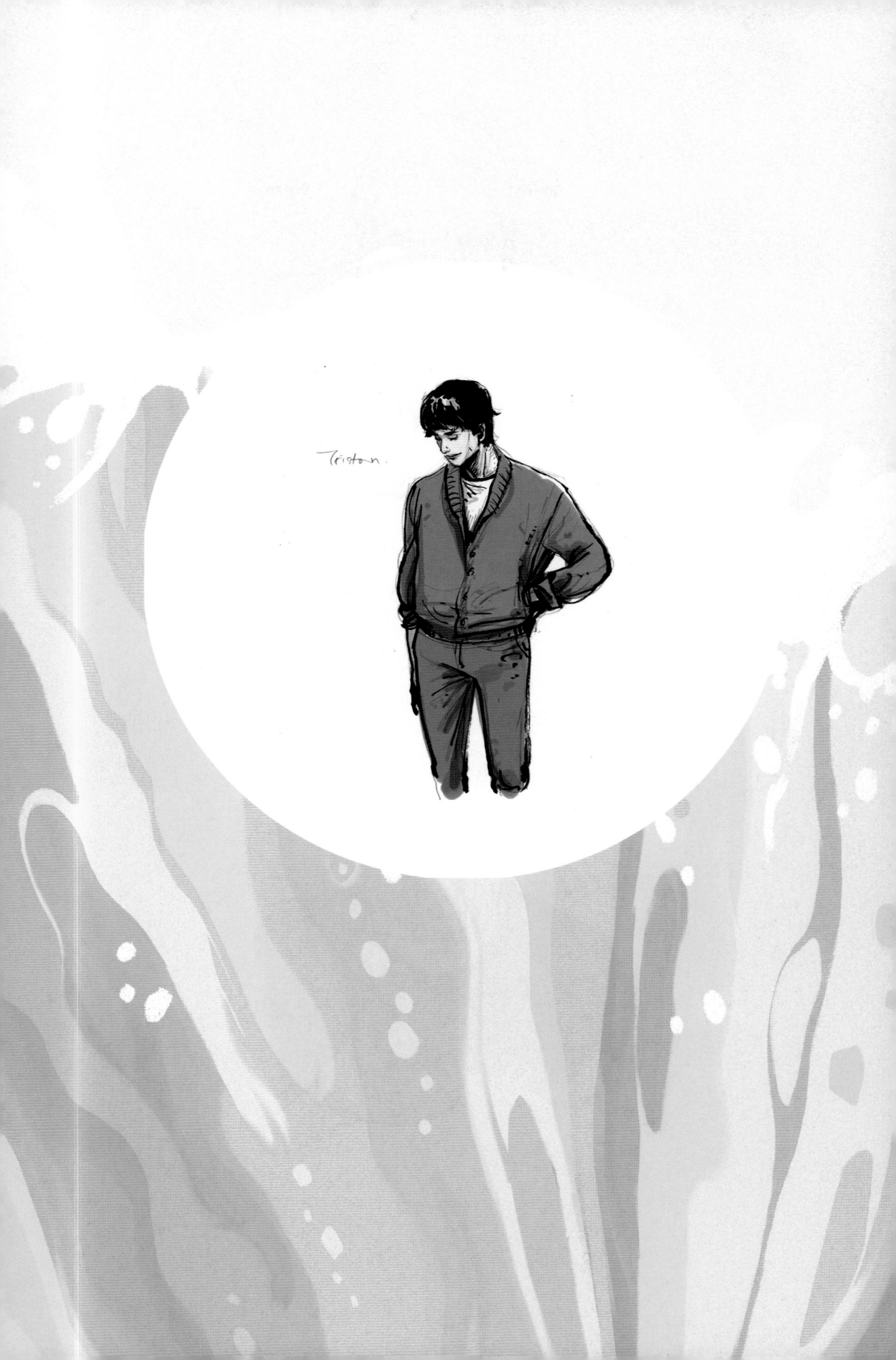
Tristan.

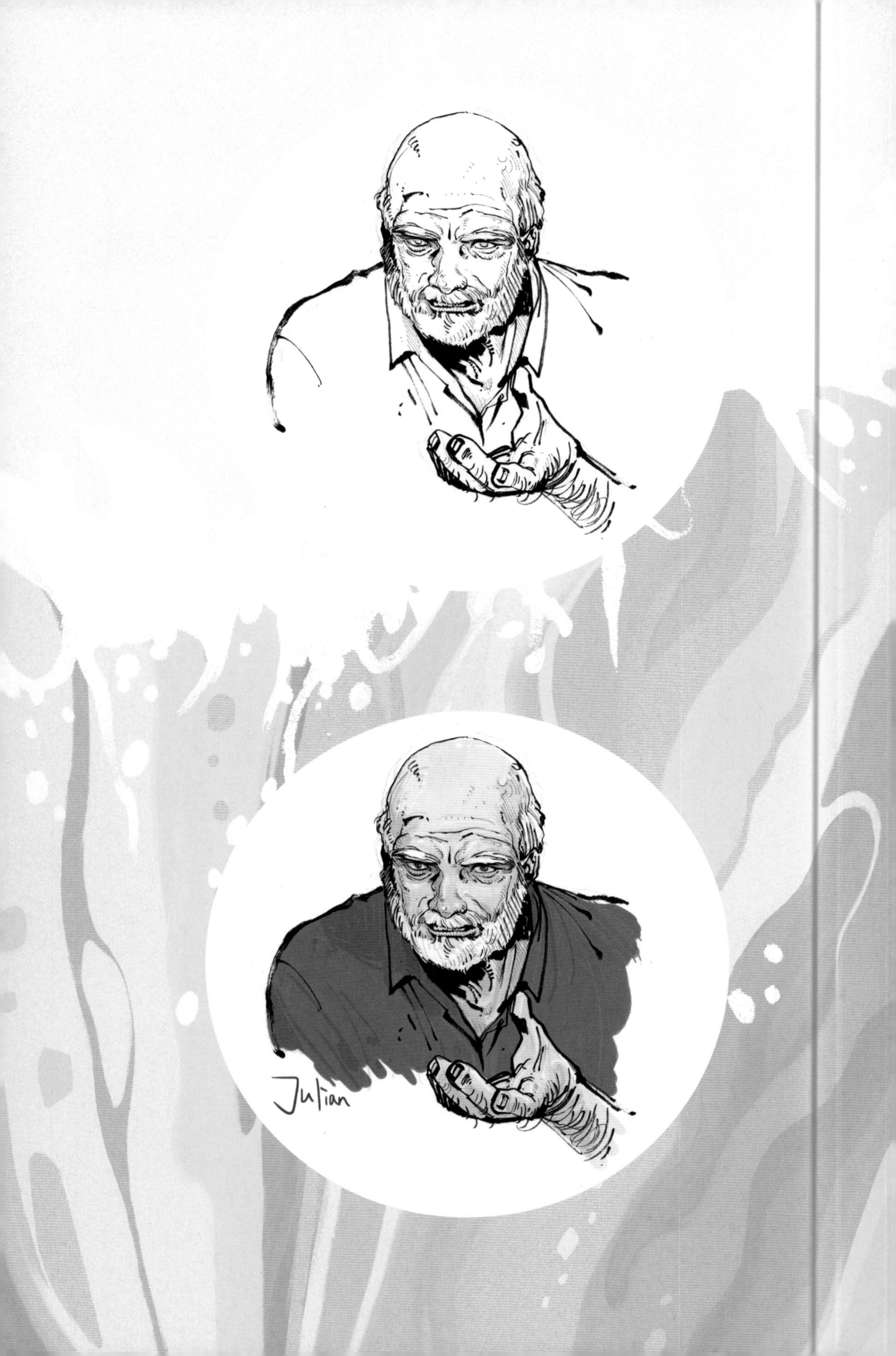
Julian

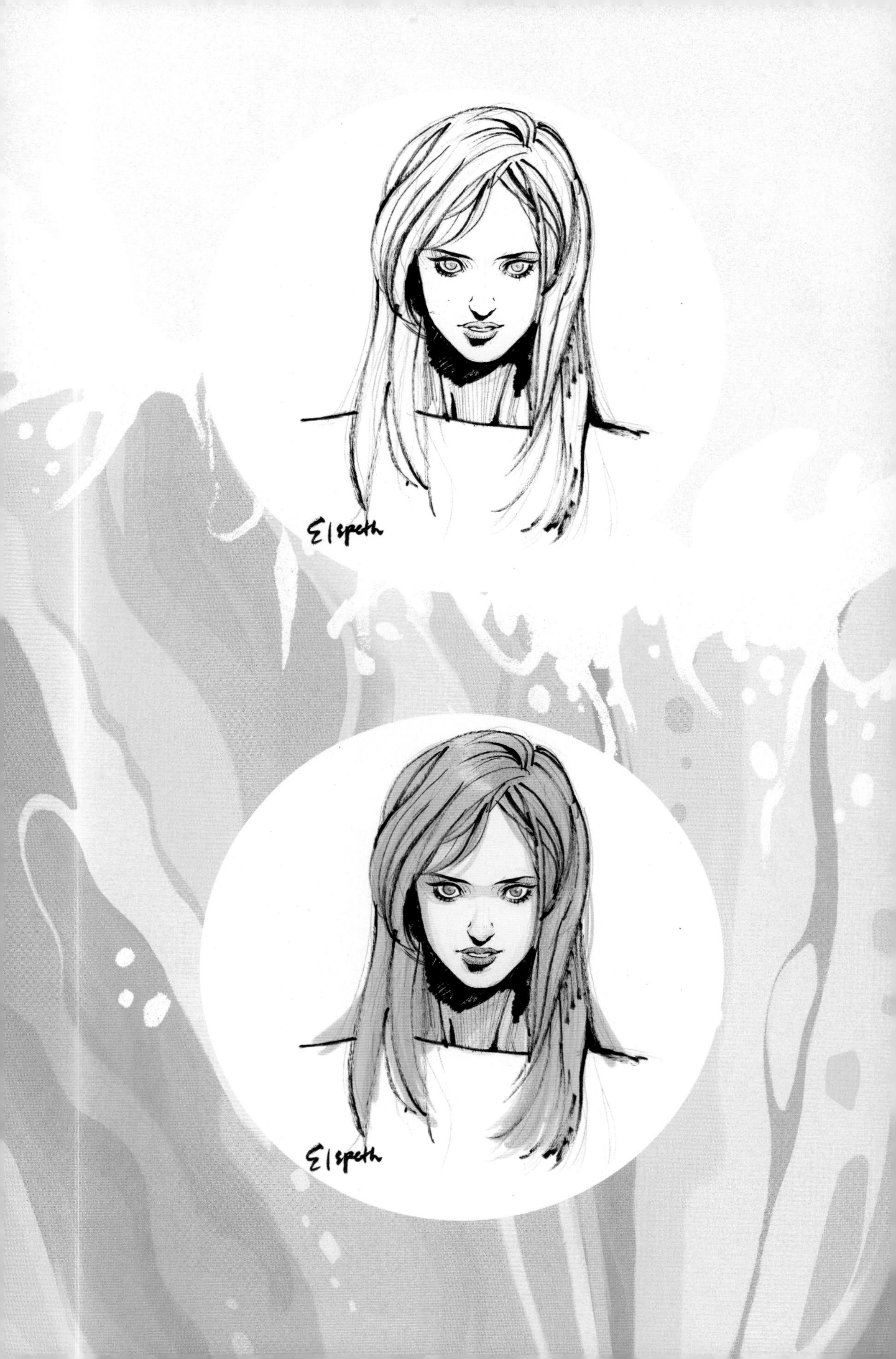
Elspeth
Elspeth

COVER GALLERY

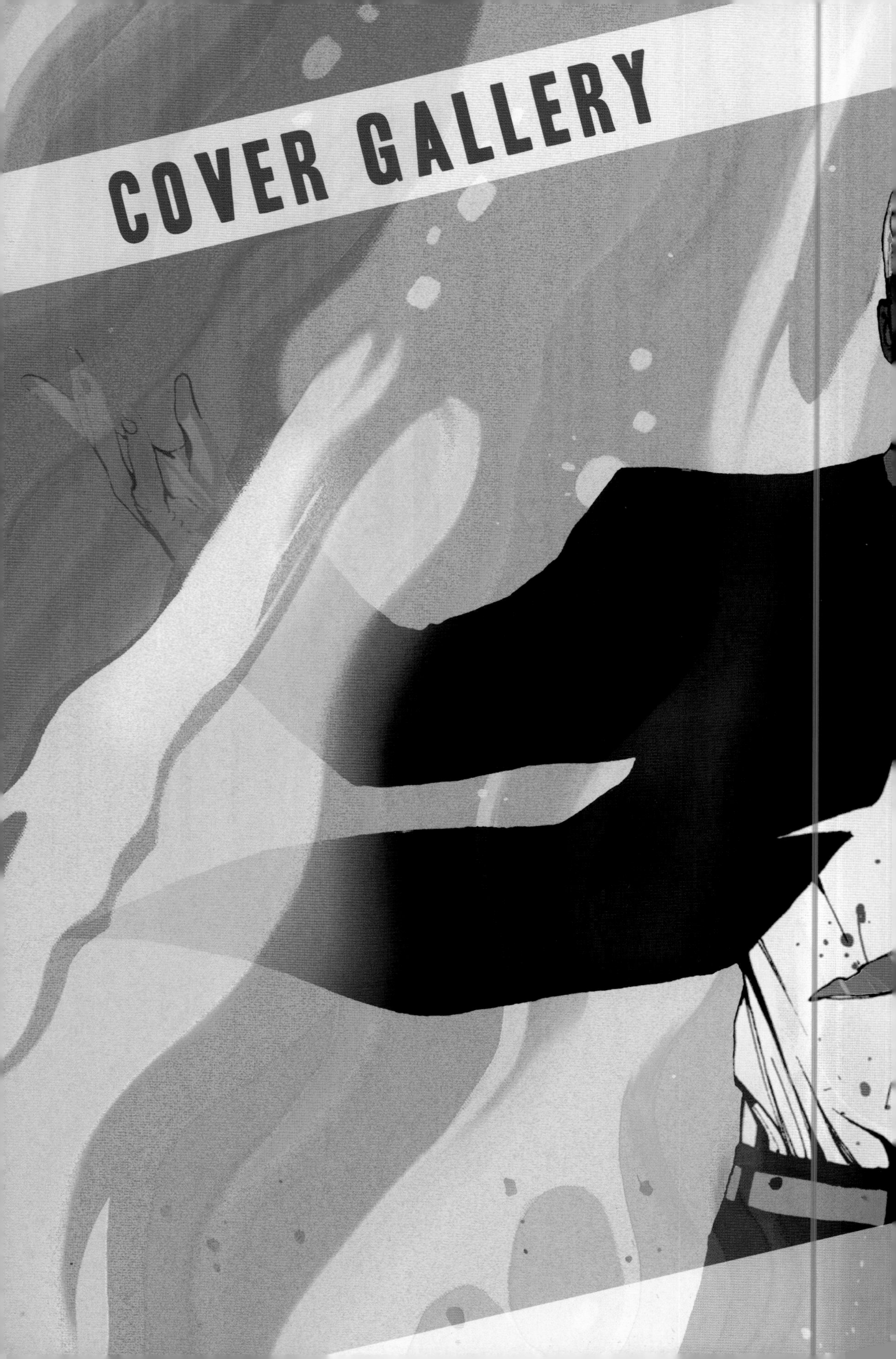

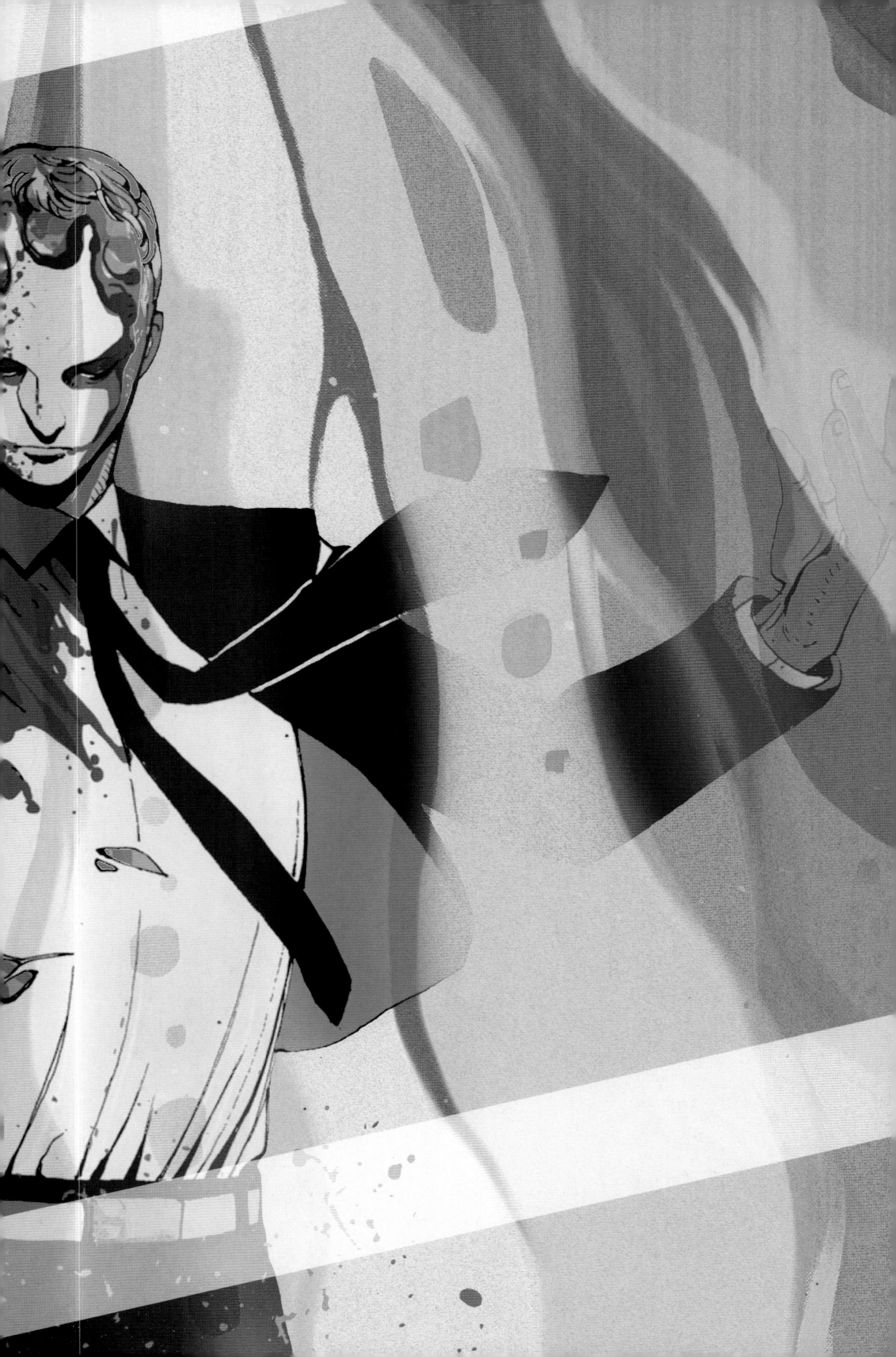

ISSUE ONE: GOÑI MONTES

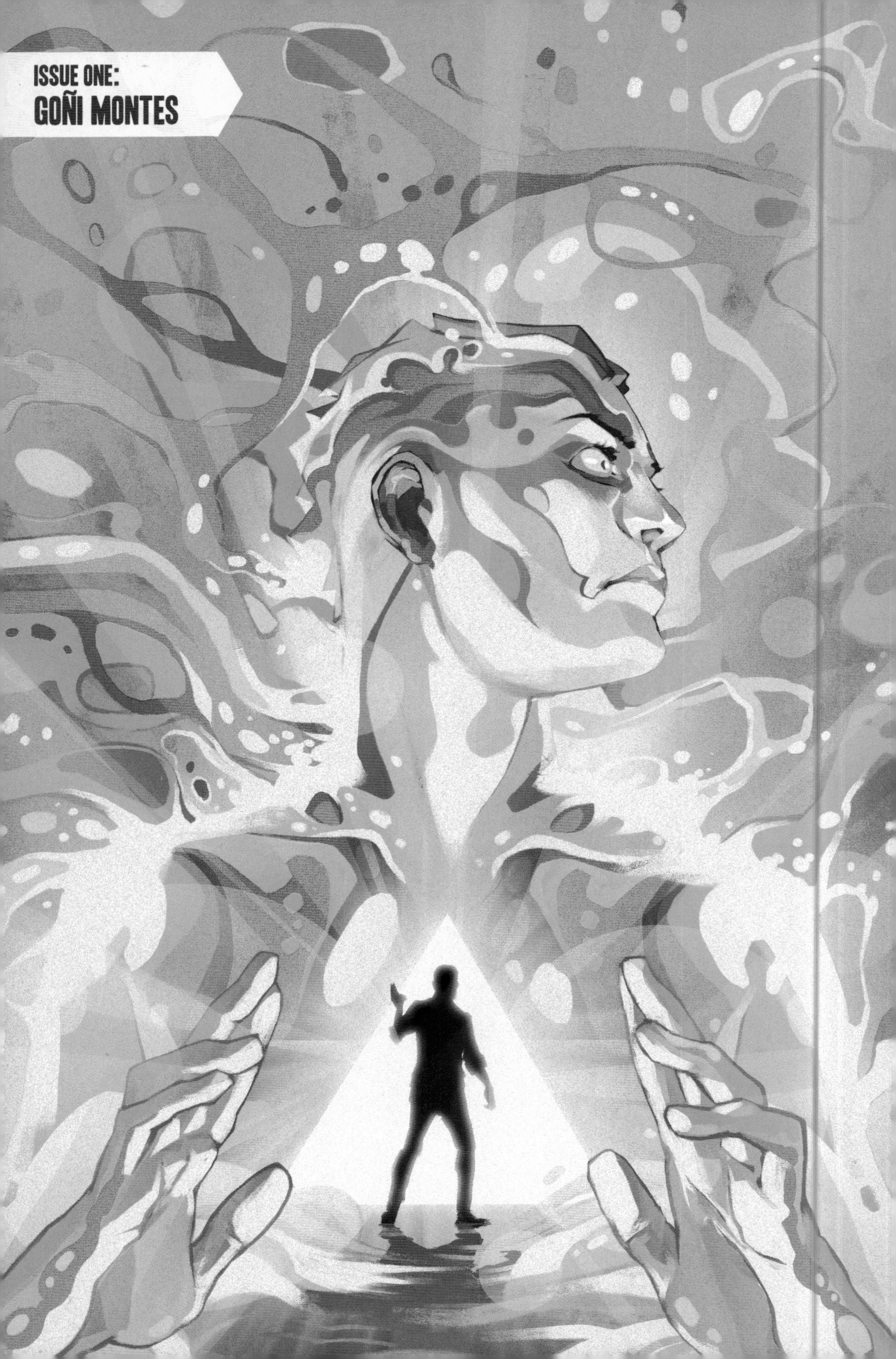

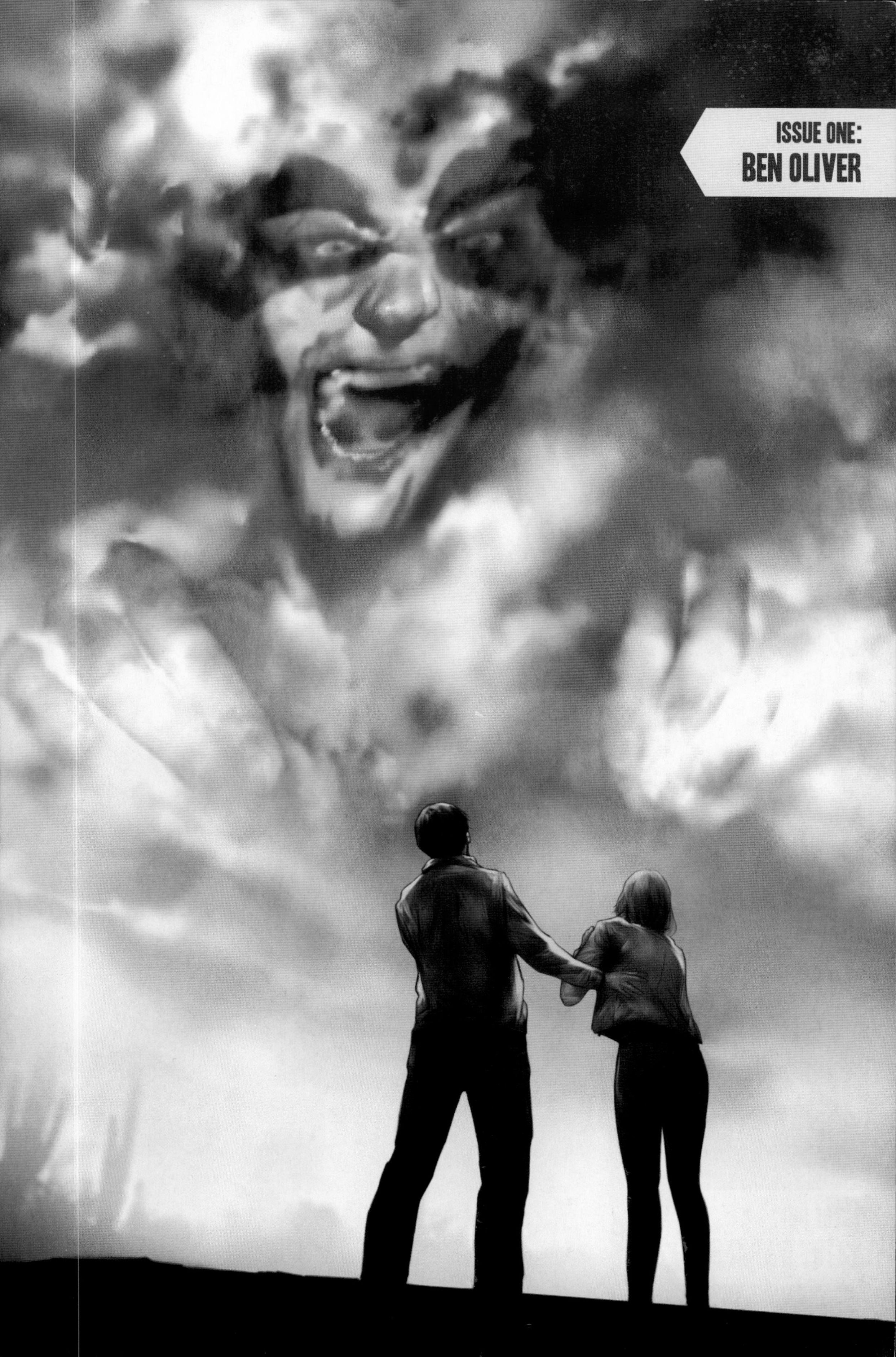
ISSUE ONE:
BEN OLIVER

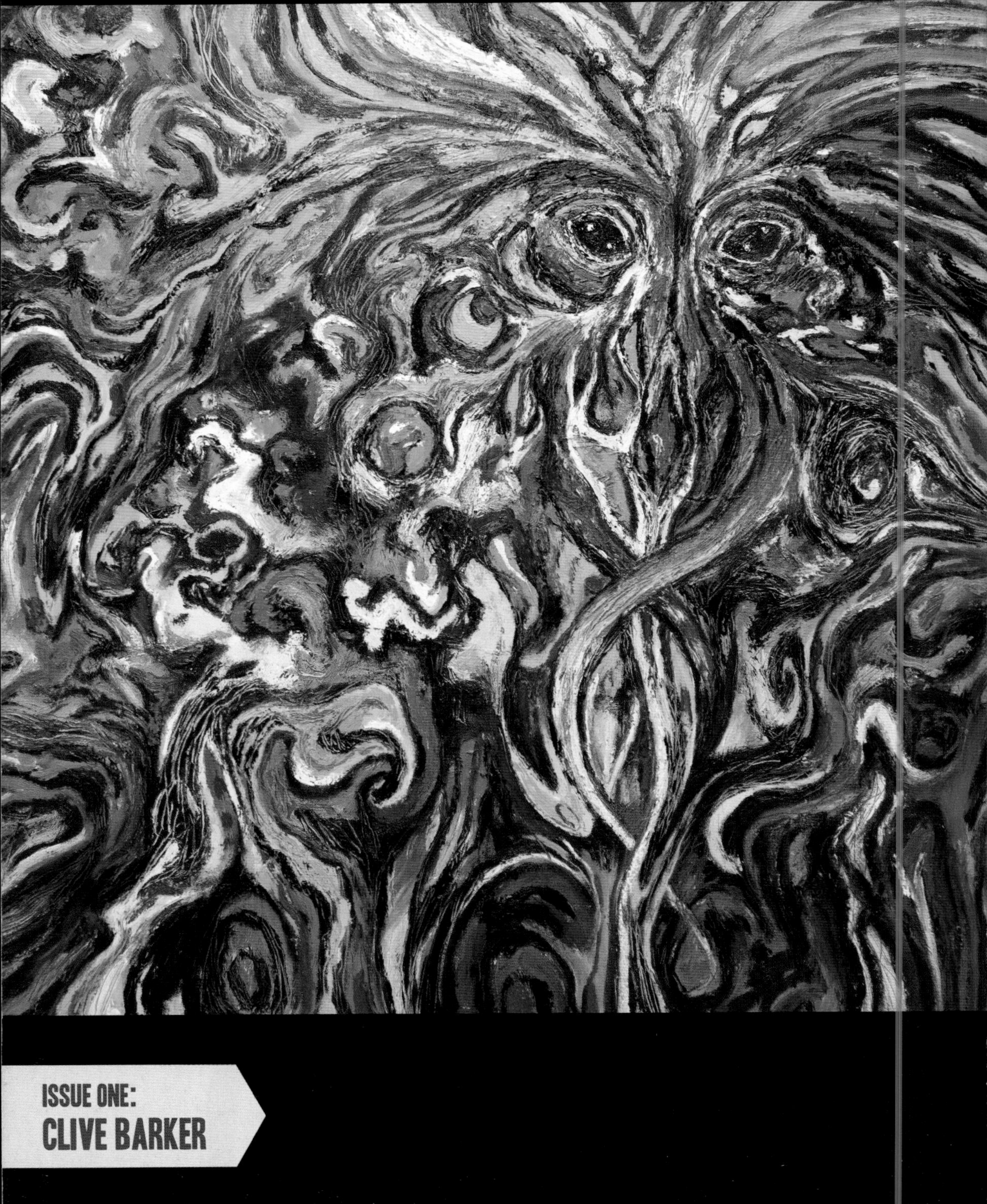

ISSUE ONE:
CLIVE BARKER

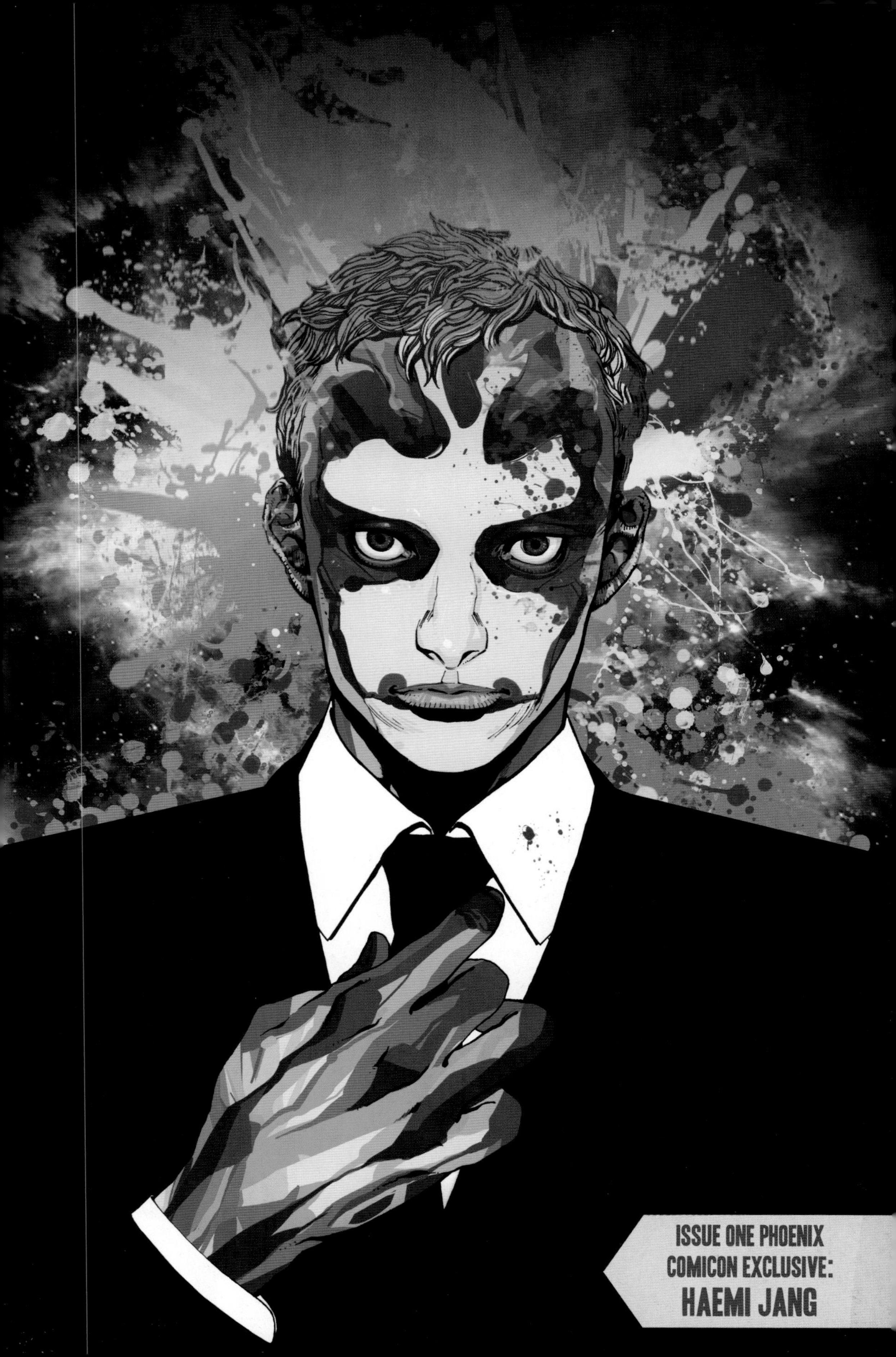
ISSUE ONE PHOENIX
COMICON EXCLUSIVE:
HAEMI JANG

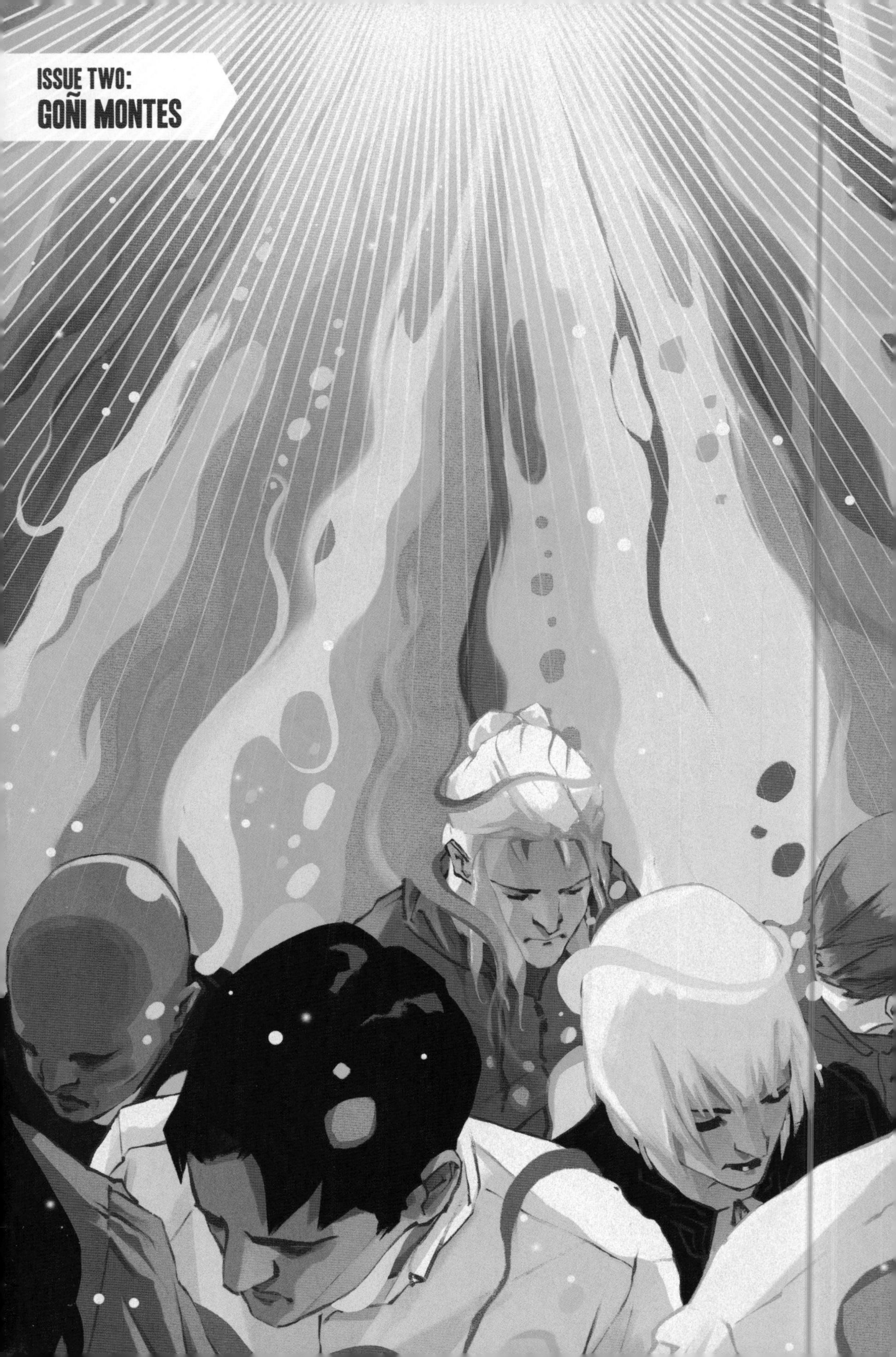
ISSUE TWO:
GOÑI MONTES

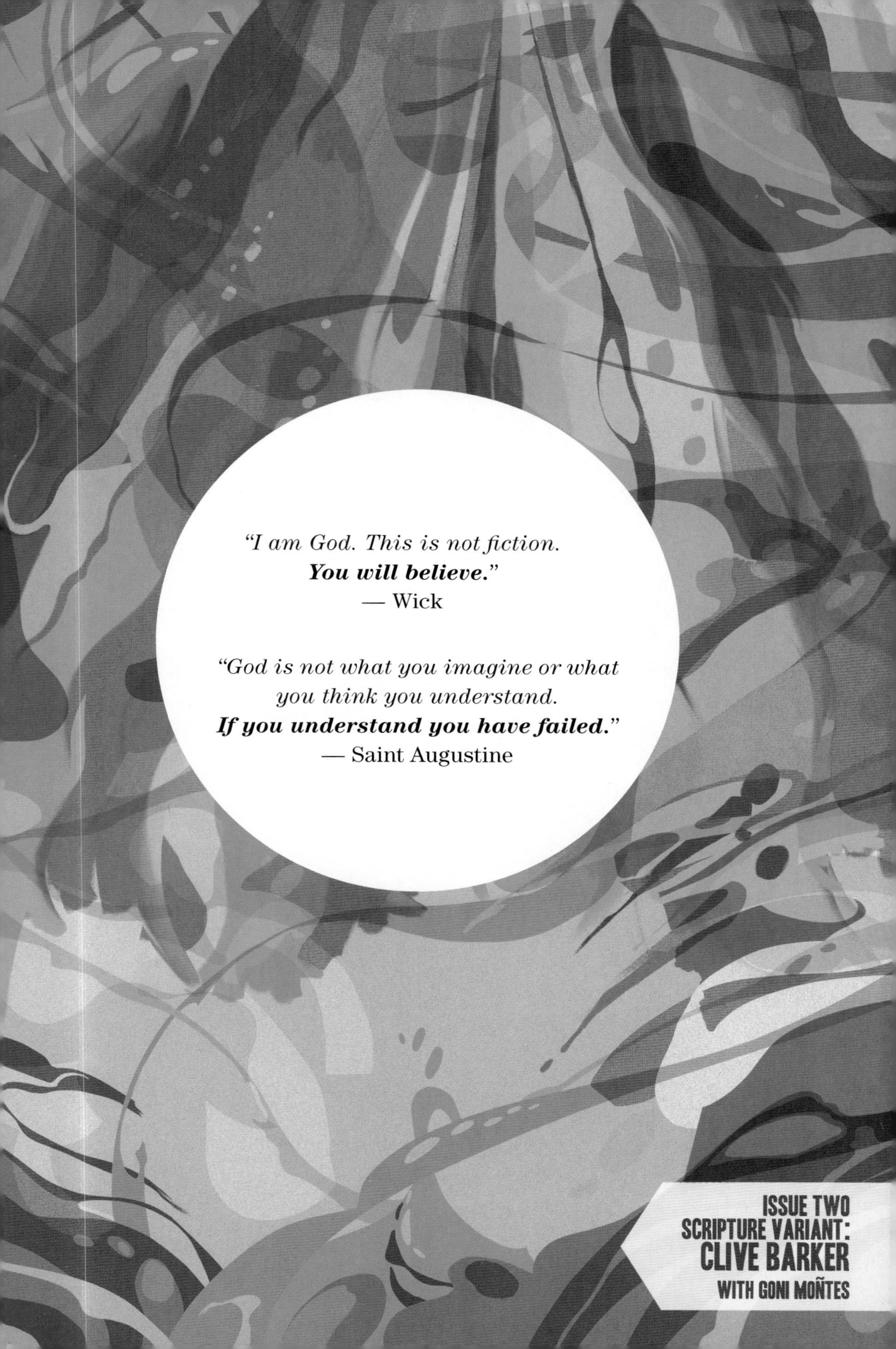

"I am God. This is not fiction.
You will believe."
— Wick

"God is not what you imagine or what
you think you understand.
If you understand you have failed."
— Saint Augustine

ISSUE TWO
SCRIPTURE VARIANT:
CLIVE BARKER
WITH GONI MOÑTES

ISSUE THREE:
GOÑI MONTES

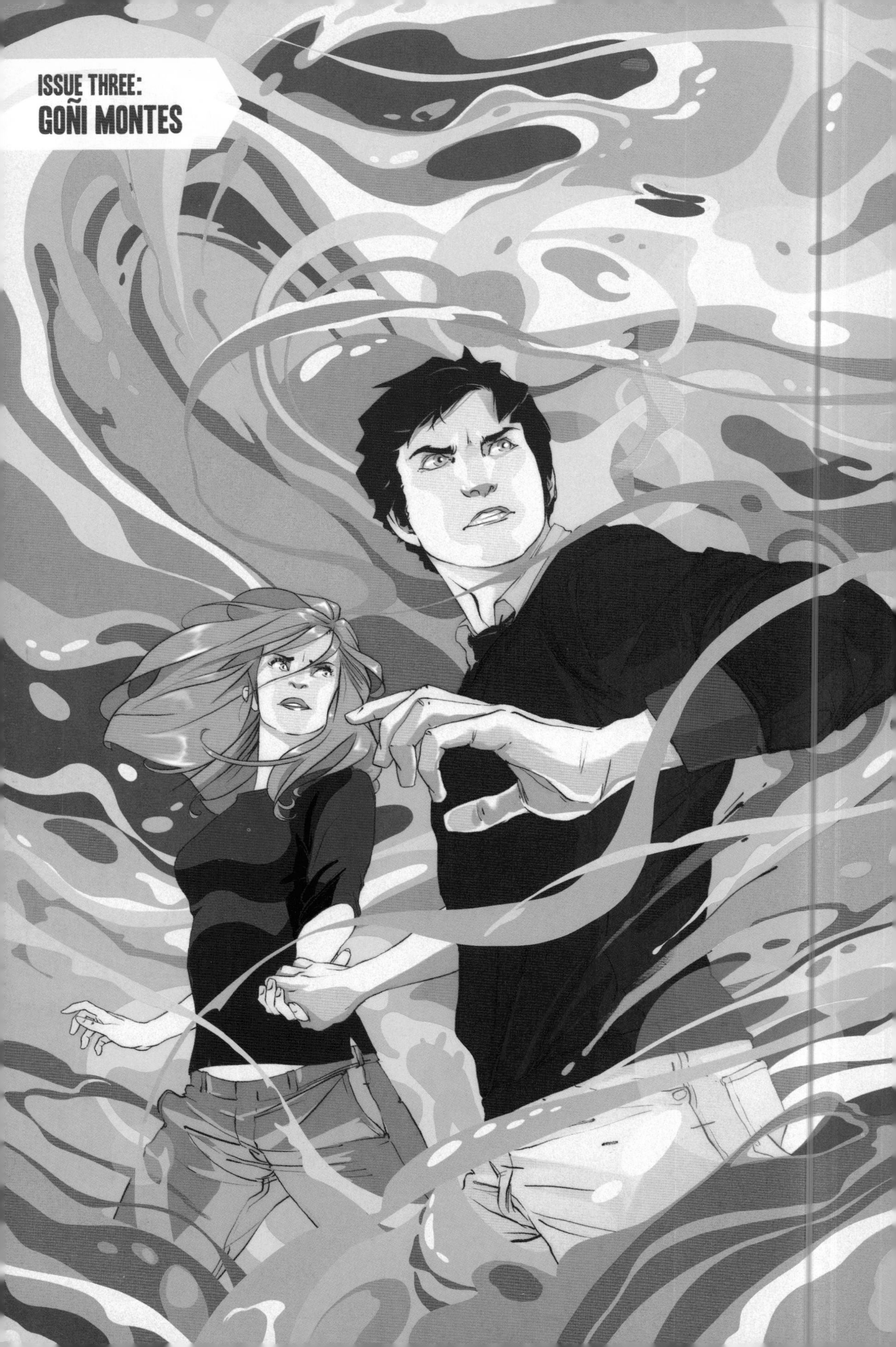

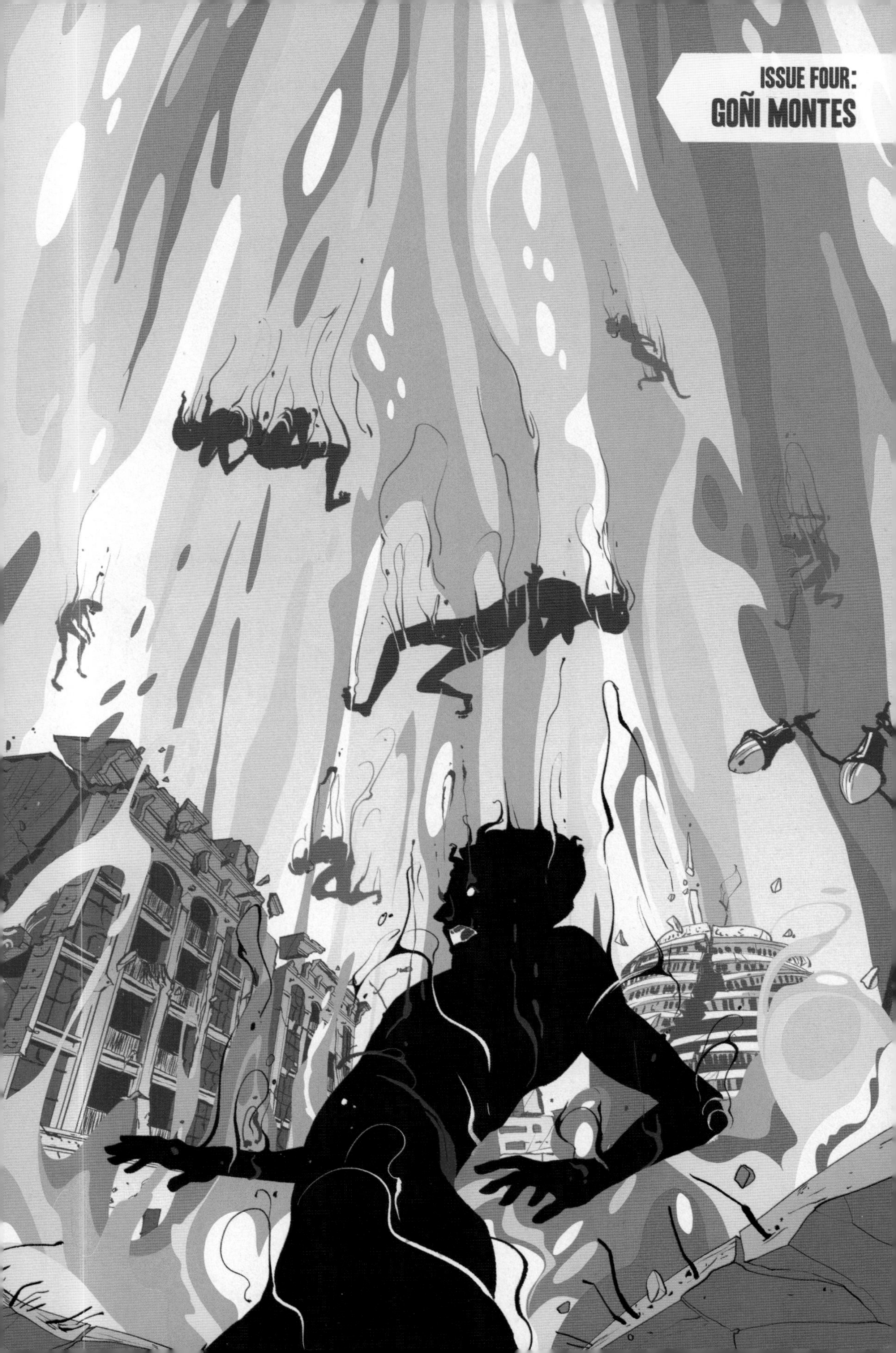
ISSUE FOUR:
GOÑI MONTES

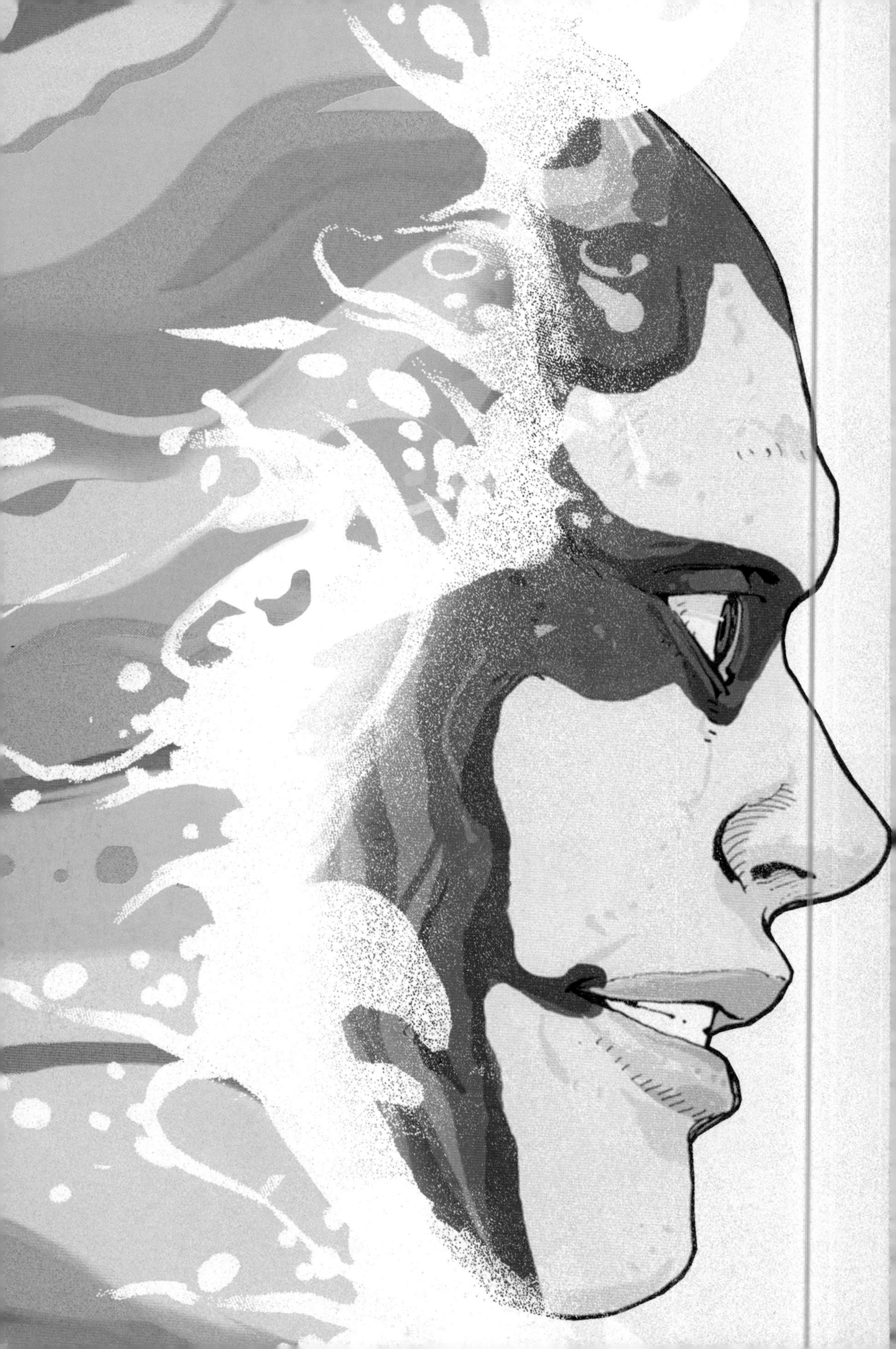